Making Money
with Your
Computer
at Home

Other Books by
Paul and Sarah Edwards

Best Home Businesses for People 50+

Best Home Businesses for the 21st Century

Changing Directions Without Losing Your Way

Cool Careers for Dummies, 2001
(with Marty Nemko)

The Entrepreneurial Parent
(with Lisa Roberts)

Finding Your Perfect Work

Getting Business to Come to You
(with Laura Douglas)

Home-Based Business for Dummies
(with Peter Economy)

Home Businesses You Can Buy
(with Walter Zooi)

Making Money in Cyberspace
(with Linda Rohrbough)

Making Money with Your Computer at Home

The Practical Dreamer's Handbook

Secrets of Self-Employment

Teaming Up
(with Rick Benzel)

Why Aren't You Your Own Boss?
(with Peter Economy)

Working from Home

Jeremy P. Tarcher/Penguin
a member of
Penguin Group (USA) Inc.
New York

Making Money with Your Computer at Home

THIRD EDITION

Paul and Sarah Edwards

JEREMY P. TARCHER/PENGUIN

Published by the Penguin Group

Penguin Group (USA) Inc., 375 Hudson Street, New York, New York 10014, USA • Penguin Group
(Canada), 90 Eglinton Avenue East, Suite 700, Toronto, Ontario M4P 2Y3, Canada (a division of
Pearson Penguin Canada Inc.) • Penguin Books Ltd, 80 Strand, London WC2R 0RL, England •
Penguin Ireland, 25 St Stephen's Green, Dublin 2, Ireland (a division of Penguin Books Ltd) •
Penguin Group (Australia), 250 Camberwell Road, Camberwell, • Victoria 3124, Australia (a divi-
sion of Pearson Australia Group Pty Ltd) • Penguin Books India Pvt Ltd, 11 Community Centre,
Panchsheel Park, New Delhi– 110 017, India • Penguin Group (NZ), Cnr Airborne and Rosedale
Roads, Albany, Auckland 1310, New Zealand (a division of Pearson New Zealand Ltd.) • Penguin
Books (South Africa) (Pty) Ltd, 24 Sturdee Avenue, Rosebank, Johannesburg 2196, South Africa •
Penguin Books Ltd, Registered Offices: 80 Strand, London WC2R 0RL, England

Most Tarcher/Penguin books are available at special quantity discounts
for bulk purchase for sales promotions, premiums, fund-raising, and
educational needs. Special books or book excerpts also can be created to
fit specific needs. For details, write Penguin Group (USA) Inc.
Special Markets, 375 Hudson Street, New York, NY 10014.

Library of Congress Cataloging-in-Publication Data

Edwards, Paul, date.
Making money with your computer at home / Paul and Sarah Edwards.—3d ed.
        p.   cm.
Includes bibliographical references.
ISBN 1-58542-445-5
1. Home-based businesses—United States—Technological innovations.   2. Microcomputers.
3. New business enterprises—United States—Management.   I. Edwards, Sarah (Sarah A.)
II. Title.
    HD2336.U5E38   2005   2005048644
        658'.0412—dc22

Printed in the United States of America
1   3   5   7   9   10   8   6   4   2

While the authors have made every effort to provide accurate telephone numbers and Internet
addresses at the time of publication, neither the authors nor the publisher assumes any responsibility for errors, or for changes that occur after publication. Further, the publisher does not
have any control over and does not assume any responsibility for the websites or their content.

Acknowledgments

We wish to express gratitude to Joel Fotinos, Mitch Horowitz, Ashley Shelby, Katie Grinch, Kristin Giorgio, Barbara Grenquist, and the others at Tarcher/Penguin who have helped to make this third edition of *Making Money with Your Compter at Home.*

We acknowledge technical writer Veronica Silva for her help in updating this edition, and Randy Caruso, Web designer extraordinaire, for providing a technical review and sage comments.

We dedicate this book to the millions of people who are searching for the way to improve their lives by taking their futures into their own hands and hope the ideas and guidance shared here will ease their way along their path.

Contents

PART I: 101 Computer Home Businesses Profiled 1

1.   ABSTRACTING SERVICE 11
2.   ANSWERING/VOICE-MAIL SERVICE 13
3.   ASSOCIATION MANAGEMENT SERVICES 14
4.   ASTROLOGY CHARTING SERVICE 16
5.   AUCTION MERCHANT 19
6.   BACKUP SERVICE 21
7.   BILLING AND INVOICING SERVICE 22
8.   BOOKKEEPING SERVICE 23
9.   BUSINESS PLAN WRITER 25
10. CLIP-ART SERVICE 27
11. COLLECTION AGENCY 28
12. COMPOSER/SOUND DESIGNER 29
13. COMPUTER-AIDED DESIGN (CAD) SERVICE 31
14. COMPUTER-ASSISTED INSTRUCTIONAL DESIGN (CAI) 32
15. COMPUTER CONSULTING 34
16. COMPUTER PROGRAMMING 36
17. COMPUTER SALES AND SERVICE 38
18. COMPUTER TRAINING 40
19. COMPUTER TUTORING 41
20. CONSTRUCTION AND REMODELING ESTIMATING
     AND PLANNING SERVICE 43
21. COPYWRITER 44
22. COUPON NEWSPAPER PUBLISHING 46

23. CREATIVITY CONSULTANT   48

24. DATA CONVERSION SERVICE   49

25. DATABASED MARKETING SERVICE   51

26. DESKTOP PUBLISHING SERVICE   52

27. DESKTOP VIDEO   54

28. DIET AND EXERCISE PLANNING SERVICE   56

29. DIGITAL PHOTOGRAPHY/IMAGE MANIPULATION   57

30. DIGITAL-RECORDING STUDIO/SERVICE   58

31. DISC/MEDIA-COPYING SERVICE   60

32. DRAFTING SERVICE   61

33. ELECTRONIC CLIPPING SERVICE   62

34. ELECTRONIC PUBLIC-RELATIONS
AND PUBLICITY SERVICE   64

35. EMPLOYEE MANUAL DEVELOPMENT
AND WRITING SERVICE   66

36. EVENT AND MEETING PLANNER   67

37. EXPERT-REFERRAL OR BROKERING SERVICE   69

38. FAX-ON-DEMAND SERVICES   70

39. FINANCIAL INFORMATION SERVICE   72

40. FORM-DESIGN SERVICE   75

41. HTML/XML PROGRAMMER   76

42. INDEXING SERVICE   78

43. INFORMATION BROKERING   79

44. INTERNET CONSULTANT   81

45. INTERNET RESEARCHER   83

46. INTERNET SERVICE PROVIDER AND WEB-SITE HOSTING   85

47. INTERNET TRAINER   89

48. INVENTORY-CONTROL SERVICES   90

49. LAW LIBRARY MANAGEMENT   92

50. LEGAL TRANSCRIPT DIGESTING
(DEPOSITION DIGESTING)   93

51. LEGAL TRANSCRIPTION SERVICE   94

52. LIFESTYLE AND HOBBY RESOURCE WEB SITE   95

53. LOCAL AREA NETWORK (LAN)/INTRANET CONSULTANT   96

54. MAILING-LIST SERVICE   98

55. MARKET-MAPPING SERVICE   100

56. MEDICAL BILLING SERVICE   101

57. MEDICAL TRANSCRIPTION SERVICE   103

58. MORTGAGE-AUDITING SERVICE   106

59. MULTIMEDIA PRODUCTION   107

60. Newsletter Publishing   108

61. Online Product Sales   110

62. Payroll Preparation   112

63. People-Tracing Service   113

64. Personal Financial Management Services/
     Daily Money Manager   114

65. Professional-Practice Management Service   115

66. Professional Reminder Service   117

67. Proofreading Service   118

68. Property-Management Service   119

69. Proposal and Grant Writer   121

70. Public-Relations Specialist   123

71. Publishing Services   124

72. Real Estate Virtual Tours and Brochure Service   126

73. Referral Service   127

74. Repairing Computers   129

75. Résumé Service   130

76. Reunion Planning   132

77. Scanning Service   134

78. Scopist   135

79. Self-Publishing   136

80. Sign-Making Service   138

81. Software-Location Service   140

82. Software Publishing   141

83. Sports League Statistics and Game Scheduling   144

84. Technical Support   145

85. Technical Writing   146

86. Temporary-Help Service   148

87. T-Shirt and Novelty Design
     and Production Service   149

88. Used-Computer Broker   150

89. Video Animator   151

90. Video and Audio Digitizing Service   152

91. Virtual Assistant/Office Support   154

92. Web Content Writer   156

93. Webmaster   157

94. Web-Site Design   159

95. Web-Site Publicist   161

96. Web-Site Promotions Specialist   163

97. Web-Site Reviewer   165

98. WEB SPECIALTY PROGRAMMER: CGI PROGRAMMING   *167*

99. WEB SPECIALTY PROGRAMMER: JAVA   *168*

100. WEB AUDIO OR VIDEO PROGRAM   *170*

101. WEB PUBLICATION   *172*

PART II: **47 Questions You Need to Answer to Start Making Money with Your Computer**   *175*

1. WHY DO YOU WANT TO MAKE MONEY WITH YOUR COMPUTER?   *177*

2. DO YOU WANT TO DERIVE A FULL-TIME OR PART-TIME INCOME FROM YOUR COMPUTER-BASED BUSINESS? DO YOU INTEND TO WORK FULL OR PART TIME?   *178*

3. DO YOU WANT TO CONTINUE WORKING IN THE SAME FIELD DOING THE SAME OR SIMILAR WORK?   *178*

    3A. ARE THERE OTHER PEOPLE DOING SOMETHING SIMILAR TO WHAT YOU WOULD DO ON A FREELANCE, CONSULTING, OR INDEPENDENT BASIS?   *179*

    3B. CAN YOUR CURRENT EMPLOYER BECOME YOUR FIRST CUSTOMER?   *179*

    3C. COULD ANY OF THE PEOPLE OR COMPANIES YOU CURRENTLY WORK WITH ON YOUR JOB ETHICALLY BECOME YOUR CLIENTS OR CUSTOMERS AS WELL? HOW MANY?   *180*

    3D. ARE THERE OTHER CLIENTS FOR WHOM YOU COULD DO YOUR CURRENT JOB ON A FREELANCE, CONSULTANT, OR SUBCONTRACT ARRANGEMENT?   *180*

4. IF YOU DON'T WANT TO, OR CANNOT, DO THE SAME TYPE OF WORK YOU'VE BEEN DOING, WHAT OTHER THINGS DO YOU DO WELL AND ENJOY DOING?   *182*

5. WHO NEEDS THE KIND OF PRODUCTS OR SERVICES YOU COULD OFFER? MAKE A LIST OF ALL THE TYPES OF PEOPLE OR COMPANIES THAT NEED THEM.   *188*

6. WHO IS YOUR COMPETITION? IS ANYONE ELSE PROVIDING SIMILAR SERVICES OR PRODUCTS?   *189*

7. HOW IS YOUR COMPETITION DOING? ARE THEY BUSY? ARE THEY TURNING AWAY BUSINESS THEY COULD REFER TO YOU?   *191*

8. WHAT SPECIALTY OR "NICHE" CAN YOU CARVE OUT FOR YOURSELF?   *191*

9. HOW WILL YOU IDENTIFY PEOPLE OR COMPANIES THAT
   NEED WHAT YOU CAN OFFER?   *192*

10. WHAT CAN YOU OFFER THAT YOUR COMPETITION DOES
    NOT OFFER? COULD YOU DO WHAT THEY DO BETTER
    IN SOME WAY?   *196*

11. HOW WILL YOU LET YOUR POTENTIAL CUSTOMERS AND
    CLIENTS KNOW ABOUT WHAT YOU WILL OFFER?   *197*

12. DO YOU KNOW ANYONE OR ANY COMPANY THAT NEEDS
    WHAT YOU OFFER RIGHT NOW? HOW MANY SUCH
    POTENTIAL CLIENTS DO YOU KNOW?   *198*

13. DO YOU KNOW PEOPLE IN OTHER FIELDS WHO WORK
    REGULARLY WITH THE PEOPLE OR COMPANIES THAT
    NEED WHAT YOU HAVE TO OFFER? SUCH PEOPLE CAN
    BECOME YOUR "GATEKEEPERS."   *201*

14. HOW MUCH MONEY DO YOU NEED TO HAVE COMING
    IN EACH MONTH?   *203*

15. HOW MUCH WILL YOU NEED TO CHARGE AND HOW MANY
    HOURS OR DAYS WILL YOU NEED TO BILL FOR IN ORDER
    TO PRODUCE THE MONTHLY INCOME YOU NEED? IS THIS
    FEE WITHIN THE RANGE PEOPLE WILL PAY YOU?   *206*

16. HOW CAN YOU SUPPORT YOURSELF UNTIL YOU HAVE
    ENOUGH BUSINESS COMING IN?   *209*

17. WHAT START-UP COSTS WILL YOU HAVE?   *210*

18. HOW WILL YOU FINANCE THE START-UP COSTS INVOLVED
    TO ADEQUATELY SET UP, EQUIP, SUPPLY, AND MARKET
    YOUR BUSINESS?   *212*

19. DO YOU HAVE A GOOD CREDIT RATING?   *214*

20. DO YOU HAVE TWO CREDIT CARDS: ONE FOR BUSINESS,
    ONE FOR PERSONAL EXPENSES?   *215*

21. HOW COMMITTED ARE YOU TO PROCEEDING WITH YOUR
    VENTURE?   *217*

22. DO YOU HAVE A SEPARATE AREA IN YOUR HOME WHERE
    YOU CAN WORK PRODUCTIVELY?   *217*

23. DO YOU HAVE THE SUPPORT OF YOUR FAMILY
    AND FRIENDS?   *219*

24. HAVE YOU CHECKED THE ZONING REGULATIONS AND
    HOMEOWNER-ASSOCIATION RESTRICTIONS TO SEE
    IF YOU CAN LEGALLY OPERATE A MONEYMAKING
    VENTURE FROM YOUR HOME?   *219*

25. WILL YOUR NEIGHBORS HAVE ANY OBJECTION TO
    YOUR DOING THE TYPE OF WORK YOU PLAN TO DO
    FROM YOUR HOME?   *220*

26. DOES WHAT YOU INTEND TO DO REQUIRE ANY SPECIAL
    STATE LICENSE?   220

27. HAVE YOU OBTAINED A LOCAL BUSINESS LICENSE?   221

28. WILL YOU BE REQUIRED TO CHARGE SALES TAX ON
    WHAT YOU OFFER?   221

29. WILL YOU SELL YOUR PRODUCT OR SERVICE YOURSELF
    OR WILL YOU SELL IT THROUGH SOMEONE ELSE?   222

30. UNDER WHICH FORM OF BUSINESS DO YOU WISH TO
    OPERATE?   230

31. HAVE YOU SELECTED A NAME FOR YOUR ENTERPRISE?   230

32. HAVE YOU OPENED A SEPARATE BANK ACCOUNT AND
    INSTALLED A SEPARATE BUSINESS PHONE LINE?   232

33. DO YOU HAVE THE OFFICE EQUIPMENT AND SUPPLIES
    YOU NEED TO WORK MOST PRODUCTIVELY?   234

34. HAVE YOU ESTABLISHED A WORK SCHEDULE FOR
    YOURSELF?   234

35. IF YOU HAVE YOUNG CHILDREN, HAVE YOU MADE
    ARRANGEMENTS FOR NEEDED SUPPLEMENTARY
    CHILD CARE?   235

36. HAVE YOU LINED UP A TEAM OF PROFESSIONALS TO
    WHOM YOU CAN TURN FOR HELP IF YOU NEED IT?   235

37. DO YOU HAVE A SUPPORT NETWORK OF PROFESSIONAL
    COLLEAGUES AND FRIENDS?   236

38. ARE YOUR CARDS AND STATIONERY DESIGNED
    AND PRINTED?   238

39. DO YOU HAVE ADEQUATE INSURANCE TO PROTECT
    YOUR BUSINESS PROPERTY AND LIABILITY?   238

40. HAVE YOU MADE PLANS FOR OBTAINING HEALTH
    COVERAGE IF YOU ARE LEAVING BEHIND THE
    HEALTH INSURANCE YOU HAD AT A JOB?   238

41. HAVE YOU WRITTEN DOWN SPECIFIC MEASURABLE
    GOALS FOR YOUR BUSINESS WITH A TARGET DATE
    AND ACTION PLAN FOR EACH GOAL?   241

42. DO YOU HAVE REALISTIC EXPECTATIONS?   242

43. ARE YOU WILLING TO READ, TAKE COURSES, STUDY,
    USE CONSULTANTS, AND OTHERWISE LEARN WHAT YOU
    NEED TO LEARN TO SUCCEED ON YOUR OWN?   243

44. WHERE WILL YOU TURN TO OBTAIN THE ADDITIONAL
    INFORMATION AND EXPERTISE YOU NEED?   246

45. ARE YOU WILLING TO EXPERIMENT UNTIL YOU FIND
    THE COMBINATION OF PRODUCTS, SERVICES, PRICING,
    AND MARKETING METHODS THAT WILL WORK FOR YOU?   247

46. DO YOU HAVE OR ARE YOU WILLING TO DEVELOP THE
TRAITS NECESSARY TO MANAGE YOURSELF AND MAKE
YOUR BUSINESS A SUCCESS?   *247*

47. ARE YOU WILLING TO STICK IT OUT AND PERSEVERE
UNTIL YOU SUCCEED?   *249*

PART III: Using Your Computer in Business   *251*

3.1. THE IDEAL HOME OFFICE   *254*

COMPUTER EQUIPMENT   *255*

PROTECTING YOURSELF FROM THE COMPUTER'S
OCCUPATIONAL HAZARDS   *264*

3.2. USING YOUR COMPUTER TO MANAGE YOUR MONEY   *269*

FINDING A SIMPLE WAY TO MANAGE YOUR MONEY   *269*

DETERMINING WHAT YOU NEED TO CHARGE AND HOW
MUCH BUSINESS YOU NEED TO GENERATE   *271*

KEEPING TRACK OF YOUR MONEY   *276*

ANALYZING YOUR PROFITABILITY   *277*

MAKING SURE YOU GET PAID   *280*

PREPARING ESTIMATED AND YEAR-END TAXES   *282*

3.3. COMPUTERIZING YOUR ADMINISTRIVIA   *283*

ORGANIZING TASKS AND RESPONSIBILITIES   *284*

EVERDAY ESSENTIALS FOR MANAGING INFORMATION
IN YOUR COMPUTER   *285*

MAKING TIME TO DO WHAT NEEDS TO BE DONE   *287*

PLANNING LARGE PROJECTS   *292*

MANAGING YOUR COMPUTER   *293*

3.4. USING TECHNOLOGY TO MARKET YOURSELF AND
INCREASE YOUR BUSINESS   *294*

GENERATING A STEADY FLOW OF BUSINESS   *296*

KEEPING TRACK OF YOUR GROWING SPHERE OF
BUSINESS CONTACTS   *297*

MAKING SURE YOUR CLIENTS AND CUSTOMERS KEEP
YOU IN MIND   *300*

CREATING A PROFESSIONAL IMAGE FOR YOUR BUSINESS   *305*

MAKING SURE CLIENTS AND CUSTOMERS CAN
REACH YOU: THE TELEPHONE   *310*

TAKING MESSAGES WHEN YOU'RE BUSY OR OUT OF
THE OFFICE   *311*

RECEIVING CALLS WHEN YOU'RE OUT OF THE OFFICE   *314*

HANDLING INCOMING CALLS WHILE YOU'RE ON THE
LINE WITH SOMEONE ELSE   317

NOT ENOUGH TELEPHONE LINES   319

3.5. USING YOUR COMPUTER TO GO ONLINE TO FIND
CUSTOMERS, COLLECT MONEY, AND GET THE
INORMATION YOU NEED TO COMPETE   326

IDENTIFYING PROSPECTS FOR A MAILING LIST OR
DIRECT SOLICITATION   332

OBTAINING CREDIT INFORMATION ABOUT CLIENTS
AND THOSE WHO OWE YOU MONEY   333

FINDING FACTS FAST FOR BUSINESS PLANS, PROPOSALS,
REPORTS, AND DECISIONS   334

KEEPING CURRENT IN YOUR FIELD   337

FINDING NAMES AND TITLES FOR YOUR MAILINGS
AND SALES CALLS   338

FINDING A SUPPLIER FOR HARD-TO-FIND ITEMS AND
LOCATING GOOD PRICES   339

OVERCOMING ISOLATION   340

GETTING BUSINESS ONLINE   341

TIPS FOR USING ONLINE SERVICES   346

Appendix : Additional Useful Web Sites   349

PART I

101
Computer Home
Businesses Profiled

I N RESEARCHING THIS BOOK, we reviewed several hundred computer-related businesses from the over 1,500 self-employment careers we have in the appendix to our book *Finding Your Perfect Work*. Of course, as new businesses emerge, we consider these as well. The task of selecting from an overwhelming set of choices and paring them down as particularly suitable required that we establish criteria for inclusion in this book.

The first screening question was: Is using the computer the core activity of the business, or is the computer an ancillary tool used for e-mail, bookkeeping, and writing? It's unusual for us to find home-based businesspeople—though we do find some—who do not use a computer, in one form or another. Our goal, however, was to identify those businesses that depend significantly on the computer. For example, a person doing Web-site design or desktop publishing clearly requires a computer at the heart of the business, while an export agent uses a computer to run his or her business and there were export agents before personal computers.

Additionally, we also included businesses in which using a computer to conduct the essential tasks involved makes the business substantially more profitable than trying to do it without one. A property-management service, for example, can be much more effective and efficient by using a spreadsheet program to track their clients' income, expenses, and tax information than by trying to rely on pen, paper, and calculators.

Beyond this logical parameter, however, several other criteria influenced our decisions, as follows:

Income Potential

G iven the title of the book, we were next interested in businesses that would offer the opportunity to provide meaningful incomes to the owners. In general, we searched for businesses in which the income potential would either be enough to categorize it as the equivalent of a full-time job, or enough to remunerate the person who does the business part time and is counting on a certain level of income to make working worth the time. The figures we've quoted for income reflect information from interviews with people in the field, or are reasonable estimates based on our knowledge and information about the field. Please note, however, that the fees and hourly rates we mention may vary due to a person's skill, experience, geographic location, and many other factors, so you will need to consider your personal circumstances in assessing your income potential.

We've also included several businesses that one might do on a less than part-time basis, but which we feel are worthwhile as add-ons to an existing business. For example, we review the business called "data conversion service," in which you assist companies that are changing software or upgrading computers and therefore need to convert massive amounts of old data to a new format without losing it. Chances are that if you're already running a related business, you could at least find clients over the course of a year who need this work and would hire you once they know that you offer the service. By adding "data conversion" to your letterhead, writing some news columns, or giving speeches or seminars, you may therefore get some business income you would not have had otherwise. This is true of all the add-on businesses we've included.

Last, we've also included a few "idea businesses." These are possible businesses that reflect the fact that computers, and especially the Internet, often generate new ways to make money. These businesses are simply ideas for businesses; they're not yet tested. As far as we know, no one is actually doing them, unlike all the other businesses we included, which a substantial number of people are not only doing but doing successfully. While some other books mix hypothetical businesses with real ones and leave you wondering which are which, we have clearly identified these businesses as "ideas" with the lightbulb icon. We've included them in the book because our experience suggests that each one could be a good business for the person who has the right mix of skills to make it work.

Reasonable Ease of Entry

Our next criterion involved selecting businesses that for the most part are relatively easy to start and do not require special academic degrees. In the majority of cases, the business depends not on a diploma but on knowledge, experience, and ability. For instance, while it may help to have a B.A. or M.A. in finance to do business-plan writing or proposal writing, the degree is not at all necessary to succeed, since one's knowledge and experience in many different areas are likely to be much more critical in getting clients and performing well in the business.

It is important to mention, however, that most of the businesses we've included do work best if you can bring some background or experience to the table. Actually, we believe that this is true for any business venture, computer based or not. The person who has previously worked in the medical field, for example, will be able to start a medical-billing business more quickly than the person who has never seen an ICD-9 code; similarly the person who has worked with numbers before is probably better equipped to open a financial-planning or billing-and-invoicing service than the person with a speech-therapy background.

In short, the experience you already have is usually proportional to how long or short a learning curve you will experience and how many barriers you will encounter along the way. If you know little about a field, you will probably need to read a great deal, talk to people in the business, and take more time getting your business off the ground. You will also be more likely to struggle through the initial stages, especially when it comes to figuring out how much time it takes to get a job done and what you can charge for your work. In fact, novices frequently underestimate how long it will take them to complete a task, or they make mistakes and spend double or triple the time they expected to spend, and so end up earning much less money per job.

Although the businesses we've included generally have a reasonable ease of entry, we caution you to fully explore the specific personal issues that may have an impact on your success. We'll address this subject more completely in Part 2.

Variety

The expanding use of computers and software in recent years into vastly differing areas of work has meant that many, many fields are now computerized to some extent. We therefore aimed to include a wide variety of ways in which people of diverse interests could make a living and work using computers. We've selected a broad assortment of professions, from writing and publishing to health, finance, real estate, allied medical fields, teaching, design, business administration, marketing, music, and various other artistic endeavors.

Demand

The demand for any business varies from community to community and from time to time. Technological change has made businesses we included in earlier editions of this book obsolete. At this writing, businesses included in this book are, to the best of our knowledge, not saturated and have a reasonable chance of finding customers.

!!! SHOULD YOU BUY A BUSINESS OPPORTUNITY? !!!

Although most home businesses are started from scratch, a variety of the businesses we discuss in this book can be started through a "business opportunity," a presumably complete blueprint you purchase from a company already in the business or that has some experience in the field. As you read this book, the question will naturally arise: Is it worth your money to buy one of these business opportunities or should you go it alone and rely on your own resources? Well, our response is that business opportunities are sometimes useful, and sometimes not, and you will need to do some homework to learn which is which. Here's why.

First, on the positive side, business opportunities, also known as "seller-assisted marketing plans," are simply a matter of people selling their expertise to help others start a business. Unlike franchises, their value is that you are seldom obliged to pay continuing fees or a percentage of your income year in and year out, nor are you required to use their company name and adhere to strict internal rules about how you run your business. With a business opportunity, all you are doing is paying someone to sell you the ways and means to start your business and operate it in a way that has supposedly proved successful. The seller of the opportunity has presumably made all the mistakes a start-up business makes and through trial and error has come up with a business that works consistently. When you buy a business opportunity, you receive the benefit of years of groundwork that, hopefully, you won't have to repeat.

However, on the negative side, we emphasize two key operative terms that we feel people need to consider if they are interested in a business-opportunity package. The first is *expertise*. We believe you must ask plenty of questions about the seller's true expertise in this business. How long has he or she been in business? Is the seller currently involved in performing the same business in another area, and if so what are the results? How much does the seller really know about this business? The second operative term is *opportunity*, meaning that you need to assess who is really getting the opportunity here, you or the seller? Is there really a market for the business large enough to fulfill your expectations and financial needs, or is the seller of the business opportunity getting the only real opportunity?

Unfortunately, since the business-opportunity market exploded in the past decade, there have been highly reputable vendors, but there have also been many others who crossed the limits of honesty and integrity in selling or pricing their packages. As a result, increasing numbers of states are monitoring the industry, with about half the states specifically regulating seller-assisted marketing plans that have a purchase over $500; a few states have lower thresholds. Most of these regulations are fairly weak, but they often require that businesses must register with the state Attorney General's Office, that each prospective customer must be given in advance an offering prospectus listing the executives of the company and stating specifically what is included in the price of the business opportunity, including any goods, services, and training. In many states, the buyer also gets a period of time, such as three days, in which to change his mind and obtain a refund of his purchase price. Last, many states bar the seller from making representations about how much income you can earn, or if allowed to do so, he or she must report how many prior purchasers of the plan have made back their initial investments.

Ultimately, our advice to you is:

1. Check out as many references as possible before buying a business opportunity. Use Dun & Bradstreet; previous buyers; current operators; state; county and city consumer-protection offices; and Better Business Bureaus (*www.bbb.org*) to find out if the company has a good reputation and record of honest dealings. Furthermore, if you live in California, Connecticut, Florida, Georgia, Indiana, Iowa, Kentucky, Louisiana, Maine, Maryland, Michigan, Minnesota, Nebraska, New Hampshire, North Carolina, Ohio, Oklahoma, South Carolina, South Dakota, Texas, Utah, Virginia, or Washington remember that a business-opportunity company that sells in your state, no matter where it is headquartered, must be registered and follow your state's guidelines. Telephone numbers and links to each of these states' sites can be found on the Federal Trade Commission Web site at *www.ftc.gov/bcp/franchise/netbusop.htm*.

2. Find out specifically what you will get with your purchase in terms of training, materials, and hardware/software. Ask also about how many other people in your area may already own the business or will be allowed to purchase it, since you want to avoid entering an already saturated market. Do your own checking in the community as well.

3. Don't hesitate to negotiate on price. Some business-opportunity companies advertise a high price but will drop it if you bargain with them.

4. Don't expect that you will necessarily be more successful by starting your business through the purchase of an opportunity than you would be if you began on your own. In fact, buying an opportunity can even be deceiving, leading you to think you can work a little less hard or that you have a backup system to support you through hard times. In reality, although you may have a blueprint for how to do your business, getting it successfully under way will still require hard work, long hours, and creative thinking to bring it into the real world of cash flow from satisfied customers.

So watch out for myths about business opportunities. Getting any business off the ground requires dedication, good personal skills, and business acumen, all of which business opportunities cannot truly provide. Also, the great number of companies selling these opportunities has in some cases saturated the country with a particular business to the point that a new entrant today would have a hard time competing profitably.

If you're on the fence about buying a business opportunity instead of starting a business from scratch, check out our book *Home Businesses You Can Buy,* for more in-depth information to help with this decision.

GROUP 1: Type of Business Category

 Word Business—The alphabet block refers to businesses that are related to word-processing, writing, and publishing.

 Numbers Business—The # sign identifies businesses that are related to number-crunching like bookkeeping and auditing.

 Database Business—A set of Rolodex cards refers to businesses that are based upon creating and maintaining a database, such as a referral service or a software-locator service.

 Graphics Business—A T-square/triangle identifies a business that is based primarily upon using graphics software like desktop video or market mapping.

 Computer-Service Business—A floppy computer disk indicates businesses that involve providing a service to help others better use or maintain their computer, such as computer consulting or a computer-repair service.

 Communications Businesses—A telephone symbolizes modem- and communication-based businesses like Web-site publication, information broker and electronic clipping services.

MS   **Multimedia Business**—Interlocked *MS* indicates that the businesses involve producing or managing multimedia content including sound, video, graphics, and animation.

CGD   **Multiple-Application Businesses**—A series of interlocking rings represents businesses that rely upon multiple applications like association management, which may involve word processing, numbers crunching, and database functions.

GROUP 2: Income Potential

Full Time—A full glass identifies businesses that have sufficient income potential to provide a full-time income. However, most full-time businesses can be operated part-time as well.

Part Time—A crescent moon refers to businesses like keeping sports league statistics or creating computerized astrological charts that are best suited to a sideline business for supplementing other income and most likely would not be able to produce a full-time income.

Add-on—A plus sign indicates a business like a disk backup service that makes an ideal add-on service to an existing business. While these businesses most likely will not produce sufficient revenue to become a full-time or even part-time, stand-alone business, they can be an excellent way to attract initial customers for a related business or as additional services you provide for your existing customers.

GROUP 3: Location of Work

At Home—A house indicates that the business can be done AT home. While you will probably need to go out of your home for client meetings, or to market these businesses or even to pick up work, you will be able to do the actual work of these businesses in your home.

From Home—A car indicates that while you can run these businesses FROM home you will actually do most of your work elsewhere. In these businesses, your home can be your base of operation, but they will take you away from home to deliver your product or service.

GROUP 4: Noteworthy Characteristic

In this last group, we have identified one major characteristic we believe distinguishes a particular business, as follows:

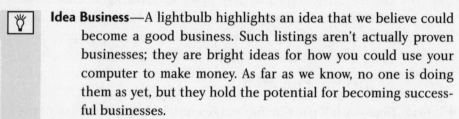

Idea Business—A lightbulb highlights an idea that we believe could become a good business. Such listings aren't actually proven businesses; they are bright ideas for how you could use your computer to make money. As far as we know, no one is doing them as yet, but they hold the potential for becoming successful businesses.

High Income Potential—These businesses can potentially produce a six-figure income without moving out of the home or adding more than one staff person.

Evergreen—These businesses have been around for many years and will undoubtedly be around for many years. We call them evergreen businesses.

Recession Resistant—These are businesses that tend to weather or even prosper during economic downturns.

Up and Coming—These are businesses that are on the rise in popularity.

Low Start-up Costs—These businesses do not require much up-front investment to get under way.

Using the Resources in This Book

At the end of each profile, we have listed resources that can be useful to you in learning about or actually operating each business. This information is intended as a starting point. Most of the resources are not specifically about how to start such a business. However, check out their Web sites and the links to other sites they provide. Some may provide you with general information and others may be useful for networking, but unless indicated, none are in the franchising business or offer actual business plans to get you started.

The resources are generally listed in the following order:

Books
Magazines/Journals
Software

Web Sites
Associations/Organizations
Training Courses
Franchises/Business Opportunities

As we stated earlier, the businesses listed here do not require an advanced degree or years of formal study. Many, however, do require expertise. With the proper background and experience, perhaps a course or two, extensive research, and initiative you can be up and running with even the most complicated of businesses, such as CGI or Java Programming, in six months' time. Also, please note, these descriptions are presented only as "thumbnail" sketches, simple overviews, of the main aspects involved in starting and running each of these businesses. They are provided as starting points from which you can begin the journey that might lead you to an exciting and rewarding home-based business.

1

Abstracting Service

Over ten thousand databases provide a continuing supply of work to abstracting services. An abstractor's job is to read articles of all types (journals, magazines, etc.) and condense the information into brief overviews of about ten to fifteen sentences for storage in a database. Researchers and browsers use the condensed information online as well as from information-oriented CD/DVD products. In addition to or instead of condensing articles, an abstractor may be required to index articles, by creating a list of key words so that a computer can locate an article quickly when a user requests a search.

In addition to database applications, abstracting services also frequently work with corporations, creating summaries of books and articles of interest to the companies' executives and technical people, as well as to their customers. Some corporations make extensive use of abstracting in order to stay up-to-date with our burgeoning information-based society.

To run an abstracting service you need to be a fast reader and have the ability to synthesize and consolidate information, as well as excellent writing skills. It also helps to have firsthand knowledge of the areas in which you work, since much of the material is specialized in scientific and technical fields. Finally, given that the profession feeds into online information services, you must also have or acquire a familiarity with database services, CD publishers, and other companies that supply and deal with information.

The best way to get business as an abstracting service is to write several samples that you can use in a portfolio to show database publishers and others. Many database publishers hire only local freelancers. To find publishers in your area, decide which type of database you want to work with and search a directory like the *Epsco Index and Abstract Dictionary* or *Gale Directory of Online, Portable, and Internet Databases* to identify publishers in that field by address. To get corporate work, contact corporate librarians and the department responsible for technical writing.

An abstractor can normally charge from $5 and up per abstract. Some abstractors charge by the hour with fees starting at $25 per hour. Specialists such as those in scientific fields can earn top money. This business is also a good add-on to an indexing service, or an editing or technical writing service.

Books

Starting an Indexing Business, Enid Zafron, Information Today, Inc., ISBN 1573870749.

An Indexer's Guide to the Internet, Lori Lathrop, Information Today, Inc., ISBN 1573870781.

Associations

AMERICAN SOCIETY OF INDEXERS, 10200 West 44th Avenue, Suite 304, Wheat Ridge, CO 80033, (303) 463-2887. While primarily for back-of-book indexers, this is the closest organization for individual providers. The society publishes and distributes to publishers without charge the *Indexer Services Directory,* a directory of freelance indexers, listing its freelance members in terms of their specific subject expertise or background. It also offers a number of publications and training courses. *www. asindexing.org.*

AMERICAN SOCIETY FOR INFORMATION SCIENCE AND TECHNOLOGY, (301) 495-0900, *www.asis.org*

NATIONAL FEDERATION OF ABSTRACTING AND INFORMATION SERVICES (NFAIS), (215) 893-1561, *www.nfais.org*

2

Answering / Voice-Mail Service

There's no shortage of answering services for businesses and professionals who need telephone coverage when they're away from their offices, but most services simply take brief messages in a cold, impersonal fashion. Therefore, a home-based business can fulfill a need by providing a truly personalized answering service that operates like a knowledgeable administrative assistant. Such an answering service is particularly useful for small businesses and individuals such as plumbers, contractors, and repairmen who often miss new opportunities by not returning a call or responding to a need immediately. Other potential clients include businesses that need or want to have a "live" person answering their phone because their customers expect it or would be put off by a pager, an answering machine, or voice mail, as well as people on the move like salespeople and long-distance truckers, military personnel, students, and, if you think about it, people in jail such as white-collar criminals, and other individuals who don't have their own phones and need a private answering line. Still other businesses need twenty-four-hour answering for orders on their 800 phone numbers.

The logistics of operating an answering service are perfect for the home-based person. Most phone companies can now set up your phone to ring differently for each incoming phone number, so you can answer the calls with whichever business greeting identifies the client being called. You can then take messages for your clients using your computer and word-processing, database, or contact-management software program that allows you to keyboard a complete record of the information. With an internal fax/modem board, you can then immediately fax the typed transcript of the call to your client's office so that the message awaits the person upon return, or you could call or page the client if immediate action is required. The advantage of this kind of operation is the level of support a home-based person can supply his or her clients. You will screen calls, decide what's important and what's not, take messages, give responses to the client's customers, and in general represent his or her business more fully than a typical answering service.

An additional option in running an answering service is to offer a sophisticated voice-mail system for new business clients who will pay you rather than purchasing and setting up their own voice-mail system when they're just starting out. Voice mail has many advantages over a traditional answering machine, since it can recite multiple outgoing messages using a menu system ("Press one for x, two for y," and so on), and it can direct incoming messages to specific mailbox locations for privacy. Running a voice-mail system requires a dedicated PC with a large hard drive (because of the space required to convert voice to digital form), a voice-mail board, and software. You may also need to reconfigure and possibly add to your incoming phone lines to handle the needs of your clients.

The fees you can charge for this business will depend on your locale and the type of clients you get, but many small businesses will pay for a high-quality answering service if you can help them win a few additional customers. On average you can charge about $35 per month for a specified number of calls—usually seventy to seventy-five—with a surcharge of 25 cents for each call beyond that number. Other calls such as "wake-up" and reminder calls for appointments are typically billed on a "per call" basis at about 50 cents per call.

The best ways to get business include networking and advertising in the yellow pages and in local business newspapers. It helps to get clients to sign on for several months at a time. Additionally, referrals from satisfied clients can significantly expand your business, so you should also consider offering a promotion that gets clients to refer others to you in exchange for a discount.

Association

ASSOCIATION OF TELESERVICES INTERNATIONAL, (866) 896-ATSI, *www.atsi.org/publications/*

Software

TALKING TECHNOLOGY INTERNATIONAL, INC., makes voice-mail systems, auto dialer, and predictive dialer software, (510) 339-8275, *www.tti.net.*

Association Management Services

People love to belong. As a result they join associations, clubs, and organizations of all kinds based on the sharing of hobbies and economic interests as well as religious and fraternal affiliations. In many cases, such associations are small enough that their members can take care of all organizational and administrative needs. But when an association grows beyond the size that its volunteer officers can effectively handle, they often turn to an association management service (also called an executive director service) to provide organizational and financial continuity.

As an association manager, you will probably find yourself responsible for keeping the files on membership and dues, paying bills, sending out frequent flyers and announcements to a mailing list, and possibly writing and publishing a monthly newsletter. As you might imagine, the more services you can offer, the more you can charge, and the higher class of clientele you can command. Similarly, the more efficient you are at performing these tasks, the more clients you might be able to handle. So running an association management service requires good management skills, a flexible communication style, and in today's PC-based environment, a fair amount of hands-on skill with many kinds of software: accounting and bookkeeping packages, contact and database management systems, and word-processing/desktop-publishing programs. You will probably need to know how to manage a Web site or hire a Webmaster. You may require good writing skills because you may be required to compose press releases, newsletters, and correspondence on behalf of your association. You should have marketing skills as well in order to attract new members. Revenues for managing associations can range from $25,000 to $50,000 or even more.

If you already have a background in management, finance, or administration, some of the best ways to get into this business are to contact the presidents of professional and trade associations directly, network with professional organizations, or offer to do a seminar on administration for volunteer organizations. You could also contact state associations that are not represented by lobbyists in your state capital and offer to represent them. You can also create your own Web site with metatags and links that direct people to your site. Alternatively, you might begin this business more informally until you gain a track record by volunteering to administrate a small group you belong to yourself, and then with experience you can survey the officers of other organizations in your community to locate paid opportunities.

Books

The Encyclopedia of Associations: National Organizations of the U.S.,
Gale Research, Detroit, MI, is available in the reference section of most libraries. This set is published annually and lists literally thousands of

local, state, regional, and national associations, both large and small. It can be one of your primary sources for locating prospective clientele. ISBN: 078762229X.

Legal Risk Management for Associations: A Legal Compliance Guide for Volunteers and Employees of Trade and Professional Associations, Jerald A. Jacobs, David W. Ogden, American Psychological Association, ISBN: 1557983046.

Managing Your Future as an Association: Thinking About Trends and Working with Their Consequences, 1993–2020, Jennifer Jarratt (editor), Joseph F. Coates, American Society of Association Executives, ISBN: 088034083.

Principles of Association Management, Henry Ernstthal and Vivian Jefferson, Washington, DC: American Society of Association Executives, ISBN: 0880341750.

Organizations

AMERICAN SOCIETY OF ASSOCIATION EXECUTIVES (ASAE), (202) 626-2723, *www.asaenet.org*

INTERNATIONAL ASSOCIATION OF ASSOCIATION MANAGEMENT COMPANIES, (630) 655-1669. *www.iaamc.org*

THE SOCIETY FOR NON-PROFIT ORGANIZATIONS, (734) 451-3582, *www.snpo.org*

4

Astrology Charting Service

If you believe that your fate and destiny are determined or influenced by the stars and are willing to serve other people who believe and will pay for this information, you can use your home-based PC to run an astrological charting service. All types of people consult astrologers before making business and personal decisions, such as changing jobs, getting married, moving, making investments, and so on. Some businesses use astrologers when assessing the compatibility of new hires with their organization.

The computer is the perfect tool to track astrological databases, such as the movement of the stars and planets around the zodiac, along with a client's birthday and other relevant information.

By tapping into the astrological databases available on several software packages, you can prepare very quickly what formerly took hours of time: an astrological chart with interpretations about future events. Astrological forecasting software requires only the customer's date, place, and time of birth. With this information, it determines the configurations of the heavens at that moment and place and compiles a star chart from which a forecast is drawn. Then you can print out the client's information as a simple table or you can produce a high-quality full-color chart with beautiful graphics and designs.

It's a good idea to start your career in astrology by taking courses at local colleges or even hiring a tutor to coach you. There are also various online at-home study programs you can take.

For initial consultations of about sixty to ninety minutes, with a comprehensive astrological chart, you can charge from $80 to $150. Some celebrity astrologers, of course, are reported to receive fees in the thousands. What you can charge depends on your ability and credentials. Astrologers also work with clients on the phone and charge by the half hour, usually $30 to $50. Depending on where your callers are from, you may need to vary your rate according to the cost of living where the caller lives. For single charts you can charge from $15 to $75, depending on whether they're natal, compatibility, or forecasting reports.

When seeking new clients, the most successful marketing aims at getting people to buy a chart at special turning points in their lives, for example a birthday, wedding, or birth. It's often at these milestones that people want to know what the future holds. Word of mouth is often how you will get business, and giving free readings is a good way to begin developing a reputation. Advertising in local "New Age" publications and on the Web is also effective. You might even consider writing a regular column in a local publication.

You may want to specialize in specific areas such as financial, medical, psychological, relationship, predictive, sun sign, Vedic, and karmic astrology, or you can define one of your own. Some astrologers have even found more specialized niches such as horse racing or stock-market timing, sometimes based on their prior career or industry. Resorts and cruise ships are also worth investigating. In fact, some cruise lines offer astrology classes and readings for their guests.

Books

A Handbook for the Self-Employed Astrologer, Robert P. Blaschke, Earthwalk School of Astrology, ISBN: 096689782X.

The Astrologer's Handbook, Frances Sakoian, HarperResource, ISBN: 006272004X.

The Creative Astrologer: Effective Single-Session Counseling, Noel Tyl Llewellyn Publications, ISBN: 1567187404.

How to Start, Maintain, and Expand an Astrological Practice, L.A.B. Professional Publishing, ISBN: 0970069626, available from the Organization for Professional Astrologers.

Associations

AMERICAN FEDERATION OF ASTROLOGERS, INC., (888) 301-7630, (480) 838-1751, *www.astrologers.com*

INTERNATIONAL SOCIETY FOR ASTROLOGICAL RESEARCH, *www.isarastrology.com*

ORGANIZATION FOR PROFESSIONAL ASTROLOGERS provides an e-newsletter and *The Career Astrologer*, a quarterly forum, *www.professional-astrology.org*.

Software

Many companies produce astrology software. You can get free charts made on a number of Web sites. Astrolabe (*www.alabe.com*) offers free charts on its site and also links to other sites with free charts, (800) 843-6682.

Training

Training in astrology can be obtained from a mentor or from schools and online courses, such as:

FORUM ON ASTROLOGY (*www.forumonastrology.com*) offers an online study program.

KEPLER COLLEGE OF ASTROLOGICAL ARTS AND SCIENCES, (425) 673-4292, *www.kepler.edu*

Auction Merchant

The Internet has become a sales arena to be reckoned with, and many people are using online auctions such as eBay, Yahoo! Auctions, Amazon.com, uBid, and bidz.com to both buy and sell just about anything you can think of. Tens of thousands of individuals and small businesses make their living this way. So, if you have a product to sell, a little computer savvy, and a willingness to manage the inflow and outflow of product, you can use the Internet to market your product to the world without having to leave your house. Working as an online auction merchant can be a part-time or full-time venture.

As an online auction merchant you pay the auction site a small fee to list your product. For this fee the site acts as an electronic intermediary by listing your wares. You can operate a business with little overhead and enjoy a volume of sales that you might expect in a well-trafficked commercial location.

When you sell at an auction site you don't need to maintain a Web site or a database. You follow the process established by the auction site. For your part, you have to create descriptions of your products, manage your inventory, track sales, and, most important, satisfy your customers. So it's best to specialize in selling what you know or what you're willing to learn about.

To sell via an auction site you need an up-to-date computer, high-speed Internet access such as cable, DSL, or satellite, or wireless, a digital camera to take photos of your product, and good lighting and a backdrop for photographing your products. Products can be shipped through the postal service or a courier service. You'll want to check out which method gives your customers good service at a reasonable cost. Typically, the seller offers the buyer a choice of shipping method and the buyer pays the shipping charges in advance.

To receive payment for your goods sold at auction you can accept credit cards and/or use an online third-party banking system, such as Pay Pal, which is owned by eBay, or Western Union's BidPay at *www.bidpay.com*. BidPay, however, at this writing does not accept accounts using Master-Card.

To help manage the details of auction selling, you can use third-party selling tools like Vendio (*www.vendio.com*) and Marketworks (*www.auction works.com*). These services automate the auction process, by sending out end-of-auction e-mails and uploading your photos. They also can track buyers and keep stock of inventory. There are many of these tools available so research what they do, if they come with technical support, and what the cost is.

It is important to describe in detail what you are selling and to include a good photograph. If you are selling used articles, honestly describe any flaws or blemishes.

A way of sustaining an online auction business is to price your goods competitively and provide excellent customer service. Ratings that come from customer feedback are displayed on the auction's site and can make or break your business. Building up favorable feedback ratings as soon as possible is a good way to jump-start your business. You should keep track of buyers and stay in touch with them by advising them of sales and promotions and by special newsletters.

Books

eBay for Dummies, Marsha Collier, For Dummies, 2004,
  ISBN: 0764556541.

eBay Hacks: 100 Industrial-Strength Tips and Tools, David A. Karp,
  O'Reilly, ISBN: 0596005644.

eBay Power SellerI, Debra Schepp, Brad Schepp, McGraw-Hill Osborne,
  ISBN: 0-07-225869-1.

The New Basic Sellers Guide to eBay, plus other related books by Skip
  McGrath are available at *www.auction-sellers-resource.com*.

Starting an eBay Business for Dummies, Marsha Collier, For Dummies,
  ISBN: 0764515470.

Sell It on eBay, Jim Heid, Toby Malina, Peachpit Press, ISBN: 0321223764.

Web Sites

www.auctionbytes.com
www.auction-sellers-resource.com
www.auction-resources.com

Backup Service

People in most businesses take little or no precautions when it comes to backing up their computers. They fail to think about the financial loss and operational problems they would incur if their files were damaged or destroyed due to fire, theft, or hardware failure. Even businesses that make backups usually don't do it on a regular basis nor do they keep their backup files off site for safe keeping. So if you are a technically oriented computer buff, and especially if you already have a computer consulting, training, or repair/maintenance service, you could have a ready-made group of clients for whom you could provide backup services as a profitable addition to your business.

You can run a backup service in any of several ways. Some services go to the client's place of business and perform the backup on site, using a portable external hard drive or tape drive, taking the data away to a vault or to their home office for safekeeping. Other backup services do the work over the phone lines in the evening when the client's business is closed, using remote communications software and Internet connections to back up the data to a hard drive on their home computers. Depending on your client's needs, you can perform the backup as frequently as every night or as seldom as once a month. Still another idea is to provide data archiving and backup using CD-ROM.

The technology for backup services is continually improving, with many new devices on the market that offer high-speed backups and complete accuracy. Additionally, communications software such as *PCAnywhere* allows the backup process to run quickly and smoothly. Data-compression programs can cut a file down to a quarter of its original size, thereby saving valuable tape or disk space.

Potential clients for a backup service range from the administrative departments of large companies in need of regular backups or off-site safe-keeping to small businesses and stores, doctors' offices, and others who don't want to spend the time or don't have the expertise. The way this service is priced varies. Some charge a flat monthly fee; others charge by the megabyte; still others by the minute. You can also beef up your fees by adding other services such as encryption of data and maintenance services such as defragmentation and cleaning of hard drives, virus checking, laser-printer maintenance, and renting out hardware for companies with temporary problems or growing needs.

We recommend this business and its allied services largely as an add-on to any existing computer business because, from the research we've done, the costs of marketing and operating a stand-alone backup business are apparently not worth the income. The business can be good, however, if you have clients for whom you already provide related computer services. Also, you may expand this business by offering other computer preventive maintenance services, such as checking for viruses, cleaning the heads of floppy disk drives, and defragmenting hard disks.

Books

How to Back Up Your PC, Patrick Bultema, Fresno, CA, Mike Murach & Associates, ISBN: 0911625631.

Software

The Remote Backup Business Kit, (800) 945-4491, (901) 850-9920, remote-backup.com/bizkits/

7

Billing and Invoicing Service

As vital to a business as billing is, many small businesses and independent professionals get behind schedule in getting their bills and invoices mailed out to their clients. Often this is because a lot of small businesses still do invoices inefficiently by hand, but most are simply too busy to stay on top of their bookkeeping needs. This reality opens the door for the person who can specialize in billing and invoicing and who understands how to bring in the cash when a company needs it.

The best way to operate your billing service is to arrange a regular daily or weekly pickup, either by fax or in person, of all your client's transaction reports. Then, using any one of today's sophisticated billing software packages, you keyboard each transaction received, update the customer's total balance, and print out the invoice for mailing. Finally, as checks are mailed in either to your address or directly to the business, you record the payment and do any account maintenance required. In the case of tardy payments, you might also perform "soft" collections such as issuing reminder invoices or calling the customer in accordance with your state laws on dunning.

A billing and invoicing business is easy to start and requires only a small investment in equipment. You will need a computer and printer to print invoices, and one of the professional billing and invoicing software packages such as *TimeSlips* (for Windows and for Macintosh).

Although you don't need to be an accountant to perform billing and invoicing, at the minimum, you should be very organized and efficient, have excellent math skills, and be familiar with your computer and software. Additionally, we believe this business works best as an add-on to an existing bookkeeping or other business service where you are already providing work for a client who can afford to hire you. The risks of the business include not getting enough clients to keep your business profitable and spending too much time getting the invoices done to make it worth your time.

The fees you can charge for billing and invoicing depend on the type of clients you find and the time it takes you to do the work. If your client is a small professional practice, such as a design firm or law office, you can probably charge an hourly fee between $15 and $30 dollars. On the other hand, some billing services are able to negotiate to take a percentage of any unpaid invoices that they manage to collect through their efforts.

Software

Timeslips software, by Best Software SB, Inc., (800) 285-0999,
(770) 492-6414, *www.timeslips.com*

8

Bookkeeping Service

Every business requires bookkeeping, so this is one field for which there will always be a need; but the need for outside bookkeeping services is changing. The number of small businesses is growing, but low-cost and easy-to-use accounting software makes bookkeeping an increasingly do-it-yourself function. However, many business owners will still need the help of a bookkeeper because they encounter problems using their software. For example, if they are using a single-entry system, their bank statements and check register may not balance. So enter the bookkeeping "consultant."

Traditionally, a bookkeeping service performs the tasks of doing the books, up to the point where an accountant can step in to interpret the financial information for the client and provide business and tax-planning advice. These tasks include keeping a client's financial records (accounts receivable and payable), reconciling bank statements, doing payroll and invoicing, and preparing financial reports (profit/loss statements and balance sheets) for tax or accounting purposes

Many excellent software packages are available today to fully computerize a home PC-based bookkeeping service, including *QuickBooks* by Intuit (*www.intuit.com*), and *Peachtree* (*www.peachtree.com*) and others.

To succeed in this business you must enjoy doing detailed, accurate, and reliable work. Although you don't need a degree in accounting or a professional designation to be a bookkeeper, you can increase your credibility by taking bookkeeping courses and become certified.

You can charge between $15 and $60 an hour depending on where you live and the industries you work with. Some bookkeepers charge by the job or transaction—checks, invoices, deposits, purchases. Some clients prefer being billed on a monthly or weekly basis. When you bill at a flat weekly or monthly rate, make sure to have a letter of engagement that defines what you will be doing and when you will be charging for extra work.

You may want to specialize in a particular industry, for example law firms, medical practices, retailers, or any other industry well represented in your area. Your most likely clients are businesses with fewer than six employees.

One of the most effective ways to build your business is by face-to-face networking with business and trade organizations—for example, your local chamber of commerce. You may get work by referral and by doing work for CPA firms, other bookkeeping firms, and financial planners. In today's competitive marketplace it is wise to have your own Web site. A yellow pages listing will enable you to be found on Web directories like switchboard.com and anywho.com. Consider placing ads on local directory sites like Yahoo Get Local and SuperPages. You can also visit retail stores and services within a twenty- to thirty-minute drive from your home.

Books

Starting and Building Your Own Accounting Business, Wiley, ISBN: 0471351601.

How to Open Your Own In-Home Bookkeeping Service, Julie A. Mucha, available both in print and as an e-book, (619) 449-0675, *www.inhome bookkeeping.bizland.com*

Web Sites

www.accounting-and-bookkeeping-tips.com, operated by the Universal Accounting Center, sells a home-study bookkeeping and accounting course (*www.universalaccounting.com*), (800) 343-4827.

www.aipb.org/accounting_bookkeeping_tax_links.php offers over 150 links to free tax and accounting information.

Association

THE AMERICAN INSTITUTE OF PROFESSIONAL BOOKKEEPERS, (800) 622-0121, *www.aipb.org*

Business Plan Writer

A business plan writer helps develop a road map for where a business is headed, laying out the estimates and projections of expenses and revenues that will predict whether the business is feasible. If you understand what's involved in the financial, marketing, and administrative aspects of taking a business idea from concept to reality, you have the general business know-how (accounting, bookkeeping, and marketing) to become a business plan writer. While business plan writers depend heavily on word processing and spreadsheets, helping a client successfully develop a business plan is as much a communications process as a writing task. You need to be able to see a business situation both from the owner's point of view and the potential funding source's outlook. Good business writing, grammar, and organizational skills are necessary, too.

Most experts advise that you develop plans on your own. Your clients are paying you to develop a plan that will stand out in terms of presentation, organization, and unique focus on the company. Specialized software is available to help the business plan writer analyze and present alternative projections for a business, use spreadsheets, and develop "what if" scenarios. These programs are helpful in helping you organize the content of a business plan, but we do not recommend that you use them exclusively to develop the plan. The best business plan writers create a unique plan for each client.

New businesses provide a good market for business planners, but often the best clients are those businesses that are well established and are seeking funding to expand. Other occasions when a business plan can be a necessity are when a business wants to franchise or to be acquired.

Business plan writing can be lucrative. Fees can range from $2,000 to $5,000 or more for each plan. Proven business plan writers can charge as much as $25,000 for working on a major project for a company seeking new financing. Typical gross earnings can range from $20,000 to $100,000 per year.

Developing a professional relationship with bank-lending officers and organizations like Small Business Development Centers that work with new entrepreneurs and who can refer business to you is one of the best ways to market yourself. Networking through trade and business organizations can also be effective, as well as giving speeches or teaching courses on starting and running a business. Showing a sample of your own business plan or other plans you have developed can be more important than having a brochure. Presenting courses at local educational institutions in writing business plans and small-business development may result in clients. Your students are likely to be entrepreneurs who may hire you to help them with their plans.

Books

Business Plans Kit for Dummies, Steven D. Peterson, Peter E. Jaret, For Dummies, ISBN: 0764553658.

The Ernst & Young Business Plan Guide, Eric S. Siegel, Brian R. Ford, Jay M. Bornstein, Wiley, ISBN: 0471578266.

The One Page Business Plan, Jim Horan, ISBN: 18913150-09-9.

The Successful Business Plan: Secrets & Strategies, Rhonda M. Abrams, Eugene Kleiner, ISBN: 0966963563.

Software

BizPlanBuilder (Jian Tools for Sales) *www.jian.com*

Business Plan Pro (Palo Alto Software), *www.palo-alto.com*

Plan Write, Business Resource Software, Inc., *www.brs-inc.com*

Tim Berry's Business Plan Toolkit (Palo Alto Software), *www.palo-alto.com*

Government Resources

Small Business Development Centers, located throughout the United States, are usually affiliated with educational institutions and sometimes chambers of commerce. They usually specialize in certain types or sizes of small businesses. To find one near you, a list is found at *http:sbdcnet.utsa.edu/sbdc.htm.*

10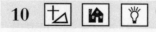

Clip-Art Service

Now that desktop publishing and Web-site development are predominant parts of business, trade, and professional communications, there is a need for generic and specialized illustrations that publishers can turn to when they need inexpensive and quick artwork. Many published pieces require visual material, from spot illustrations to large, colorful scenes, to accompany the written word or simply to spice up the layout.

If you have an artistic bent and are interested in learning to use design and drawing software, starting a clip-art business can earn you some extra income. You might focus your talents on doing specialized artwork, such as religious or technical drawings, or you might try to develop a unique style of art that you can then self-syndicate or sell to a clip-art software publisher. You can also purchase clip art from artists and dealers, perhaps to supplement what you create.

The challenge in running a clip-art business is marketing your work. If you want to go big-time, you might consider packaging your diskette or CD-ROM of clip art and selling it retail in as many outlets as you can get. Alternatively, you could pursue the smaller self-publishing route and market your art on your and others' Web sites, often called galleries, as well as advertising your work in computer magazines or publications. You could also sell subscriptions for a year-round clip-art service and provide monthly CDs of new art. Your clients could include advertising agencies, graphic designers, in-house art departments, and any organization that produces regular newsletters or other publications using illustrations.

There is no standard pricing for clip art in the industry, but if you have a distinctive or unusual style, you might be able to earn from a few extra thousand dollars per year to much more.

Book

Books, Books, Books: A Treasury of Clip Art, Darcie Clark Frohardt, Libraries Unlimited, ISBN: 1563082659.

Collection Agency

Many businesses rely on collection agencies to collect on delinquent accounts, and there is no reason to think this need will diminish. In fact, during tough economic times, collections become even more vital. According to the *Los Angeles Times,* the amount of business that collection agencies receive goes up 20 percent during recessions.

Today the collection business is changing in ways that give a home-based collection service a distinct advantage in serving small businesses. While large collection agencies cannot afford to take on smaller accounts, or give up on some small accounts after three letters, a home-based service can take on such business and, by operating efficiently, obtain reimbursements for its smaller clients and still make sufficient money to prosper.

To succeed in this business you need to have good communications skills and the ability to write a good collection letter. You must also be able to walk a fine line between being firm and understanding when you deal directly with the people who owe money. Above all, you must know the laws in your state about collections, and you may need a state license and a bond. In addition, you must operate within the Fair Debt Collection Practice Act.

The quickest way to develop your business is to solicit professionals and businesses by phone or in person, including medical practices, small retail stores, and even nonprofit associations that have conducted donation campaigns. Health-care providers are an especially good market for a collection agency because three out of every four dollars sent out for collections are for hospital and medical bills not covered by insurance. Other markets include day-care providers, cable TV operators, companies who sell infomercial products on installments, and the growing number of spouses who need help collecting child-support payments.

Specialized software is used in the collection business. *Debtmaster,* by Comtronic, is a popular program. You will also want a good printer because the professional quality of your letter can have an impact on a forgetful or negligent payer.

You need to become versed in the requirements of the the Fair Debt Collection Practices Act,which you can find at *www.ftc.gov/os/statutes/ fdcpa/fdcpact.htm.*

Home-based collection agencies earn up to $60,000 a year, although the typical average is $30,000 to $50,000. The competition is steep in this field, but by finding your niche, you can make a good living at it.

Books

How to Start a Home-Based Collection Agency, Robert H. Bills, Eatonbrook Publishing, ISBN: 0972843000.

Starting Your Own Collection Business!, Michelle Dunn, *www.mad agency. com/ebook-order.html*

Software

Debtmaster, Comtronic Systems, (509) 674-7000, *www.comtronic.com/*

Composer/Sound Designer

You hear sound everywhere . . . on television and cable programs, commercials, promotional videos, training videos, CD-ROM and multimedia programs, computer games—even on the Web. Never before has such a wide variety of music been used in so many media. Where does all this music come from? It can come from you. Whether you're an accomplished, trained musician or composer or an intuitive, creative lover of music, today's computer-based music-making technology makes it possible to compose and record music right at home and with sound quality technically equal to that of the best recording studios. And with the growth of markets that require fresh, new sounds we feel that this is an excellent climate for home-computer-based composers.

The home-based digital studio doesn't require extensive soundproofing or costly renovations to living quarters. Many successful composers work out of a spare room, a garage, basement—or even a bedroom. The reason for this is that, due to today's technology, you can write music that will be performed electronically by electronic keyboards, sound modules, and sound cards. An entire symphony for sixty-six "instruments" can be written and realistically performed electronically and recorded without a single microphone. Now, if you're interested enough to be reading this, chances are you already know something about digital recording, so we won't get into much detail about the technology. The best way to get business always starts with a good demo. Put together a short demo of at least five short examples of your best work—three to five minutes total. Select pieces that show your range or specialties. The better you demonstrate your originality, the better your chances of getting work. Another thing producers, directors, and other prospects look for is range. Even if you specialize in one style of music, create your demo to reflect the range you cover—e.g., fast, mid, and slow tempos and emotional ranges including exciting, calm, uplifting, and dramatic. When your demo is complete, put together a biography that includes a brief description of your experience, credits, and working style. Invest in nice-looking labels for your demo and make sure your bio is well designed and is easy to read.

For advertising and commercial work send your package to local advertising agencies, cable television stations, radio stations, and independent producers. It is helpful to call each of your prospects in advance to get the name of the person responsible for selecting music. For sound track work, your choices are myriad. For corporate and "industrial" productions, send your package to the directors of media services or corporate communications departments of the larger corporations in your region. Again, be sure to call first to get the proper name and department. For multimedia work, your choices include corporate communications directors, independent producers, and multimedia production houses. Check the latest edition of *Songwriter's Market*, published yearly by Writer's Market Books, for more prospective outlets for your work.

The income you can earn as a home-based composer varies considerably. When you're first starting out, you may even find yourself doing some work for free. Composers we spoke with vary greatly in terms of how they bill for their services. Longer projects, such as a sound track for a program ten minutes or longer, are usually on a complete-project basis. Shorter pieces such as commercial jingles are usually billed on a per-piece basis. Composing for a living is a difficult undertaking, but we do know people who are doing it. You may wish to offer composing services in conjunction with a desktop video or multimedia production business. As your composing credits and contacts pile up, you can make the switch to full-time composing if you wish.

Books

Songwriter's Market: Where & How to Market Your Songs (annual), Writers Digest Books

Organizations

ASCAP (American Society of Composers and Publishers), *www.ascap.com*

BMI (Broadcast Music International), *www.bmi.com*

13

Computer-Aided Design (CAD) Service

From architecture to printed circuit board design and from fashion to product engineering, the expanding field of computer-aided design (CAD) has completely changed the way inventors, builders, electricians, plumbers, and creators of all kinds visualize new ideas. For example, using computers, scanners, and specialized software, a fashion designer can scan in a fabric pattern, place it on a dress design, and sketch a model in 3D all on the computer screen. Similarly, an interior designer can construct an office or conference room, paint colors or scan in wallpaper for the walls, and reconfigure the placement of furniture until the most attractive combination is achieved. And a civil engineer can produce a layout of every street in a city and show the effect on traffic of installing a new set of lights at a busy intersection.

As CAD software has matured, the days of drawing a set of lines to define a wall are gone. Now you indicate a wall and your task is to tell the software how high a wall, how far off the ground, and what colors and texture it should be on either side. Automatically the software is making a list of how much lumber, sheetrock, and paint the contractor will need to produce that wall. In a separate window, the wall you just built is displayed in 3D, with the lights that you just placed washing down on it. The software now does the hard work.

Depending on your background and interest, you might explore establishing a CAD-based service specializing in any of many design fields: architecture, civil engineering, electrical or plumbing layout, fashion, interior design, landscaping, mechanical engineering, and many others. One of your skills will need to be relating CAD to the needs of your clients.

To be in this business, you will need, however, to invest in the hardware and software that is up-to-date for your field. For printing out blueprints or designs you'll require printers designed for this purpose.

This career may require specialized training for a few months, but you can find such training in many technical schools and community colleges. The opportunities for success are enormous if you can offer special expertise in a particular field and you know your way around the hardware and software. CAD designers can be paid $50 and more per hour for developing computer models of a design, blueprints, and even three-dimensional animated sequences that simulate the item—be it a building, a room, or a product being used. This is also one field where the technology is rapidly changing, so you will need to stay abreast of changes in the field on a continual basis.

Book

Learn Autocad 12 in a Day (Book and Disk) Ralph Grabowski, ISBN: 1556223390. Grabowski has other titles including *The Illustrated Auto-CAD 2005 Quick Reference*, an annual.

Software

ArchiCAD, (617) 485-4203, *www.graphisoft.com*

AutoCAD offers a number of products, including a Light version of *Auto-CAD*, an *Architectural Desktop*, and an *Inventor* version, among others: *http://usa.autodesk.com*.

14

Computer-Assisted Instructional Design (CAI)

Computer-Assisted Instruction (CAI) is used to teach practically any field to almost anyone. You might think of CAI as the equivalent of a textbook or a self-study course, except that the information is designed as interactive software to be delivered on a computer screen, often enhanced with graphics, diagrams, simulations, and quizzes that make the instruction more interesting and useful.

CAI programs are used to teach nursing, carpentry, technical repair, employee safety, sales techniques, accounting, and many other skills. Other CAI programs help people learn home repair, crafts, foreign languages, and even cooking. In short, whatever people may want to know, a CAI program can be designed to teach.

Furthermore, unlike writing other kinds of software publishing, you do not need to be a programmer or know how to do custom programming to be a CAI designer. So if you have a strong background or expertise in a specific area that other people may want to learn, then consider becoming a CAI designer. Only your expertise and ability to teach are necessary. Most CAI packages are developed using special software programs called authoring systems and provide you with templates for designing screens, drawing diagrams, or illustrations, and writing any accompanying text. The authoring systems then help you sequence the material and tag screens indicating such things as optional material, points where readers may skip ahead, and interactive question/answer material.

The best way to get into this business is to ask yourself what expertise you can share or what market might benefit from a CAI course you could develop. Once you have targeted an area, find out which authoring system works best for you. Each system is slightly different in its approach to CAI and what it requires to run on your hardware. Then you can approach companies directly and offer to create a customized CAI tutorial for them to use in teaching their employees the material. Or you can develop a CAI program and market it directly to companies via telemarketing, flyers and/or your own Web site. Another option is to develop your program and offer it as shareware (see "Software Publishing") through the distribution channels used for such kinds of programs. What you can earn as a CAI designer will vary, depending on the nature of your tutorials, the market niche you select, and how much you charge for your product.

Book

Hypermedia Learning Environments: Instructional Design and Integration, Piet A. M. Kommers, Scott Grabinger, Joanna C. Dunlap, Lawrence Erlbaum Associates, ISBN: 0805818286.

Organizations

AMERICAN SOCIETY FOR TRAINING AND DEVELOPMENT, (703) 683-8100, (800) 628-2783, *www.astd.org*

INTERNATIONAL SOCIETY FOR PERFORMANCE IMPROVEMENT, (301) 587-8570, *www.ispi.org*

15

Computer Consulting

Most homes and businesses today have computers and while some people have a basic understanding of how to work with computers, there are many more that need assistance. As a computer consultant you might work in a single area or multiple areas of expertise. For example, you might specialize in analyzing a business's needs and recommending hardware and software best suited to that business. Many computer consultants focus themselves in a particular niche market. For example, your area of expertise may lie in offering software support for an application that is no longer supported by the company that created it but is still used widely. Consulting related to information technology is in demand at the time of this writing.

Technical knowledge and expertise is obviously a must for the person interested in becoming a computer consultant. The most successful consultants today will, in fact, have both a broad knowledge of the field and a specialty that distinguishes them from other consultants.

Most computer consultants start out by doing a few small jobs and then build their business over time with word-of-mouth referrals. If you are a generalist and have an interest in working in many areas, however, you would benefit by getting certified by a vendor or software publisher. This can require a significant investment of cash and time but can be a key to building your business.

Networking is an excellent route to build this business. Making yourself visible by helping people at computer and software user-groups, answering questions on online computer services and local bulletin board systems, and joining business networking groups are several good avenues. Publicity, direct mail, and yellow-page listings and ads are among the many ways computer consultants market themselves. You should also have a Web site that is effective in promoting your business.

Today there is a trend by some companies to outsource their information technology projects to offshore companies in places like India, Russia, China, or Israel. These are usually million-dollar projects but can sometimes provide an opportunity for a solo consultant who can act as a U.S. local project manager. If you speak the language spoken in the offshore country, you can attract these clients. The local consultant can help the overseas contractor understand the needs of the client. Of course, companies who have had unhappy, costly experiences with outsourced projects are apt to look with favor on working again with a U.S. consultant.

Computer consultants typically charge $75 an hour, but some get less than $15 an hour and others can charge as much as $250 an hour. What you can charge depends on the area in which you specialize, the industry that you work in, community size and location, the size and kind of clients you serve, and the length of the project. You can also work through a broker who finds you in return for 20 to 30 percent of your hourly rate.

Books

The Computer Consultant's Workbook, Janet Ruhl, Technion Books, ISBN: 0-9647116-0-5.

Getting Started in Computer Consulting, Peter Meyer, Wiley, 1999, ISBN: 0471348139.

MCSE Consulting Bible, Harry M. Brelsford, Wiley, ISBN: 0764547747. (MCSE means Microsoft Certified Systems Engineer.)

How to Become a Successful IT Consultant, Butterworth-Heinemann, ISBN: 0750648619.

Organizations

INDEPENDENT COMPUTER CONSULTANTS ASSOCIATION, (800) 774-4222, *www.icca.org*

Web Sites

www.govcon.com is all about government contracting for computer consultants.
www.realrates.com: Janet Ruhl's Computer Consultant's Resource Page with tips, results of compensation surveys, and more

Training and Certification

INSTITUTE FOR CERTIFICATION OF COMPUTER PROFESSIONALS, (847) 299-4227, *www.iccp.org*

THE SECURITY PORTAL FOR INFORMATION SYSTEM SECURITY PROFESSIONALS is an extensive list of IT certification programs with links to them: *www. info syssec.com/infosyssec/itcert.htm*. Training can be obtained from local colleges, universities, private training schools, and vendors.

16

Computer Programming

The demand for computer programmers continues to grow, and the Bureau of Labor Statistics identifies programming as one of the fastest-growing occupations. Much of the demand for programming is being provided by freelancers because as companies reduce the number of core employees, more programming work is being "outsourced" to outside contractors. Technology is changing rapidly, and it makes good business sense to contract the work to people with the most up-to-date skills rather than hire and keep such people as full-time permanent staff. Clients sometimes need off-the-shelf programs customized to meet their needs, and they hire freelance computer programmers to do this work.

Programmers begin by developing an understanding of the tasks that clients want the computer to perform, how much data needs to be processed, and in what form it is needed. Once programmers have a full understanding of what needs to be done, they design and write code to fit the platform used by the clients, or they may modify commercial programs for PCs that will do the job to the customers' satisfaction and pocketbook. Then they test, debug, and implement the software, including training personnel to use it.

Ideally you should have two to five years of programming background in several languages and platforms if you want to strike out on your own. This experience will help you know how long it takes to complete various projects so you can make accurate estimates of what you will need to charge your clients. Most programmers find that not only do they need to be able to write code, but they must also be familiar with a variety of software and hardware. You also need to be able to understand and speak knowledgeably with clients about their business needs so that you can do what they want and inspire trust in your abilities. This means that it helps to have a background in databases, accounting, and general business because the potential for business probably will revolve around one of these fields. Besides your technical expertise, you require excellent communication and customer service skills. You must learn quickly and keep up with changes and new technologies within the industry.

Programmers' fees generally range from $30 to $75 to more than $125 per hour for experienced professionals. Many programmers working forty or more hours per week are able to bill over $100,000 per year.

Making personal contacts through business and trade associations, getting referrals through computer stores, and teaching classes on programming for business people are effective ways to attract business. Creating a Web site that markets your skills and has Metatags and links will direct potential clients to your site.

Books

The following publishers offer a selection of books related to computer programming: OReilly, *www.oreilly.com*; and Sybex, 1151 Marina Village Parkway, Alameda, CA 94501-1013, (510) 523-8233, *www.sybex.com*.

Magazines and Newsletters

ADVISOR PUBLICATIONS publishes a group of magazines such as *Access-Office-VB Advisor, E-Business Advisor, File Maker Pro Advisor, Foxpro Advisor, Lotus Notes & Domino Advisor,* and *Security Advisor.* From its Web site, it offers Microsoft certification and other online classes, *www.adviser.com.*

DR. DOBB'S JOURNAL, written by professional programmers for professional programmers: (415) 358-9500, *www.ddj.com/ddj*

SOFTWARE SUCCESS, 11300 Rockville Pike, Suite 1100, Rockville, MD 20852-3030, (877) 266-7075, *www.softwaresuccess.com*

Organizations

ASSOCIATION OF INFORMATION TECHNOLOGY PROFESSIONALS, *www.aitp.org*

ASSOCIATION FOR COMPUTING MACHINERY, the world's largest educational and scientific computing society offers local chapters and a large number of special-interest groups: (800) 342-6626, *www.acm.org.*

THE INSTITUTE OF ELECTRICAL AND ELECTRONICS ENGINEERS (IEEE) COMPUTER SOCIETY, part of IEEE, is the world's largest technical professional organization: (212) 419-7900, *www.ieee.org.*

SOCIETY OF INFORMATION MANAGEMENT, (312) 372-6540, *www.simnet.org*

INDEPENDENT COMPUTER CONSULTANTS ASSOCIATION (ICCA) has many local chapters: *www.icca.org.*

INSTITUTE FOR CERTIFICATION OF COMPUTING PROFESSIONALS, (800) U-GET-CCP/ (847) 299-4227, *www.iccp.org*

Courses and Training

VATTEROTT COLLEGE offers an associate degree in computer programming and network management entirely over the Internet at *www.vatterott global.com.*

Web Sites

JANET RUHL'S COMPUTER CONSULTANT'S RESOURCE PAGE has a survey of rates: *www.realrates.com.*

JOB BOARD OF THE NATIONAL ASSOCIATION OF COMPUTER CONSULTANTS. Independent programmers and other computer consultants can post their résumés, *www.isjobbak.com.*

17

Computer Sales and Service

Although there's no shortage of retailers and mail-order companies selling computers, the market for computer systems and peripherals is still huge. And since many people and companies need extensive assistance or prefer to work one-on-one with a consultant when they buy a system, opportunities for a home-based computer sales and service business are good.

There are two keys to being successful in this business. First, even if you generalize and work with many clients, we recommend that you have a specialization in one or more specific areas such as a certain kind of office system, or in one technology such as intranetworking or accounting. Having an area of expertise adds value to your service and gives you a market cachet that many others lack. Second, you should be able to provide a wide range of services to your customers, including system customization, software installation, and ongoing support. In this sense, you want people to consider you more as a computer consultant than as a salesperson.

Getting into the sales and service business is actually quite easy, given that the field of hardware suppliers is teeming with companies looking for business. You begin by contacting manufacturers and vendors of computer equipment around the country and finding out about bulk pricing options for prebuilt systems or parts that you can assemble into a system yourself. If it suits your business, you might also arrange to become an exclusive agent for a manufacturer as a Value Added Reseller (VAR) for their equipment or software, a useful approach if you specialize. Becoming a VAR also adds to your credibility and sometimes gives you a higher profit margin, since you are usually selling a complete package to a customer rather than just one component of a system.

To obtain clients, you can advertise in the yellow pages and do telemarketing directly to businesses. However, your most effective methods should focus on getting business to come to you; and so networking both face-to-face and through the Internet and online services, giving speeches, and encouraging referrals will save money and time. As with any computer consultant, your satisfied customers are your best source of new business, since customers prefer to know that you have been successful in helping others.

Earnings for a sales and service business can be considerable and vary depending on the sale. Furthermore, you can also charge hourly fees for consulting, customization of software, and other services that businesses often need when they buy equipment.

Trade Shows

COMDEX, (800) 915-9804, *www.comdex.com*

CONSUMER ELECTRONICS SHOW, *The Consumer Electronics Association, ce.org*

18

Computer Training

Learning to use computers and software programs and getting around on the Internet are necessary aspects of running a successful business. Rather than wasting time reading manuals and groping in the dark in cyberspace or with new software programs, many companies recognize the value of bringing in professional trainers to teach executives and support staff the basics of word processing, spreadsheets, databases, networking, and specialized or customized software.

Computer trainers generally teach groups of individuals in a classroom style on the premises of a company. They may also teach public computer seminars or offer corporate training classes off the company premises. Classes can range from small groups of two to six individuals to workshops with twelve to twenty people paired up on PCs.

Stand-up training and presentation skills are essential for a computer trainer. You must be able to command your audience's attention, communicate instructions clearly, and handle group dynamics. A background in teaching or educational design is useful, as this helps you know how to sequence and present new information to people in "chunks" so that they can understand and assimilate it efficiently. Some computer trainers specialize in software applications that are used mainly in particular industries such as law, construction, health care, and so on. Others learn multiple software packages so that they can service a wider audience. Either way, a computer trainer must be an expert both in the software and how it is used in a specific business.

Computer trainers often charge by the hour for their services, and the hourly rate ranges from $36 to $200 or more. Income potential may run from $40,000 to more than $100,000. This is a business that is easily expanded without significantly increasing overhead because you can subcontract with other trainers to teach your classes once you are selling more training than you alone can deliver. You need to price your fees at just the right rate so that the client perceives a savings over and above what it would cost their employees to sit at their desks and try to learn on their own.

Directly soliciting companies that need computer training and speaking before business and professional groups are effective ways to obtain work doing in-house training. Direct-mail and print advertising will most likely be necessary if you intend to offer and fill public seminars. Another alternative is to arrange to teach courses under the sponsorship of business or educational institutions that will promote and administer the seminars. Some manufacturers certify trainers for their software, and this certification qualifies you for referrals to their customers. Having your own Web site with testimonials can also be effective.

Books

The Accidental Trainer: You Know Computers, So They Want You to Teach Everyone Else (Jossey-Bass Business and Management Series), Elaine Weiss, San Francisco, Jossey-Bass Publications, ISBN: 0787902934.

The Complete Computer Trainer, Paul Clothier, Computing McGraw-Hill, ISBN: 0070116393.

The Computer Training Handbook: How to Teach People to Use Computers, Elliott Masie, Rebekah Wolman, Lakewood Publications, ISBN: 0943210372.

The Computer Trainer's Personal Training Guide, Gail Perry, Bill Brandon, Paul Clothier, Shirley Copeland, Patty Crowell, New York, Que Corp., ISBN: 1575762536.

Newsletter

Quick Training Tips, free e-mail newsletter, the Micro Computer Trainer, Systems Literacy, Inc., (973) 770-7762, *www.quicktrainingtips.com*

Training

THE AMERICAN SOCIETY FOR TRAINING AND DEVELOPMENT offers a train-the-trainer certificate program: (703)683-8100/(800)628-2783, *www.astd.org/astd.*

19

Computer Tutoring

While there are many computer trainers and training companies, independent computer tutors have an advantage over other methods of becoming computer literate because they bring the training to their clients and customize it to their needs. Computer tutors generally work on the clients' premises, providing in-depth, one-on-one, or very-small-group coaching. They may go into a company to help an office automate, assisting with setting up the entire computer system and teaching the responsible employee to use both the hardware, software, and the Internet. Increasingly, those who are learning to use their first computer or upgrading to new versions of software and equipment, as well as parents looking for tutoring for their kids, may turn to a computer tutor.

Many successful tutors specialize in working with particular industries like law firms, health professionals, construction companies, and so on. Alternatively, they may specialize in particular software applications like spreadsheets, database management, or desktop publishing and graphics software as well as the Internet. And then there are those tutors who provide tutoring to private individuals or families.

To be a successful computer tutor you must have a thorough knowledge of at least one software program that a sufficient number of people need to learn. Some software manufacturers actually offer training courses and will certify you to teach their software. Once you're certified, the manufacturer may also become a referral source for clients. You also need to be thoroughly familiar with the operating system that the software program is used on. It is important that you stay up-to-date with new technology and the updates of the software applications you teach, including new versions and the latest patches. You must also be familiar with the field in which you decide to work so you can understand your clients' particular needs and uses for computer technology. Finally, you need to have tact, patience, and good communication and presentation skills and be able to convey technical ideas in a nonthreatening, easy-to-understand style. To get work as a computer tutor it helps to be able to develop winning proposals as well as create good training materials.

Income potential for a good computer tutor is excellent. Fees range from $35 to $125 an hour. Yearly incomes can range from $40,000 to $125,000.

Giving speeches about computerizing a business and networking through professional, trade, or business associations in the field you choose to serve are among the best routes to building your business. You can also place brochures in displays or flyers on bulletin boards at computer and office-supply stores. Becoming certified in the software that you intend to teach can mean receiving referrals from the manufacturer.

Franchise

COMPUTERTOTS teaches children to use computers: (703)759-2556, (800)531-5053, *www.computertots.com.*

See book and newsletter resources in "Computer Training."

Construction and Remodeling Estimating and Planning Service

Since such a large percentage of people wants to save money by doing their own home-improvement projects, why not create a home-repair and -improvement business that goes into customers' homes or offices not to do the work yourself, but to teach your customers how to do the job properly or to help them through jobs they're stuck on? This type of service can be an add-on to expand an existing contracting or repair business. You might call your business Do It Yourself Plumbing [Carpentry] Assistant, We Help You Do It Carpentry, or Fix It Yourself Consulting.

You can charge much less than someone who actually does the repair and still help clients feel that they've saved money since they've received professional advice in helping them complete their current jobs, as well as learning for future tasks. You can also add on other services, such as providing special supplies or materials they may need. The computer aspect of this idea is that you can use costing software to provide cost estimates for your clients. And, you might offer a finder's service by which you locate the best sources and prices for construction materials using a database that you develop from various supply sources in your area.

Your fees might range from $35 to $50 per hour plus any extra services the customer requests. The best methods to get customers may include advertising in local community newspapers and yellow pages, direct mail, and particularly networking with salespeople in building supply stores who can pass your business card to people who are purchasing materials and inevitably ask how to do the work properly. You might also create your own Web site. For a person already in the home-construction or -repair business, this service can also be an excellent way to make money from lost query calls when the people decide they can only afford to do the job themselves.

Software

Golden Seal, (888) 272-1008, *www.turtlesoft.com*

Timberline's, headquarters (503) 690-6775, *www.timberline.com*

Copywriter

Businesses and organizations often have a need to sell their products or services using written materials that represent them to the world, from advertising slicks and brochures to direct mail sales letters. Newsletters and Web sites—everything that businesses put out not only needs to be written clearly and concisely but also must capture attention, impress, and motivate the reader to buy or to call for further information. And with the cost of direct mail and advertising today, it is extremely important that the writing for such materials sparkle.

As a result, small-business owners rarely have the time, talent, or know-how to prepare such sparkling materials themselves. Since they usually don't need (and often can't afford) to employ a full-time copywriter to do it for them, they instead turn to freelance professional copywriters.

Copywriters prepare the text and sometimes the design for a wide variety of materials, including ads, brochures, Web-site content, instructional manuals, media kits, grant proposals, feature stories, catalogs, company slogans, company annual reports, consumer information booklets, captions for photographs, ghostwritten magazine articles, product literature, annual reports, product names and packaging labels, marketing communication plans, speeches, telemarketing scripts, video scripts, storyboards, and much more. The copywriter's clients may include major corporations, independent professionals, small manufacturers, banks, health clubs, consumer electronics firms, direct-mail catalog companies, and newsletter publishers.

A strong background in grammar and communications is essential in whatever language you will be working. You need to be a logical, organized thinker who can take information and craft it into a theme or message. The successful copywriter can write clear, concise, and compelling copy.

Copywriters use word-processing and sometimes desktop-publishing software to produce their work. CD-ROM disks loaded with reference material are a boon for copywriters because they allow them to find in a flash millions of well-known quotes, look up rules of usage, or enjoin clip art to their material.

Copywriters charge by the hour, by the day, or by the job. By the hour, fees range from $15 to over $150 depending on the copywriter's experience. Serious freelance copywriters typically gross from $25,000 to $40,000 a year during their first two years, but can increase their income to $80,000 to $175,000 a year in later years when they become "real pros" and write for major companies.

If you are interested in copywriting as a career, the best way to build your business is to develop samples of your work to show to everyone you know. Also, begin networking through business organizations, especially in industries with which you are familiar, and develop affiliations with related professionals such as graphic designers, desktop publishers, photographers, copy shops, and printers who can refer business to you.

Books

Advertising Copywriting, Philip Ward Burton, NTC Publishing Group, ISBN: 0844232068.

The Copywriter's Handbook, Robert W. Bly, Henry Holt and Company, ISBN: 0805011943.

Cybertalk That Sells, Herschell Gordon Lewis, Jamie Murphy, NTC/Contemporary Publishing, ISBN: 0809229234.

Phrases That Sell: Ultimate Phrase Finder to Help You Promote Your Products, Services, and Ideas, Sally Germain, Edward W. Werz, NTC/Contemporary Publishing, ISBN: 0809229773.

Positioning: The Battle for Your Mind, Al Reis, Jack Trout, Warner Books, ISBN: 0071373586.

Secrets of a Freelance Writer: How to Make Eighty-five Thousand Dollars a Year, Robert W. Bly, Henry Holt and Company, ISBN: 0805047603.

Tested Advertising Methods, John Caples, Prentice-Hall, ISBN: 0130957011.

Words That Sell, Richard Bayan, NTC/Contemporary Publishing, reprint edition, ISBN: 0809247992.

Write on Target: The Direct Marketer's Copywriting Handbook, Floyd Kemske, Donna Baier Stein, NTC Publishing Group, ISBN: 0844259144.

Organizations

AMERICAN MARKETING ASSOCIATION, (312) 648-0536. *www.ama.org*

DIRECT MARKETING ASSOCIATION, (212) 768-7277, *www.the-dma.org*

EDITORIAL FREELANCERS' ASSOCIATION, (212) 929-5400, *www.the-efa.org*

INTERNATIONAL ASSOCIATION OF BUSINESS COMMUNICATORS, (415) 544-4700, *www.iabc.com*

Magazines and Newsletters

Creative Business, (617) 451-0041, *www.creativebusiness.com*

Writer's Digest Magazine, (800) 333-0133, *www.writersdigest.com*

Software

Ideafisher and Writer's Edge, *www.ideafisher.com*

Zillion Kajillion Clichés, Eccentric Software, (800) 436-6758, (206) 760-9547.

Web Sites

Freelance Online: *www.freelanceonline.com*
Resource Central: *www.resourcehelp.com*
Useit.com: Jakob Nielsen's tips and resources for writing for the Web, *www.useit.com*
Writers Weekly, *www.writersweekly.com*
Zuzu's Petals Literary Resource, *www.zuzu.com*

22

Coupon Newspaper Publishing

Have you recently received a booklet, flyer, newsletter, or magazine composed of advertising coupons for local business services? If so, you are undoubtedly familiar with the concept of this business idea.

Thanks to desktop publishing technology, you can start a business publishing and distributing advertising newspaper service. Your goal in this business is to sell space in your coupon booklet to small businesses that will benefit by having a chance to advertise at relatively inexpensive rates to a clearly targeted audience. You operate the business by contacting local businesses, helping them compose ads or discount coupons, and then putting the coupon booklet together using your computer, desktop-publishing software, and a laser printer. Once the booklets are printed, you can either drop them off in bins at stores where neighborhood people can take them for free, distribute them by hand, or you can purchase a specific mailing list or develop one yourself that you use to mail the booklets.

The earning potential in this business is good. For example, as a sideline or add-on business, you can make around $600 in just a few days by taking an 11-by-17-inch page, breaking each half into eight equal parts, or sixteen blocks total, selling each square to local retailers, doing the ad design and pasteup, getting them printed in two colors, and distributing five thousand copies by hand over a holiday weekend. Or as a full-time venture, you can create a twelve-page coupon newsletter (with three coupons per page) every month for thirty-five advertisers in it at $150 each and you could generate $5,250 in gross revenue, while your production costs could be very little. One angle that you may wish to pursue if you are interested in this business is to organize your booklet around a specific niche, such as wedding services (florist, caterer, bridal boutique, wedding makeup, etc.), cleaning services (carpets, windows, Venetian blinds, air ducts, etc.), health (chiropractors health-food stores, diet programs), or new parents (diaper service, day-care center, parenting class, children's-clothing store, etc.). Advertisers pay in advance, and if you do this as an add-on business you can reserve one of the coupons for your own business. This way you not only make a profit; you get free advertising!

The two major qualifications for operating this business include good telephone sales skills and desktop publishing savvy. However, it would also help to have some retail business experience, knowledge of marketing and advertising, and excellent writing and visual skills, since your clients may expect your assistance in designing an effective advertisement or coupon.

It pays not to skimp on equipment when you start this business. You will need a fast computer with a large-capacity hard drive, a monitor that allows you to see complete pages clearly, word-processing and desktop-publishing software including clip-art programs, and a high-quality laser printer. You should also have a scanner that allows you to scan in photos, logos, and other items that retailers may want you to reproduce.

The most difficult aspect of the business is to sell space for the first issue, since most businesses will repeat their ads several times if your prices are reasonable and the ads are even slightly successful. Your selling points, however, can be that the material is hand-delivered to a guaranteed number of targeted customers, you sell to no two competing businesses in a given booklet, and their coupon appears in a well-designed, two-color publication.

Check the books and Web sites dedicated to desktop publishing, typography, and principles of advertising.

Creativity Consultant

How often do you hear about a business wishing it had a winning idea for a product, a press release, an ad campaign? How often do you hear executives and entrepreneurs say, "If only I could find the right angle . . . the missing piece . . . the new idea"? It's not unusual for most of us to find ourselves groping for something clever, only to find our thoughts hopelessly mundane.

Well, for the person who enjoys developing creative ideas, why not make use of today's new idea-generating software, package yourself as a creativity consultant, and sell your services to companies looking to brainstorm their way to the winning product idea, marketing campaign, or service? Although it may sound strange, creativity is fast becoming the science of the future, as businesses explore every avenue to expand revenues or cut expenses.

What makes a creativity consultant different from an ordinary consultant is that this person specializes in using specific tools and techniques to jar people into thinking differently and to abandon their inhibitions and customary habits, such as constant nay-saying or nitpicking. In fact, the creativity consultant intentionally aims to produce unusual and silly ideas, since these are often the basis for brilliant, cash-producing winning products.

Not so strangely, computers have now become one of the tools used by creativity consultants. One program, *IdeaFisher* by Fisher Ideas Systems, Inc., allows you to generate ideas for marketing strategies, advertisement and promotional materials, new products and product improvements, speeches, articles, stories and scripts, solutions to problems, names for products, services and companies, or any other task requiring the creation of new ideas. The results can be interlinked with a personal information manager program to follow through on an idea.

We've been told by public-relations and advertising firms that they don't want their clients to know that their best ideas come as a result of using *IdeaFisher*, for fear that their clients might conclude they don't need them anymore. But although anyone can buy and learn to use such software themselves, learning it takes time, so a creativity consultant who specializes in using such software can be a cost-effective way for many companies seeking to design an ad campaign, problem-solve an issue, name a product, or create a new business.

It would probably be easiest to market this service if you are already doing consulting, business-plan writing, copywriting, or other work that brings in business clients on a regular basis. Nevertheless, don't automatically nay-say this business; be creative and see if you can make it work!

Books

Cracking Creativity, Michael Michalko, Ten Speed Press, ISBN: 1580083110.

Creativity Games for Trainers, Robert Epstein, McGraw-Hill, ISBN: 0070213631.

Flow, Mihaly Csikszentmihalyi, Perennial, ISBN: 0060920432. Other titles by the author: *Creativity*, ISBN: 0060928204; *Finding Flow*, ISBN: 0465024114.

The Mind Map Book, Tint Buzan, Plume, ISBN: 0452273226.

Six Thinking Hats, Edward de Bono, Back Bay, ISBN: 0316178314.

Software

IdeaFisher, (949) 650.4211, *www.ideafisher.com*

The Idea Generator Plus, (800)678-7008, (510)644-0694, *www.project kickstart.com*

24

Data Conversion Service

If you have a good technical background in data storage and retrieval, you may enjoy a business in data conversion. This business encompasses four types of activities: converting data from one software platform to another, transferring disk-drive storage to CD-ROM, converting archival data, and converting databases for use on the Internet.

Companies and professional offices occasionally change software and then must convert their word-processed documents, spreadsheets, and databases to the new software so that they will be continuously usable. As an expert in this service, you implement the needed conversion and assist in making sure that no data is lost, destroyed, or improperly converted. While many software packages have the built-in capability to perform conversions, most are imperfect and therefore require a certain amount of supervision and manual intervention. For example, in transferring a large spreadsheet, some cell definitions and macros that the user may have defined in the original software may not translate accurately into the new program without a knowledgeable professional tweaking them just right to allow the conversion to proceed. Similarly, converting large and complex databases often requires hand-holding to be sure that data is not scrambled or lost.

Conversion of data into CD-ROM provides another market for this business. As many companies expand their information requirements and resources (databases, research materials, and so on), they surpass the capabilities of ordinary hard-disk storage and retrieval, and need to put their data on CD-ROM disks. Therefore a conversion service can assist in the evaluation of the appropriate technologies and in the actual data transfer itself as well.

As you might imagine, both of these services require an excellent command of hardware and software, as well as a fair amount of expensive equipment such as scanners, tape drives, disk drives, etc. In particular, you need to be completely confident and competent in your ability to complete conversions successfully, as you run the risk of making serious errors and/or losing valuable data and you could be held liable for damages. Regardless of your skill level, obtaining liability insurance is smart.

Converting data can be a profitable add-on business for computer consultants or trainers specializing in spreadsheet programs, databases, and in high-performance hardware. Your fees can range from $35 to $125 per hour for skilled advice and work.

Software

FileMerlin. Available on sites from the Web, such as *www.acii.com/fmn.htm.*
Priced according to types of conversions.

MediaMerge for PC, eMag Solutions, (800) 364-9838, (404) 995-6060, *www.emaglink.com.* The company also produces MMUNIX for Unix.

25  Databased Marketing Service

Although mailing-list services have been around for a number of years, a rapidly expanding extension of the business is developing that can be called a databased marketing service. In brief, the general concept behind this business is to make mailing lists and direct-marketing lists much more precise so that mailings or telemarketing offers can be more closely customized to the actual needs of customers. This is done by learning more about customers and their purchasing habits and customizing lists accordingly. The benefits of a databased marketing service are therefore twofold: first, to provide highly targeted mailing lists that have substantially higher returns than even a qualified list, and second, to learn how to project the psychological and demographic profile of potential new customers in order to expand a list.

Databased marketing grows out of the increasing sophistication of both database-management software to cull information and mail-merge software to facilitate personalized mailings to customers. It reflects the need to reduce the costs of marketing and to improve a company's ability to perform "narrowcasting," whereby they can find the market for their product among the smallest audience of likely customers (the opposite of mass marketing). Databased marketing also points to the growing recognition that every customer is an individual and has personal needs and desires. It therefore allows a business to locate niches faster and to understand customers better so that they can address them with exactly the right products and services at the right time.

Getting into databased marketing will be easiest if you have a background in marketing, sales, or computers, but anyone who has worked with database software can probably enter the field without much difficulty. You will need a personal computer with a large hard drive and one of the professional database-management programs such as *Paradox*, Microsoft *Foxpro*, or Microsoft *Access*.

Your clients can include any businesses that have their own mailing lists and need assistance in developing, targeting, managing, and regularly contacting their lists. You might also be able to perform subcontract work from mailing-list services and mailing-list brokers who can benefit by allowing you to massage their mailing lists to create more accurate marketing databases. In such cases, you can likely command $50 to $100 per hour for your professional expertise in developing mailing-list databases.

Books

The Complete Database Marketer: Second-Generation Strategies and Techniques for Tapping the Power of Your Customer Database, Arthur M. Hughes, Probus Publishing Co., ISBN: 1557388938.

Targetsmart! Database Marketing for the Small Business (Psi Successful Business Library), Jay Newberg, Claudio Marcus, Oasis Press, ISBN: 155571384X.

Organizations

AMERICAN MARKETING ASSOCIATION, (800) AMA-1150, (312) 542-9000, *www.marketingpower.com*

26

Desktop Publishing Service

Desktop publishers provide services for organizations of all kinds that need printed material both for their internal and their external communications. While some DTP companies do any kind of work that comes their way, others carve out their own niches and specialize by serving only particular industries or doing only particular types of documents like newsletters, proposals, books, or directories. Some specialize even further, doing only newsletters for law firms or catalogs for mail-order craft companies.

You must also have a sense of design and layout and a feel for fonts, illustration, printing, and paper. Additionally, if you are creating or editing text for your clients' documents, you obviously need the ability to write good copy, edit, and proofread. You can of course, also use the services of a fellow home-based copywriter, technical writer, or proofreader.

Desktop publishers may charge by the hour, by the page, or by the job, depending on the client and the job. Hourly rates vary between $15 and $75. Page rates, appropriate for shorter publications like newsletters, are between $25 and $50. You will see desktop publishers bidding for jobs on online job banks like *elance.com* at $2 to $4 a page. Very often these are offshore service providers who live in countries such as India or China. Rates can vary considerably depending on the nature of the work, the time frame of the assignment, the degree of special expertise required, and other factors. You may want to check out these Web sites that provide pricing information:

- *www.brennerbooks.com.* Brenner Books conducts national surveys and posts hourly rate ranges by state.
- *www.the-efa.org/services/jobfees.htm.* The Editorial Freelancers' Association posts rates reported by its members.

To do this kind of work, besides an-up-to date computer, laser printer, and scanner, you'll also need software such as *QuarkXpress, Adobe Page-Maker, Adobe PhotoShop* and *Adobe Illustrator,* to name a few.

Effective ways to get business as a desktop publisher are to directly solicit small businesses, independent professionals, and nonprofit organizations and to advertise in the yellow pages and local newspapers. Contacting businesses directly through their Web sites can also be effective. You should consider having your own Web site, since many clients search the Web for this type of service. Also consider being listed in online directories, such as that of the Editorial Freelancers' Association, (*www. the-efa.org,* (866) 929-5400). The business has become competitive, so networking and word of mouth through professional and business organizations are critical to your success.

Books

How to Open and Operate a Home-Based Desktop Publishing Business, Louise Kursmark, Globe Pequot Press, ISBN: 0762722509.
An extensive collection of the many books on desktop publishing can be found at *www.desktoppublishing.com.*

Web Sites

www.desktoppublishing.com/open.html is a portal for desktop publishing.
www.desktoppublishers.com offers a comprehensive array of news, analysis, features, and reviews on the latest products and services on the market.
www.dtpjournal.com provides news, best practices, buyer's guide, and tips.

www.jumpola.com is a list of links for designers and marketers by author Chuck Green.

www.dmoz.org/Computers/Desktop_Publishing

Training and Certification

Courses on desktop-publishing software and related drawing, photo-editing, and Web-page-design programs are widely available at community colleges; computer, trade, and art schools; and in continuing-education programs. Many of these programs issue certificates.

Courses in how to use major desktop software programs are provided by the companies that make these products—for example, Adobe (*www.adobe.com*) and QuarkXPress (*www.quark.com*).

27

Desktop Video

The rapidly growing field of desktop video has made as dramatic an impact in the world of video production as desktop publishing has on the world of print. Essentially, desktop video refers to using computer technologies to edit and add effects to full-motion video at a fraction of the cost of more traditionally shot and edited video programming. Desktop video is actually a wedding of video and computer technology and can be considered to be a branch of the larger field of multimedia production. The following are some of the types of applications made possible with desktop video:

Presentation Videos—creating low-cost videos for use in presentations that would previously have relied on still slides and overheads.

Computer Graphics—integrating computer-generated graphics and special effects into video productions.

Video Production Services—turning raw videotapes shot from a camcorder into professional-looking productions good enough for broadcast television.

Creating Television Commercials for Local Cable Companies—producing professional-quality commercials for local businesses at a fraction of their normal cost.

Self-Publishing Special-Interest Videotapes—producing how-to and local-interest videotapes.

Corporate Video—producing full-motion video for marketing, sales, training, and annual reports.

Video-on-Demand for Web Publishing—Any of the above can now incorporated into a Web site where they will be instantly available to be played using various software applications. There are two ways to go: traditional linear editing and total computer-based nonlinear.

Linear video production uses your PC to essentially enhance the way video has always been produced. Your "raw" footage remains on your source videotapes, and you use your computer to add effects and otherwise manipulate images as you edit them.

Nonlinear desktop video production utilizes much more of your computer's processing ability for much more dramatic results. Your raw video footage is immediately stored in the digital domain, usually to a hard disk (that is, unless you shot the footage with a digital camera in the first place). All editing then takes place within your computer. A nonlinear system costs more in computer hardware but eliminates the need for editing VCRs, outboard edit controllers, and effects. Nonlinear systems require the fastest PCs available, a high-end multimedia video card, an editing program such as *Adobe Premier*, and a VCR onto which you can download your finished programs.

Once you get to know your equipment and establish your reputation, the income potential can be very high. To do well in this business, you should have good visual abilities as well as computer know-how. Networking and directly soliciting clients needing the type of work you specialize in are the best routes to building the business. You can also establish a multimedia Web site on which you can post short clips of your work.

Books

Desktop Video for the PC, Robert Hone, Prima Publishing, ISBN: 0830645241.

Operating a Desktop Video Service on Your Home-Based PC, Harvey Summers, Windcrest, ISBN: 0830645241. Although the technology is out-of-date, the business section remains helpful.

28

Diet and Exercise Planning Service

You've probably heard about statistics showing that millions of Americans are overweight and, for one reason or another, usually cannot maintain a diet or exercise program. But have you ever thought about creating a business concerned with helping people through a computerized diet and/or exercise program custom-tailored to their needs?

A wide array of software is now available for such businesses as "personal nutrition planners" or "body designers." There are programs that analyze a person's eating preferences and habits and then recommend a specific nutritional plan to follow; programs that contain thousands of recipes with a complete breakdown of calories and nutritional content; and programs that can track a person's exercise workouts and help maximize their utility. While most of these programs are commercially available for the home market, many people don't have the time to learn to use them and would gladly pay a consultant to help them find the right diet and exercise program for their specific needs, be they to lose weight or to build muscle mass.

You don't need to be an expert to run this business, but a strong personal interest in the field and a background in nutrition and/or exercise will boost your professional credibility. To get clients, you might begin by advertising in local and community papers and on bulletin boards in fitness centers, supermarkets, and other public locations. With luck, you will also find that word of mouth from satisfied customers is a major way to bring in new business.

Fees for your service will depend on the extent of your work for a client. You might prepare a one-time diet or body-building plan for $50 to $250 or even more, but you might also offer monthly, quarterly, or biannual updates for maintenance diets or workout programs coupled with your ongoing personal support and motivation.

Software

Food/Analyst Plus CD database, *Santé* software for weight control, diet, exercise planning, and other products, Hopkins Technology, ISBN: 1886649111, (800) 397-9211 (U.S.), (952) 931-9376, *www.hoptechno.com*

Diet & Exercise Assistant, Handango, ASIN: B00006OAQF, (866) 426-3264, *www.handango.com*

Yahoo's Directory lists nutrition-related software under Business_and_Economy/Shopping_and_Services/Health/Software/Nutrition/.

29 | MS | 🗑 | + | 🏠 | 100,000

Digital Photography/Image Manipulation

Digital photography and digital image-manipulation technology have made profound advances. Today's digital cameras, scanners, and image-manipulation software serve a wide variety of needs on a number of different levels. On the highest level, digital photography is gaining ground on traditional photographic methods. High-end digital cameras now boast resolution equal to or better than the quality of 35mm film and don't require film developing or prepress preparation for printing. Image-manipulation software, like Abode's ubiquitous *Photoshop,* allows for complete photo retouching, image enhancement, as well as a galaxy of special effects and editing procedures. The moneymaking possibilities of these new technologies, especially using image-manipulation software, are only limited by your creative ability to find ways to use them.

If the possibilities of this kind of business intrigue you, you will want to conduct some more research into the latest digital-photography and image-manipulation technologies. The capabilities of the technology itself should open doors to creative ways in which you can use it to create a specific service. You must also purchase the necessary hardware and software. And you will need good image-manipulation software such as the earlier mentioned *Adobe Photoshop,* or *PaintShop Pro* from JASC. For greater flexibility, a scanner is required as well. If your primary market is multimedia or the Web, you will not need as high resolution a machine because usually 600 dpi is enough. If your primary market is the printed media, you may need a scanner capable of 1,600 dpi or greater.

This is a great add-on business for Web designers, scanning and digitizing services, graphic designers, and desktop video services. With the right idea it can become a thriving full-time venture as well. To obtain clients, you must first determine the exact nature of the service you wish to provide. The more targeted, the better. When you have determined your market, begin finding work by networking online in discussion groups, on bulletin boards, and in users' groups. If your service is unique, small advertisements in the appropriate trade magazines and newsletters might be helpful. If this is an add-on business, let your current clients know what you're up to and show them examples of your work. You might also consider establishing a Web site that demonstrates your capabilities.

Books

Digital Photography: A Hands-on Introduction (book with CD), Philip Krejcarek, Delmar Publishing, ISBN: 0827371314.

Digital Photography for Dummies, Julie Adair King, ISBN: 0764516647.

Web Site

Photo-Electronic Imaging online magazine, *www.peimag.com*

Digital-Recording Studio/Service

With the right software and some reasonable-quality microphones you can turn a spare room in your house into a top-quality, professional recording studio.

Depending on the physical size of the room you use, you can record almost anything, from a single voice-over narration to a small choral group. Digital-recording technology is far cleaner and quieter than its analog predecessor. This means that soundproofing is far less of a consideration than before (unless your neighbors mind the extra noise!). The market for high-quality digital recording is extremely large and includes small advertising agencies, local radio and television stations, independent multimedia producers, and desktop video producers, composers, musicians, actors, publishers of books on tape and instructional audio programs, church and civic groups, and many more. If you purchase a portable DAT (Digital Audio Tape) recorder, you can double your potential business by recording events, speeches, concerts, ambient location sounds, news, and interviews "in the field."

The technology required to set up a digital-recording studio is rather straightforward. In addition to your computer, you will need a high-quality sound card that allows you to record sound to your computer's hard disk as well as translate the stored material so it can be played back in real time. You will also need software such as Digidesign's *ProTool,* which will allow you to record sound onto your hard disk, then edit it. You can record multiple tracks, then quickly and easily cut, paste, splice, loop, compress, equalize, and otherwise manipulate the material to your liking. This software also enables you to "mix" multiple tracks, which eliminates the need and expense of traditional analog mixing boards. There are also all-in-one hard-disk recording systems available from manufacturers such as Akai and Alessis that include a dedicated computer, hard disk, sound card, and recording/editing software.

To find customers for your digital studio, first identify which market you wish to serve. Although the best results come from servicing one market well, you can go after a number of markets when you're first starting out, then see which responds the most positively. This will also allow you to find out which kinds of clients and work you enjoy the most. No matter which market you target, you first have to produce a demo of your capabilities. Keep your demo short, about five minutes, and include a wide variety of recording situations, such as a short narration, solo instrument, instrumental group, sound collage, or ambient "soundscape" and a larger musical group, if your physical space permits. To find work from small advertising agencies, local radio and television stations, and publishers of books on tape and instructional audio programs approach them directly, preferably by phone. Find out who is responsible for audio production and try to develop a relationship with that person. For independent multimedia producers and desktop video producers, try networking online in user groups and professional forums. To find composers, musicians, and actors in need of recording services, place ads in local newsletters and publications that cater to these people. Also try leaving flyers in music stores and local theaters.

Most audio studios we know charge by the hour. The rate you charge should be commensurate with the capabilities you offer. For straightforward, high-quality digital recording and editing you can charge up to $50 or more per hour. More complicated recording projects like those that require SMPTE lockup, many tracks with multiple effects can be billed from $60 to $125 and up per hour.

Books

The Audio Workstation Handbook (Music Technology Series), Francis Rumsey, Newton, MA, Focal Press, ISBN: 0240514505.

The Billboard Guide to Home Recording, Ray Baragary, New York, Watson-Guptill Publications, ISBN: 0823083004.

Magazines

Mix, (800) 532-8190, *www.mixmag.com*

31

Disk/Media-Copying Service

Copying CDs, DVDs, and other media can be an additional source of revenue for software companies, computer consultants and tutors, and someone providing backup services as well as someone already in the audio- and video-copying business. As a disk-copying service, you can handle any combination of the following tasks for a software developer for an agreed-upon price:

Duplicate CDs or other media
Attach labels
Prepare retail boxes (fold, make inserts)
Put discs, manuals, warranty sheets, etc., in boxes
Attach Universal Product Code labels to boxes
Shrink-wrap boxes
Put retail boxes in shipping boxes
Prepare shipping documents
Ship merchandise and send copies of shipping documents to clients
    for invoicing

Your clients would be software companies that fall in between those large enough to have their own staff to carry out these functions and very small companies that can only afford to handle these tasks themselves. There are thousands of software publishers that may do a few thousand or even tens of thousands of orders a month split between various products. These production runs are simply not long enough to support a large-scale minimum-wage staff. Other companies use disks as marketing tools to acquaint customers with their products. Others use disks to teach clients how to use their products.

The best part of this income generator is that it's extremely easy. Tasks like attaching labels and assembling boxes can be done, for example, while you're watching TV or waiting for dinner to cook. Also, the entry cost is low. You will need to pay attention to details and correctness and demonstrate a sincere ambition to satisfy the customer, however. Using specialized software for this purpose you can format, copy, verify, and serialize disks and print labels at the rate of better than one a minute on an inexpensive computer. Dedicated duplicator machines costing thousands are also available, but an ordinary computer can be outfitted with four disk drives so that it can produce as many as three hundred disks per hour. One person can manage six to ten computers.

Typical prices for duplicating disks in quantities of one hundred to one thousand are approximately $.70 to $1.75 each.

Prices may or may not include a label and disk sleeve. Additional charges can be made for packaging, customized printing of labels, and binding.

Software

Easy Media Creator, Roxio, (408) 367-3100, *www.roxio.com*

Power2Go, Cyberlink, *www.gocyberlink.com*

Instant CD/DVD, Pinnacle Systems, (650) 526-1600, *www.pinnaclesys.com*

32

Drafting Service

Personal computers can automate much of the drafting work required for architecture and mechanical engineering. Computers make it possible to do this work at home.

Home-based drafting services work with companies that aren't large enough to employ someone full time to do their drafting in-house. For example, small contractors doing room additions and swimming-pool contractors often hire a drafting service to turn a design into a rendering for customers.

You need a background in drafting or architectural design. Training in drafting is available through a community college, or it can be learned through practical experience. Most of the work can be done at home, and there is usually not a great deal of competition. The work can be seasonal, however—swimming pools in the summer, remodeling during good weather.

During these peak times, everyone wants renderings immediately, so you may be working under the pressure of deadlines. You also must make sure to get deposits up front before doing this type of work.

Pricing for work may be by the square foot or based on flat rates. Gross earnings may reach six figures. The best way to get business is through personal contacts with contractors or homeowners.

Book

AutoCAD Bible (with CD-ROM), Ellen Finkelstein, Wiley, ISBN: 0764536117.

Association

AMERICA DESIGN DRAFTING ASSOCIATION, (731) 627-0802, *www.adda.org*

Software

QuickCAD, Autodesk. (415) 507-5000, *www./usa.autodesk.com*

33

Electronic Clipping Service

In today's competitive world, businesses and professionals need to keep up with the constant flow of information about their field, their competitors, and their own products. Each day hundreds of periodicals, newspapers, and journals publish articles that might contain useful data, product reviews, and inside information about competitors that many businesses simply miss.

An electronic clipping service is one answer to this dilemma and a fascinating business for those who enjoy reading and learning about many fields. As a clipping service (also called an alert service), you track articles in many publications that are of interest to your clients. In the past, this service was performed manually, and so a clipping service would subscribe to hundreds of publications and someone would read through them and actually cut out the appropriate articles.

A clipping service can be entirely computerized, employing online databases and fast searches using the keywords and phrases that a client gives you. Any wire-service story or article that uses those keywords or phrases is then delivered in original form or in an abstract to your computer or in print through the mails. In this way, you can help a business stay current with every article that mentions whatever subjects they want to follow. A clipping service can also offer broadcast monitoring, particularly with many broadcasts being simultaneously available on the Web.

To run a clipping service, you must enjoy sleuthing and finding information, as well as having a solid expertise in computerized searching, using free services like Google's News Service (*news.google.com*) and Excite's Newstracker (*www.newstracker.com*) as well as subscription ones like Ebsco, Dialog, and Lexis Nexis's ECLIPSE. One aspect you need to be aware of, however, is that you may need to pay copyright fees for any articles that you clip or copy. You may be able to make good use of newer Real Simple Syndication (RSS) either using aggregator software yourself or being a recipient of sites providing RSS.

Clipping services usually charge a flat monthly fee that takes into account the costs they will incur on behalf of their clients for using online services. These costs depend on how many documents the client is likely to receive and which database services you will be using, since you pay for these according to the amount of time you spend online, and each service varies in its per-hour fees.

Books

The Lexis Companion: A Complete Guide to Effective Searching, Jean McKnight, Addison-Wesley Publishing Co., ISBN: 0201483351.

Also see the resources listed under "Information Brokering."

Electronic Clipping Services

DIALOG INFORMATION, (919) 462-8600/(800) 3-DIALOG, *www.dialog.com*

EBSCO INFORMATION SERVICES, (205) 991-6600, *www.ebsco.com*

LEXIS NEXIS'S ECLIPSE, (800) 227-4908, *www.lexisnexis.com*

Looksmart.com lists popular news electronic news clipping services: *http://search.looksmart.com/p/browse/us1/us317916/us147927/us269888/*.

Electronic Public-Relations and Publicity Service

The number of Web publications, newsletters, and news services continues to grow and may outnumber that of traditional print media. Even more significantly, a growing number of businesspeople, educators, civil employees, and consumers are turning to online publications as their first choice for news, learning about new business and social trends, technological and product updates, even entertainment. All these publications must meet the burgeoning demand for new content.

We see a steady growth in the demand for this type of service because there are actually two markets who need the service: (1) online media who publish information and (2) those who create the information—the companies, individuals, government and civic organizations, and anybody else who benefits from having an audience find out about what they are doing or have done. If a software company creates a new accounting program that's easier to use and more powerful than what's currently available, that's worthwhile news to anyone who needs the product. Online publications whose content deals with computers, technology, or accounting know this, and they are always looking for news of this kind. As an online public relations and publicity specialist, your job is to bring the news to the publication for the benefit of its readers. The other beneficiary is the software company who created the product. The more people who know about the product, the more people are likely to buy the product. It is always the information provider who will be your client and pay for your services. Your services will include e-mail press releases, company profiles, articles for online publication, e-mail letters, and electronic media kits that can even include multimedia content such as video, audio, graphics, and animation.

By specializing in electronic public relations and publicity you create a niche for yourself that allows you to stand out from the many established PR firms and publicists who do not concentrate on the online world. The online publications and media are also rather different from those of the print media. New publications and media are constantly springing up, and the technology required to deliver the information they offer changes frequently. By making the online world your specialty, you will have the time, focus, and expertise to stay abreast of the latest developments. This will make you a valuable resource for your clients.

To do well in electronic PR and publicity you need to be creative, to write well, and to be eager to learn about and enjoy the challenge of a quickly changing business landscape. It is helpful if you have public-relations or corporate-communications experience, but it's not essential. In terms of equipment, besides a good computer, you will need a reliable Internet Service Provider (ISP), bulk e-mail software, contact-management software, and a database program to keep track of clients, publications, etc.

Within your specialty as an electronic PR and publicity service, you can concentrate even further in terms of the type of clients you serve. Areas of concentration include high-technology companies, manufacturers, entertainment companies, nonprofit organizations, even celebrities.

Earning potential is similar to that of tradition PR agencies. As an independent practitioner, you can expect to earn from $35,000 to $75,000 or more annually. Online networking is a good way to pick up clients. You might also try contacting large PR agencies and asking them to outsource their online PR work to you. You can also contact companies directly, either through a direct "snail mail" or a targeted e-mail campaign.

Books

Effective Public Relations, Scott M. Cutlip, Allen H. Center, Glen M. Broom, Prentice-Hall, ISBN: 0135412110.

Public Relations on the Net, Shel Holtz, American Management Association, ISBN: 0814471528.

Public Relations: Strategies and Tactics. Philip H. Ault, Warren Kendall Agee, Glen T. Cameron, Dennis L. Wilcox, Allyn & Bacon, ISBN: 0205360734.

List

IDG LIST SERVICES provides e-mail lists of high-tech users who have agreed to accept promotional e-mailings: (888) IDG-LIST, (508) 370-0808, *www.idglist.com*.

Software

ARIAL SOFTWARE offers electronic news distribution directly to high-tech editors: (307) 587-1338, *www.newstarget.com*.

Association

PUBLIC RELATIONS SOCIETY OF AMERICA, (212) 995-2230, *www.prsa.org*

35 |ABC| |🗑| |+| |100,000|

Employee Manual Development and Writing Service

One specialized area of business consulting is helping companies write comprehensive, informative, and legally passable documents that serve as their employee manuals. Nearly every company that employs more than ten or fifteen people will want to have available standard and consistent information that spells out for employees the policies and procedures for performance appraisals, sexual harassment, vacation and benefit terms, regulations on safety and substance abuse, dress codes, employee development, and many other issues.

Most of this work can be done using standard word-processing and desktop-publishing software, but one company, JIAN Tools for Sales, has also developed a software package specifically for this purpose. Called the *Employee Manual Builder,* the software provides formats and templates that allow you to create manuals more easily and accurately.

The qualifications for running this business should include a good background in human resources, organizational behavior, and personnel development. You also need to have at least some knowledge of the various federal and state government laws about equal-opportunity employment, harassment, hiring and firing regulations, insurance requirements, and so on. Excellent writing skills and personal-communication habits are also critical, since you will be working directly with company presidents and directors of personnel.

Fees for this service can be quite lucrative, ranging from $5,000 to $20,000 or more, depending on the length of the document and amount of time you need to spend developing the material with the executives. Such manuals are often vital pieces in a company's public-relations and hiring procedures, and are therefore worth their cost.

The best ways to get business include networking in professional organizations and among business planners and consultants who specialize in working with small companies. You might also consider sending out direct-mail announcements to companies in your area, being sure to follow up with a call and samples of your work. This business is a good add-on business if you already operate a consulting or business-planning company.

Because of the legal aspect of these manuals and the frequency of lawsuits filed against employers, you will want to have a contract for any job you take that eliminates and minimizes your liability in the event of an employment lawsuit. You might also wish to have errors-and-omissions insurance to protect you against any mistakes you might make in developing manuals.

Software

DescriptionsNow, CCHKnowledge Point, (707) 762-0333, *www.knowledge point.com*

Employee Manual Builder, JIAN Tools for Sales, Inc., (650) 254-5600, *www.jian.com*

OfficeReady Office Policy Manual, KMT Software, *www.templatezone.com*

36

Event and Meeting Planner

An event and meeting planner is someone who plans business and social events as a profession. Event planners are highly trained and professional individuals who know where to find high-quality goods and reliable services at the best prices. Whether it's catering services or clowns, musicians or multimedia equipment, the event planner has names and numbers of suppliers at his or her fingertips. If you enjoy planning and organizing events of all kinds and have an excellent track record for getting things done without forgetting even the slightest detail, this business may be the one for you. Although the field is very competitive, a good event planner can work steadily with a variety of companies that need to attend trade shows or put on sales conferences, product announcements, seminars and training workshops, and even employee parties.

The most effective event planners use their computers to make sure that the job is done efficiently and well. Software such as project management and scheduling programs, database programs, and contact managers all allow an event planner to keep track of the many behind-the-scenes arrangements of an event, thereby avoiding slipups and mistakes.

Getting started in this business is easiest if you have a public-relations or communications background and perhaps have done event planning for a company, volunteer organization, or association before. If you don't have a background, you might wish to work with an existing company to get experience. You should also join your city's convention and visitor bureau as a membership often entitles you to inside information about trade shows and a free listing of your company's name in any materials they send out to prospective attendees.

Another aspect of event planning is contest organizing, in which you help companies set up sales contests for the general public. To do this, you need to be familiar with your state's laws about contests, and it also helps to have a statistical background so you can deal with the mathematics behind designing successful contests. Fees for event planning vary greatly depending on the nature of the event, the locale, and the going rate for the area. Fees can range from $40 to $60 per hour and up to thousands of dollars per event.

Books

The Business of Event Planning, Judy Allen, Wiley, ISBN: 047083188X.
An accompanying book by Judy Allen is *Event Planning: The Ultimate Guide to Successful Meetings, Corporate Events, Fundraising Galas, Conferences, Conventions, Incentives and Other Special Events,* ISBN: 0471644129.

How to Start a Home-Based Event Planning Business, Jill Moran, Globe Pequot, ISBN: 0762724862.

Web Sites

www.bizbash.com
www.conworld.net
www.expoworld.com and *www.expoworldcanada.com*
www.conventionbureaus.com
www.majorexhibithalls.com is an online directory to the world's largest, most prestigious Exhibition Hall Facility Web sites.
www.findspeakersandbureaus.com
www.tourismbureaus.com

Software

MeetingTrak, www.gomembers.com

Yahoo's Small Business directory lists multiple sources of event-planning software.

Association

MEETING PROFESSIONALS INTERNATIONAL, (972) 702-3000, *www.mpiweb.org*

37

Expert-Referral or Brokering Service

An expert-referral service matches businesses that need highly specialized professional help with the people who can meet their needs. Companies often turn to freelance outside experts for ad hoc consulting services rather than keeping expensive experts on staff. The expert-referral broker therefore puts the two parties together as needed for either a short-term job or an ongoing consulting or training contract. For example, an expert service might provide a client with a direct-mail specialist, a lawyer with specific expertise in exports, a materials engineer specializing in plastics, or a toxic-waste manager. Whatever the situation, the expert would then perform a job for the client or teach specific skills to their employees.

Success in this business depends on creating a pool of reliable, respected experts you can count on and attracting companies that are looking for such truly specialized assistance. It helps to have been a consultant so that you have a good understanding of the nature of the consulting business and what a client expects. Calling on your own contacts is the best way to get started, but you can also use telemarketing and/or direct-mail pieces addressed to the directors of corporate departments you can help, such as engineering, manufacturing, finance, human-resource development, training, etc.

Start-up costs to become an expert location service are low, and income potential is good. Referral services generally take a cut of the fees paid to the expert, typically between 20 to 35 percent. Expert-referral services can earn from $50,000 to $150,000 a year. If you operate your business like a brokerage you bill your client directly and then pay the consultant a daily rate. Daily rates vary, but if you were using a training consultant, you might charge the client $1,000 a day. You could pay the trainer $750 and as the broker keep the difference of $250 as your fee.

To get started, besides a computer you need contact-management, database, or personal-information software and other basic business software and office equipment. Because you will need to write contracts with your clients, you may wish to explore the many prewritten contract software programs available.

Books

The Encyclopedia of Associations, Gale Research, Detroit. Published annually.

How to Start and Manage a Personnel Referral Service Business, Lewis & Renn Associates, Inc., ISBN: 1579160476.

Web Site

National Consultant Referrals, Inc., *www.4consulting-services.com*
www.referrals.com
Also see Part 3.5 for information about using the Web to locate prospective clients.

38

Fax-on-Demand Services

A fax-on-demand service is an exciting marketing and information concept that is both a tool for anyone with a home office to consider and a home business in itself. The technology required to turn fax on demand into a business consists of multiple telephone lines, a modified computer with a special fax board, and customized software that makes the system into an automatic fax-delivery machine that can assist with sales, marketing, customer support, and "fax publishing" for large numbers of clients. Large companies are setting up such systems in-house to speed customer requests for information while reducing their costs of providing it. A fax-on-demand service can provide this for smaller companies and professionals.

Generally a fax-on-demand service works as follows. First, a typical system holds up to one thousand extensions that the fax-on-demand service "leases" to other businesses or individual professionals who want their clients or employees to have information available twenty-four hours a day and seven days a week. These people can call the fax-on-demand service at any time, listen to a synthesized voice telling them what's available, or punch in an extension they've already been told to ask for, and they then leave their fax numbers on the computer. A few seconds later, the computer calls the person back and immediately faxes several pages of up-to-date product literature, a newsletter, or whatever document the lessee wants delivered.

Here are a few examples of the possible uses of a fax-on-demand service. A bank can give customers the special phone number to call to obtain current information about its daily loan and investment rates; busy retailers, wholesalers, and manufacturer's agents can have their prospects and customers call the service for product information; while away at another job, plumbers or carpenters can enable new callers to obtain rate information and schedules; a restaurant can have customers call the number to receive a copy of that day's menu; and a mail-order company can offer more in-depth or up-to-the-minute product descriptions than their catalog does for customers who want more information on an item.

The fax-on-demand software can also be programmed to perform automatic broadcasting services whereby faxes are delivered to large groups of people on a regularly scheduled basis. Such services are useful for companies that need to communicate regularly with sales reps or employees to update them on products or specials, and for associations and trade groups that must communicate with members or associates around the country.

Fax on demand is a good add-on service for answering service and voice-mail businesses, as many of today's voice-mail systems also have a fax-on-demand option or component.

Fax on demand can also be used in conjunction with a 900 number as a way of selling information such as a newsletter or a specialized report. Buyers get charged on their telephone bill for the material they receive by fax with no postage stamps and no collections on your part.

Running a fax-on-demand service requires an initial investment for the hardware (including a scanner needed to scan in the documents that your clients want to have available on the system) and software to record the incoming calls, track them, and bill your clients. You may also choose to use an 800/888-number or 900-number phone line for incoming calls and additional lines for outgoing faxes. The major challenge is marketing this fax delivery system and discovering the many uses that businesses and individuals can make of it. One important concept to keep in mind is that your customers, too, can make money through the service; for example, a restaurant can lease a line from you and charge people for calling in to receive a special recipe by fax, or a plumber might send faxes to do-it-yourselfers for a small fee.

Revenues from this business vary greatly, depending on the number of clients you can get and how extensively they use the system. Some services charge by the page from 3.5 to 6 cents a page depending on volume. Others charge a fee per month for each client to cover incoming calls with unlimited fax responses. Some services place a cap on the number of faxes allowed without additional charges.

A fax-on-demand service has potential as an add-on business for an answering/voice-mail service or a consultant who may work with businesses in marketing or sales.

Software

FaxFacts Fax on Demand, Demonstration, (888) 332-6742, *www. copia.com*

Impact Fax Broadcast, Black Ice Software, Inc., (603) 673-1019, *www.black ice.com*

Financial Information Service

Large numbers of baby boomers are nearing retirement age and are concerned about advice regarding their money for retirement. Those who have invested for retirement are faced with a myriad of choices. People need help sifting through the competing alternatives as well as a predictable glut of information focused on this lucrative market.

Financial planning was once considered a service mainly for the wealthy. But more and more people need help in making sound decisions about what to do with their money. Financial planning has taken off. Selling financial products is one way to go in this growing field, but you may also serve as someone who analyzes your client's situation and then strategize with him or her to develop a plan that they carry out. To pursue a career in financial planning, you need to decide what credentials to obtain. Some financial-planning credentials are available only to those with a specific education. For others, the credentials are relevant to specific services or products. You should research options about what credentials to acquire carefully. The two principal credentials are:

- Certified Financial Planner (CFP), which is perhaps the most general and useful for someone just starting out. Granted by the Certified

Financial Planner Board of Standards, it requires a bachelor's degree, passing an exam, and experience. Educational requirements are specified by the College for Financial Planning.

- Chartered Financial Consultant (ChFC). If you have an insurance background, taking eight courses from the American College plus passing an examination administered by the college will qualify you for this.

After receiving one of these credentials, you can go on to obtain certifications in various specializations including estate planning, insurance analysis, investment analysis, investment consulting, investment management, mutual funds, and retirement planning.

Although you don't need an MBA to operate in the financial arena, you do need a solid background in the financial markets so you know where to look for information and how to get the inside story on investment opportunities. You need to be a good listener and be able to communicate effectively with your clients. Your clients must feel that you are someone who is trustworthy. You should be familiar with software that can handle the analysis of business data or be able to develop your own spreadsheets and formulas for projections about a company's future profitability. You must be able to access pertinent information that is available on the Internet and be conversant with numerous online databases like Dow Jones News/Retrieval, Disclosure II, Company Analyzer, and TRW Business Credit Reports to do research and analysis. Finally, you might be a member of a local bulletin-board system, from which you can get tips and information by chatting with others.

The one caveat about providing financial information and services is that you must be extremely careful about how you promote your business to avoid conflicting with the federal and state licensing and regulatory laws. You must maintain a reputation for honesty and integrity, in addition to your credibility as a researcher and information mogul.

Some financial planners charge a fee either by the hour, per project, or they charge a rate based on the value of the assets they manage. Hourly rates range from $50 to $150 but can go as high as $350. Those who bill based on the client's net worth typically charge a percentage of the client's portfolio value.

Some planners charge a commission based on the investment products they sell. Others charge both a fee and a commission. They charge an hourly rate for their advice and also a commission on the products they sell. A typical gross annual billing is about $90,000 based on billing $100 an hour, eighteen hours a week, fifty weeks a year.

The best way to get business is word of mouth, since this is a field in which trust counts a great deal. One way to begin your business is to offer free information to friends or a few clients over two or three months until you can begin charging them comfortably once they see how much information you can obtain. From there, you can build up a larger list of accounts using their referrals or endorsements. It is advisable to have your own Web site. With a Web site, you can get leads from database directories that are maintained by national organizations that consumers use to locate a professional.

In addition to a personal computer setup, you will need a high-speed modem, a laser printer, and a good spreadsheet or word-processing package that allows you to generate tables, charts, and graphs in your reports to clients.

Books

Deena Katz on Practice Management for Financial Advisers, Planners, and Wealth Managers, Deena Katz, Bloomberg Press, 2001, ISBN: 157660084X.

Getting Started as a Financial Planner, Jeffrey H. Rattiner, Bloomberg Press, 2000, ISBN: 1576600351.

Getting Started in Financial Consulting, Edward J. Stone, Wiley, 2000, ISBN: 0471348147.

So You Want to Be a Financial Planner, Nancy Langdon Jones, AdvisorWorks, 2001, ISBN: 0971443610.

Storyselling for Financial Advisors, Scott West, Mitch Anthony, Dearborn Trade Publishing, 2000, ISBN: 0793136644.

Magazine

Financial Planning Interactive, www.fponline.com

Associations

FINANCIAL PLANNING ASSOCIATION (FPATM), online new planner community, (800) 322-4237, *www.fpanet.org*

NATIONAL ASSOCIATION OF PERSONAL FINANCIAL ADVISORS (NAPFA), fee-only planners, (800) 366-2732, *www.napfa.org*

SOCIETY OF FINANCIAL SERVICE PROFESSIONALS (SFSP), (610)526-2500, *www. financialpro.org*

Software
For Billing

Centerpiece, portfolio management software, Schwab Performance Technologies™, (919) 743-5000, *www.schwabperformancetechnologies.com*

For Financial Planning

Money Tree Software has a suite of programs: (877) 421-9815, *www. moneytree.com.*

FPLAN Professional Advisor, First Financial Software, Inc., (800) 719-8761, *www.fplan.com*

Training and Certification

AMERICAN COLLEGE offers distance education: (888) 263-7265, *www. amercoll.edu*

CERTIFIED FINANCIAL PLANNER BOARD OF STANDARDS (CFP®). The Web site provides a directory of education programs located throughout the United States: (888) 237-6275, 303-830-7500, *www.cfp.net.*

COLLEGE FOR FINANCIAL PLANNING, (800) 237-9990, *www.fp.edu*

40

Form-Design Service

If you are thinking about starting or are currently operating any kind of desktop publishing or graphic-design business, take note that you can expand your customer base and income by also offering a professional form-creation and -design service. The market for this business includes companies and services of all kinds that have special needs for forms such as invoices, purchase orders, customer forms, questionnaires, or other paper documents they may use frequently and need to print in large quantities. An important area of form design is designing computer forms for on-line use where receptionists or operators keyboard information into grids on the screen.

Form design is in some ways akin to the field of ergonomic designing, in that it's becoming recognized by many businesses as a previously over-looked factor in reducing errors, increasing efficiency, and ensuring that a business transaction is properly done. A poorly designed form can take a salesperson much longer to fill out or cause an employee to process infor-mation incorrectly and thereby cost the company money.

With a personal computer and specialized software you can design professional-looking forms on screen with many graphic options from which to choose. The created form can then be printed out in high-resolution type on a laser printer or linotronic machine or transferred directly to a file as a graphic image that can be stored online by a com-puter system.

To market yourself as a form designer, you should have a good back-ground in graphics, type design, and color. You also need to have good communication skills so that you can interview your clients to understand their needs and create the best form for them.

Fees for form designing range from as little as $25 to hundreds of dol-lars for complex jobs that require color separations and special printing.

Software

FormDocs, Free trial: (978) 686-0020, *www.formdocs.com*

HotDocs, LexisNexis™ Group, (800) 500-3627, 801-354-8000, *www.hotdocs.com*

Adobe® Form Designer, *www.adobe.com*

Association

BUSINESS FORMS MANAGEMENT ASSOCIATION, (503) 227-3393, *www.bfma.org*

41

HTML/XML Programmer

HTML (Hyper Text Markup Language) is the international language of the Web. HTML allows text, graphics, video, and audio to be combined in a Web page or site, and then posted on the Internet where it can be accessed by anyone with a browser and a connection. Programming in HTML has grown with the size of the Web itself. Now XML (Extensible Markup Language), which makes it easier to share information between computers, is coming on strong with annual growth estimated over 100 percent since 2001.

Although HTML and XML are programming languages, they are easy to learn. Anyone with an aptitude for computers and logical thinking can become fluent.

Often, people who are not outright experts in the language, such as graphic designers, Webmasters, MIS staff, corporate communications people, wind up doing their own programming when developing their Web sites.

As an HTML/XML expert, you will be able to provide sophisticated solutions to your clients and save them a great deal of time and aggravation in the process. Because of your focus on the language, you will always be aware of the latest developments in features and capabilities. You will be on top of all the capabilities available and will be able to incorporate them into your clients' Web sites.

You will need an up-to-date computer system and familiarity with the latest versions of HTML and XML. You will need a good Web editor, such as Macromedia's *Dreamweaver* (Windows) or Adobe's *PageMill* (Mac). In addition to your programming skills, part of the value you will offer to your clients is your up-to-the-second knowledge of the Web and HTML programming developments. Your best source for this information is the Web itself. Use search-engine databases and online service providers to keep yourself in tune with the industry.

Good strategies for finding clients include networking with the graphic designers in your area who design Web sites. Contact local ISPs (Internet Service Providers) and tell them what you do. You can even contact corporate communications and media services departments of corporations you find online and ask them to outsource their HTML programming to you.

You can charge on an hourly basis or by the project. Rates vary widely depending on the complexity of the project you are working on. When you start out, see what the market will bear from that point forward.

Books

HTML 4 for Dummies, Ed Tittle, Natanya Pitts, Wiley, ISBN: 0764519956.
HTML for the Web with XHTML and CSS, Peachpit Press, ISBN: 0321130073.

Learning XML, Erik T. Ray, O'Reilly, ASIN: 0596000464.

Sams Teach Yourself Web Publishing with HTML & XHTML in 21 Days, Laura Lemay, Rafe Colburn, Sams, ISBN: 0672325195.

XML in a Nutshell, Elliotte Rusty Harold, W. Scott Means, O'Reilly, ISBN: 0596002920.

XML Weekend Crash Course, Kay Ethier, Alan Houser, Wiley, ISBN: 0764547593.

Association

HTML WRITERS GUILD, *www.hwg.org*

Indexing Service

Indexers create indexes for nonfiction documentation to help readers find information quickly. They identify meaningful keywords within the text of the copy and flag them to be included in the index. Some indexers work with print publishers, while others create indexes for the Web and the field of online computer database users. Many authors do not have the time or desire to index their own books, and some publishers don't want them to, so publishers frequently hire independent indexers. (The indexer is often the same person who also prepared the abstract of the article, which this book covers under the category of "Abstracting Service.")

Indexers must have a knack for determining how readers will seek out information and be able to create user-friendly indexes. Whichever kind of indexing you do, you must be a detail-oriented person and enjoy working with words. It also helps to have a background in the subject areas you are indexing or a broad-enough general knowledge and interest to ferret out central ideas and relevant information. The computerization of this business comes in the form of software that allows you to build an index using specialized software that helps you categorize, alphabetize, and keep track of page references.

Book indexers charge from $3 to $10 per printed book page that they read to produce an index, or from $30 to $60 per hour and sometimes more.

The best way to get business is to contact the publishers or database services directly and send them a sample of your work. Many database publishers only work with local indexers, so to find database publishers in your area, decide what type of databases you could work with and then search a directory like the *Epsco Index and Abstract Dictionary* or *Gale Directory of Online, Portable, and Internet Databases.* To locate book publishers for whom you might work, check into *Writer's Market* by Writer's Digest or *Literary Marketplace* published by Bowker. Indexers can obtain referrals by joining a chapter of the American Society of Indexers. Major cities have chapters, and its annual conference attracts publishers with whom indexers can connect.

Books

The Art of Indexing, Larry S. Bonura, Wiley, ISBN: 0471014494.

Directory of Indexing and Abstracting Courses and Seminars, American Society of Indexers, ISBN: 0936547170, *www.asindexing.org*

A Guide to Indexing Software, Linda K. Fetters, Maria Coughlin, Ty Koontz, American Society of Indexers, ISBN: 0936547278.

Marketing Your Indexing Services, Anne Leach (editor), American Society of Indexers, ISBN: 0936547286.

Running Your Indexing Business, American Society of Indexers, ISBN: 0936547324.

Indexing from A to Z, Hans H. Wellisch, H.W. Wilson, ISBN: 082420882X.

Association

AMERICAN SOCIETY OF INDEXERS, (303)463-2887, *www.asindexing.org*

Training

UNITED STATES DEPARTMENT OF AGRICULTURE, Graduate School, (888) 744-GRAD, *http:grad.usda.gov/index.html*

43

Information Brokering

Our society is drowning in information, yet finding the particular information we need when we need it is increasingly a challenge. In the past ten years, the new career of information broker, or information-retrieval service, has developed to meet this challenge. Like a detective, the information broker tracks down any information a client needs, be it market research for a company investigating a possible new product idea, a legal search about government regulations for a law firm, or an erudite biography search for a movie producer. Going far beyond what even a specialized librarian does, the information broker does far more than look up information in books and periodicals. The main tools for the professional information broker are interviews with experts and tapping into any of the thousands of databases on online computer systems that hold millions of documents in their original form or as abstracts (summary form). In fact, with so many databases and online systems, each with its own set of passwords and methods of use, today's information broker does best by specializing in a particular type of research such as high technology, business, manufacturing, or whatever.

To do well in this business, you do not necessarily need a degree in library science, although it may help some people. You must have, however, an absolute love for information and a never-say-die attitude in sleuthing through whatever sources you need to find what your client wants. You must also have an ability to sell your service, since many people are not used to paying for information; still others consider it a commodity available free on the Internet. And last, it helps to be somewhat familiar with the many online information services available, at least to the point of knowing how to do a computer search cost effectively and how to get help when you need it.

Information brokers typically charge between $20 and $100 per hour, or hire themselves out on a monthly retainer for businesses that have frequent needs for information searches. Typically full-time brokers gross between $17,500 and $75,000 per year. Some brokers command fees up to $200 an hour and produce significantly more income. Networking and personal contacts in organizations, such as trade and business associations in the industries or fields in which you specialize, are the best sources of business. Speaking and offering seminars on information searching at meetings and trade shows or writing for trade journals can also be effective.

To be in this business, you will need an up-to-date personal computer with broadband Internet access, a large-capacity hard disk for storage of information you retrieve, a fax capability to receive copies of original documents, and a good printer for your reports to clients. Do not forget that you will also need to pay monthly fees to all the online information services to which you subscribe.

Books

Building & Running a Successful Research Business, Mary Ellen Bates, Reva Basch, Cyberage Books, 2003, ISBN: 0910965625.
The Invisible Web: Uncovering Information Sources Search Engines Can't See, Chris Sherman, Gary Price, Independent Publishers Group, 2001, ISBN: 091096551X.
Super Searchers Make It on Their Own, Suzanne Sabroski, Reva Basch, Cyberage Books, 2002, ISBN: 0910965595.

Magazines and Newsletters

INFORMATION TODAY, INC., publishes a number of magazines and newsletters: (609) 654-6266, *www.onlineinc.com*

Association

ASSOCIATION OF INDEPENDENT INFORMATION PROFESSIONALS, (225) 408-4400, *www.aiip.org*

Training

AMELIA KASSEL offers various training programs: (800) 544-5924, (707) 829-9421, *www.marketingbase.com*

Many colleges and universities of library science have courses on information searching open to outside students. Information Professionals Institute, (972) 732-0160, offers seminars with industry leaders: *www.burwellinc.com*

44

Internet Consultant

Most businesses of any size, governments, and nonprofits employ the Web in a growing number of ways. Although they understand the Web's advantages, many businesses and organizations lack the in-house capability to achieve their goals and thus are candidates for the services of an Internet consultant.

Internet consultants are somewhat different from computer consultants. Internet consultants are specialists whose domain is, of course, the Internet and its component parts. Additionally, Internet consultants also must have a feel for marketing and communications. Most companies turn to the Internet to add strength to their marketing and to improve the efficiency of their communications. Specifically, Internet consultants help companies and organizations understand and implement Internet-based solutions in areas such as:

Internet connectivity and access
Intranet/Internet connectivity
E-commerce
Internet communications and transactions such as e-mail, video conferencing, interactive forms, secure transactions, digital money (or e-cash).
Internet applications such as Archie, Veronica, FTP, telnet, gopher, WWW, WAIS
"Netiquette" and rules for proper and appropriate network usage
Search-engine optimization
How to research, including finding addresses, databases, vendors, and service companies

If you believe your experience with and knowledge of the Internet and your understanding of the basics of marketing and general business knowledge would be of help to a company getting its feet wet in the cyberpond, you may have what it takes to be an Internet consultant. Your potential clients will include businesses that are either considering putting up Web sites, or have just done so. Potential clients also include companies and organizations that have had a basic Web site up for a while but wish to expand their Internet presence. You can prospect for clients in both the virtual and actual domains. Virtually, start by putting up your own Web site that explains your experience, services, and areas of expertise. Then publicize your site through targeted e-mail and online networking. Avoid "spamming," which is overtly advertising yourself. Rather, contribute useful information and try to establish yourself as an expert. Networking at your local chamber of commerce and other civic and business organizations is also quite helpful. You can also host free Web seminars for prospective clients in public meeting rooms, etc. Write articles on relevant Internet and business issues and get them published in business, computer print, and online magazines. These activities will establish you as an expert to whom people will want to turn.

A successful, well-known Internet consultant with a track record can charge $200 per hour or even more. But if you're just starting out, your rates need to be much lower. The range for Internet consultants with a year or two of experience usually starts at $40 and up. Contact other Internet and computer consultants and try to find what they charge, then set your prices accordingly. Set your prices somewhere in the middle of the figures you are quoted.

Books

Telecommunications in Business: Strategy and Application, John Vargo, Ray Hunt, McGraw-Hill/Irwin, ISBN: 0256197873.

Web Sites

Internet.Com, the Internet and IT Network, *www.iworld.com*
Internet World Online Magazine, *www.internetworld.com*
Web Developer's Virtual Library is a site that contains an extensive list of bookmarks, reference material, and software useful to Web consultants: *www.wdvl.com.*

Association

INDEPENDENT COMPUTER CONSULTANTS ASSOCIATION, (800) 774-4222, *www. icca.org*

45

Internet Researcher

The Web can be an unruly place. Oftentimes a search through the Web for information will yield a jumbled and confusing array of results. It's touted as the ultimate research tool and information resource, and it really is, but unless someone has a great deal of experience in conducting searches and performing research, or an unlimited amount of time to follow a sometimes endless series of links, finding exactly the information one needs on the Web can be a daunting task.

One of the services most helpful to researchers on the Web today is what's known as "Meta" sites. A Meta site is a Web site devoted to a specific or single type of information. An example of a successful Meta site is Brint (*www.brint.com/interest.html*). It is one of the most information-rich, useful places on the Web for business and technological issues and is searchable for any business topic of interest. It is also organized into a comprehensive series of links by subject matter such as Journals & Magazines (links to business-related magazines and research journals), IS Professional Careers (links to positions offered, career trends, etc.), International Business Technology (links to worldwide business entities and organizations, travel resources, international media), and much, much more. Know this.com (*www.knowthis.com*) is a Meta site that is a knowledge site for marketing interests. These Web sites offer little in terms of original content but, rather, offer visitors well-organized, comprehensive lists of resources and "links" to other useful sites, all pertaining to a single area of interest.

Running a Meta site can serve several functions in terms of *your* business interests. If you develop a site that appeals to a large number of people, you can sell advertising space, or you can look for sponsors: companies who sell products or services to the market you attract. For example, a Meta site that provides an exhaustive series of links to sports teams, sport statistics databases, season schedules, sports news sources, sport equipment manufacturers, etc., would be a great site for beverage bottlers, sports publications, or even professional sports teams to sponsor. A Meta site is also an excellent way to promote a primary business such as an Internet consultancy or Internet trainer, Web writer, Web-site reviewer, Web publication, Web promotions expert, or Web program. Such a site will establish your credibility in any of these areas and draw attention and perhaps even publicity to you and your business.

To start a Meta site, you must, of course, select an area of concentration. Choose a subject that you're interested in, even passionate about. You'll be spending a lot of time conducting research for site content, so if you have a high level of personal interest, your research will go more smoothly. Then meticulously search the Web to make sure that there aren't too many such sites in existence. Now you're ready to begin some serious research. The value of a Meta site is that it saves visitors to your site a considerable amount of time in performing their own research. The time you save them must, however, be invested by you. Your job at this point is to sift through the countless thousands of Web sites that do not provide substantive information on your area of concentration and compile a listing of those that do. You must also categorize lists of relevant sites into meaningful categories. The better and deeper your own research, the more value you will offer to your site's visitors. Check other Meta sites to see how much information they offer and how the information is organized. You will also have to actually design and post your site on the Web. There are many Web designers who can offer you some excellent solutions at fairly reasonable prices. Check for designers online and also ask your local Internet Service Provider if they can design a Meta site for you, or if they can recommend someone who can. If you want to build up high traffic quickly, you may also wish to engage the service of a good Web publicist or promotions specialist.

Books

Building & Running a Successful Research Business: A Guide for the Independent Doing Internet Research, Steve Jones, SAGE Publications (November 3, 1998), ISBN: 0761915958.

Find it Online, Facts on Demand Press, ISBN: 1889150290.

Searching and Researching on the Internet and the Web, Ernest C. Ackermann, Karen Hartman, Franklin Beedle & Associates, ISBN: 1887902716.

Magazine

InfoWorld Online Magazine, www.infoworld.com

Web Site

http:archive.ncsa.uiuc.edu/SDG/Software/Mosaic/StartingPoints/Network-StartingPoints.html. This Metasite contains hyperlinks to many common Internet-based information resources.

46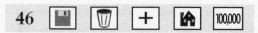

Internet Service Provider and Web-Site Hosting

The Internet and the Web are not a nebulous collection of sites that exist in a mysterious dimension called cyberspace. What we call "the Web" is actually a complex network of servers (host computers) linked together through routers and high-speed communications lines that share common protocol languages. Every site you've ever accessed on the Web actually resides on a server somewhere on the network. These servers, in many cases, aren't the large mainframe or minicomputers you might imagine. That site you browsed last night may well have been "served" on a PC. And you might be surprised to find out that these servers don't reside on the upper floors of corporate high rises or communication towers. There are more than a few servers on the Web residing in people's living rooms and dens. For a monthly fee an internet service provider provides access to the Internet. The service provider gives you a software package, user name, password, and access phone number.

Running a server on the Web as a home business has a number of clear advantages. Your income is derived from "renting" space on your server. The larger the Web site, the more space it takes up and the more you can charge for rent. In addition to occupying space, Web sites also generate "traffic." The more a site is accessed and viewed, the greater its traffic. Higher traffic takes up more "bandwidth." Bandwidth is the second resource you have to sell as a server and the greater a site's traffic, the more you charge for it. The great thing here is that once a site resides on your server, all the income you derive from it is passive. It's like owning real estate; you can charge rent for its use.

The technical requirements for running a server are straightforward. Besides a computer, you need a high-speed connection to the Web. You will need to lease a special line from your local phone or cable company to gain greater bandwidth. Bandwidth is the essential commodity in Web hosting. The more bandwidth you can offer, the more competitive you will be. You'll need to do some research into this area because we don't have the space to devote to it. Configuring a server and maintaining it can get rather technical. You may want to consider hiring a consultant to get you up and running and to be a phone call away in case of problems.

Web-Site Hosting

Reseller programs make it possible for a business to rent a Web server from an already established Web hosting company and then market it as their own. When you become a reseller you are independent of the Web hosting company and run your own company. Most resellers get paid based on the number of new clients that they attract per month, and then on a recurring basis for each client they retain.

The first thing you need to think about is what services you want to resell. Do you for example, only want to resell Web hosting? You can in fact, resell most aspects of a Web-hosting operation. For example, you can offer clients connections and backbones, servers, and e-commerce storefronts. There are some resellers who prefer to farm out as much as possible so that they can concentrate on the business end of things. Other resellers offer additional features that a regular Web-hosting company might not provide, such as Web design services.

Once you've decided what services you want to resell, it's time to choose a program, and there are many programs out there to choose from. It's wise to go with a company that's been around for a while and has a proven track record. There will always be companies that promise higher returns, but when all is said and done, it is usually the companies that have lots of experience who can deal with the snags that are bound to arise in the day-to-day operations of your business.

If you decide that you want to run a full-service Web-hosting company, there is more to consider than the servers you need to host your clients' Web sites on. Connectivity is one of the most important components to consider. You'll need a redundant connection to an Internet backbone if you want to run a well-connected Web-hosting company. Avoid choosing a provider that only has a single connection. Go for a provider with multiple connections. If a single connection goes down, then so do all your clients' Web sites. If a provider with multiple connections has a problem with one connection, there are others available as backup and your client sites won't be affected.

Software is another factor to give serious consideration to. Your servers require an operating system, so it's wise to pick a system that will be compatible with yours and meet your needs. You may want to offer e-commerce services to your clients, and you need software that can handle this.

Solid technical support is also critical. Unless you have the technical expertise, make sure that you choose a reseller who can offer you top-notch support.

Once you have the technical side of your business in place, attracting customers is the next step. Initially, it's probably wise to appeal to small businesses and individuals. They're usually working on tight budgets and don't want or expect intensive hosting services. These smaller operations are likely to have fewer requirements, and you will have a chance to get your feet wet before getting in over your head. All it takes is one client, and you are in the Web-hosting business! You may want to consider hiring a consultant to get you up and running and to be a phone call away in case of problems.

If the idea of actually owning a physical server and leasing a connection seems overwhelming, you can offer Web-site hosting on a virtual server. A virtual server is where you don't have a physical computer—you just "rent" space on somebody else's and configure it to resell to clients as Web-server space. The only disadvantage to this is that you are at the mercy of another's space limitations, service schedule, and general business fortunes. If the owner of the physical server upon which you rent space goes out of business, so do you, at least temporarily.

Once you've got your server and high-speed connection up, or have a virtual-server deal in place, you can market your service to a wide number of potential clients. Web-site designers and design agencies are always looking for new, competitively priced high-speed servers. Send an e-mail to every Webmaster you come across when browsing sites. It's wise to network with local Internet service providers. They generally serve their own sites, but sometimes they get full and you can take their overload. You may even want to consider a small ad in a national computer- or Internet-oriented magazine.

To determine current competitive rates for bandwidth, call your competitors and find out what they charge. Rates vary depending on where you are located.

Books

ISP Marketing Survival Guide, Christopher M. Knight, Wiley, ISBN: 0471376795.

Service Provider Strategy, Anne M. Burris, Prentice-Hall PTR, ISBN: 0130420085.

Strategies for Web Hosting and Managed Services, Doug Kaye, Wiley, ISBN: 0471085782.

Web Site

NEXT GENERATION SERVICES (successor to Boardwatch) publishes NGS Services Directories, which make it possible to find and compare services and software: */www.nextgenerationservices.com/*.

47

Internet Trainer

The Internet is the fastest-growing communications medium since television. Every day more businesses, schools, civic organizations, and so on are on the Internet. Yet, many of the people within these organizations are not familiar with even the basics of the Internet and how it can be used effectively. Many companies and organizations are turning to Internet trainers to teach their employees about the Internet and how it can be utilized to help serve the companies' needs.

The need for knowledgeable Internet experts who also have an affinity for teaching is definitely on the rise. There has been an increase in the number of both midsized and smaller firms that provide Internet training, but the market is still growing.

To set about becoming an Internet trainer, you must, of course, possess a great deal of knowledge about the Internet and how it works. You must also know the basic principles of instructional design so that you can develop cohesive course content outlines. You must also be able to relate to the students in your classes and one-on-one sessions. Your students will most likely be technical novices. There are a number of Internet textbooks you can purchase and teach from, but we recommend that you develop your own course work. This will you give you an added benefit in the marketplace.

The areas that companies are paying to be trained in include:

HTML, XML, JavaScript, and Web Authoring Tools: how to create Web pages to format documents and make them available via the Internet.

Doing Business on the Internet: how large and small organizations are using the Internet to enhance visibility, increase productivity, improve customer relations and support, reduce costs, advertise effectively, and sell creatively.

There are many other subject areas in which clients may desire instruction. If there is enough demand in a specific area, develop a course to teach it.

As an Internet trainer you may find yourself teaching large classes at your clients' facilities. You may also be asked to work one-on-one with specific employees. In either case, you will have to have your course work developed before you begin teaching. Materials you will need include course outlines that you can send to prospective clients as well as hand out at the beginning of a class or session. You will also need detailed teaching plans that outline what subjects will be covered during each session. Teaching plans are for your own use and should not be given to clients or students. You will need at least one textbook for each of the classes you teach. You can use a published textbook and include it in your teaching plan, or you can develop your own. Your own textbook need not be a professionally bound and published book. You can use a word processor and a desktop publishing program to produce the book, and then print it out on a laser printer. Take the print out to a copy shop and have them photocopy and bind just the number of books you will need for each class.

To find clients, start by developing a Web site of your own. Be sure to include a form on your site that allows visitors to request further information. In most cases, you will need to go to a client's location to do your training, so you will, at least at first, have to confine your marketing efforts to your immediate region. Networking at your local chamber of commerce and other business organizations is a great way to market locally. Try calling your local Internet service provider and arranging a deal whereby you train the business customers who request it. Since Internet training is a fairly new and specialized service, advertisements in local business publications might also bring you some results. You may also consider giving free seminars to businesses on "The Power of the Internet" or "Internet Business Solutions" to attract local clients.

Income potential as an Internet trainer is good. Hourly fees range from $50 to $175 for class instruction, and $40 to $100 per hour for individual instruction. You can also charge by class. This can vary a great deal, so find out what is being charged in your local area.

Books

Instructional Design Fundamentals, Barbara B. Seels, Educational Technology Publications, ISBN: 0877782849.

The McGraw-Hill Internet Training Manual, Ronald L. Wagner, Eric Englemann, McGraw-Hill, ASIN: 0070669376.

48

Inventory-Control Services

We first saw an inventory-control service in operation at a health-food store—a man we were acquainted with was using a bar-code reader and a notebook computer to inventory the shelves of his "mom-and-pop" store. A few months later we were giving a workshop in the second-floor meeting room of another health-food store and were telling the group about this business. The owner on the floor below overheard us and shouted up, "If any one of you wants to get into that business, I'll be your first customer!"

Many businesses need inventory control, which embraces not only merchandise in stores and warehouses but also office equipment and vehicles, as well as other kinds of equipment used by businesses, nonprofit institutions, and governments. Small businesses in particular need to know their inventory and when to reorder, but often they lack the technology or the staff to do it efficiently.

While inventory can still be done with a bar-code reader and notebook using either a database program or special inventory-control software, the technology for doing inventories has advanced in a number of ways that enhance its potential as an add-on, part-time, or even full-time business. For example:

A TimeWand II handheld code-scanning device will read "buttons" attached to vehicles or equipment that will withstand weather and handling. This product, made by Videx, will also read other types of media with bar codes.

A software package called *PC Census* eliminates manual scanning of all equipment and software attached to a LAN to produce an inventory.

A bar-code printer might be the basis of a service for colleges, small cities, or companies in which you provide printed bar codes on permits that then can be assigned to vehicles, allowing law-enforcement or parking officers to instantly identify a vehicle from the bar code placed on the windshield.

Fees for inventory services may be established for doing the inventory on a regular, recurring basis, or if you help the business computerize its inventory-control system, you can likely obtain a consultant's fee for selecting, installing, and setting up the hardware and software as well.

Hardware and Software

BEAR ROCK TECHNOLOGIES (530) 672-0244, (800) 232-7625, *www.source data.com/500/000155.html*

PORTABLE TECHNOLOGY SOLUTIONS, (877) 640-4152, *www.ptshome.com*

TIMEWAND II, VIDEX, INC., (541) 758-0521, *www.videx.com*

Law Library Management

In the course of any given day, a lawyer usually refers to many law books; so many, in fact, that law firms usually maintain their own private libraries. The problem is, books in a law library must be kept current with the continual stream of updates on the latest legal rulings, which are supplied on a regular basis by publishers. Keeping the library updated, however, is an important but time-consuming task.

As a result, medium-sized law firms and corporate legal departments that are not large enough to employ a full-time law librarian contract out the management of their law libraries to a law library management firm, which keeps the physical law library up-to-date. This business requires that you acquire or already have a background in legal reference work and have a system for keeping the library current that is flexible enough to be adapted to the needs of a variety of clients. Since many firms also do on-line computer research, you should also know how to use the online services such as Lexis, Nexis (*www.lexisnexis.com*), and Westlaw (*http:lawschool. westlaw.com/DesktopDefault.aspx*) efficiently.

Once established, this business provides steady work because updating is an ongoing enterprise. Your hours can be long, however, and the work can be repetitive. Typical gross revenues can range from $35,000 to $80,000 a year.

Networking in librarian associations and personal contacts with legal librarians can be a source of business as can direct mail addressed to the managing partners of law firms. Mail, however, needs to get through the secretary, so it needs to look like news or an announcement. We suggest having an informative, professional brochure to leave with people you meet. Also, you need a visual identity so as lawyers repeatedly see your logo you will develop name recognition. Once you have a few clients, you are likely to make many other contacts in the field while working in clients' offices.

Newsletter

Legal Information Alert, (773)525-7594, *www.alertpub.com/hplia.html*

Association

THE AMERICAN ASSOCIATION OF LAW LIBRARIES, (312) 939-4764, *www.aallnet.org*

Training

THE UNITED STATES DEPARTMENT OF AGRICULTURE GRADUATE SCHOOL offers a course in library technology, (888) 744-4723, (202) 314-3300, *www.grad. usda.gov.*

50

Legal Transcript Digesting (Deposition Digesting)

Transcript digesting (also called deposition digesting) is an important part of the complex practice of law in this country and a potentially well-paying career as well. The transcript digester assists lawyers by summarizing documents that they need to read as background for their cases.

The need for transcript-digesting services arises from the way legal cases flow through the court system. First, lawyers don't like to be surprised in the courtroom when someone takes the stand, and they are entitled to know what the opposition has as evidence. So prior to a trial, lawyers take testimony from those involved under oath in what is called a deposition. Depositions are recorded by a court reporter, and then the entire testimony is transcribed into a document, which the lawyers must study carefully before the trial. As you can imagine, the transcripts are quite long, so to save time for the lawyers, transcript digesters identify relevant points and summarize the transcript. Each page of testimony is reduced to a paragraph. Depositions are also carefully indexed for the lawyers.

Digesters can also digest trial transcripts during the course of a trial, such as when an attorney needs a transcript of a previous day's proceedings to prepare for cross-examination. In lengthy trials that can last for months, digests of prior testimony are essential. Digests are also used in making appeals.

Sometimes digests are prepared by trained paralegals. In fact, digesting transcripts is part of paralegal training, but a digest can also be done by someone who has the ability to analyze and write succinctly. And today more and more law firms, from the solo practitioner to large firms, are using outside digesting services.

Provided that you have the ability to write clearly, this is a business that takes a minimal amount of time to learn, costs little to start, and has the potential for earning good money. Typically digesters are paid by the transcript page. Novice digesters who work for an agency earn $.80 to $1 per page. Experienced digesters working on their own earn $2.50 to $4.00 per page. Ten to twenty pages per hour is typical for an eight-hour day. Gross revenues for a digester can range from $38,000 to $100,000 or more per year.

Software

SUMMATION LEGAL TECHNOLOGIES, (800) 735-7866, 415- 442-0404, *www. summation.com*

Training

MEDITEC.COM, (801) 593-0663, *www.meditec.com*

Web Site

Scopists.com, *www.scopists.com*

51 ABC 🗑 🏠 -$

Legal Transcription Service

Although most state and federal courts employ court reporters with computers at trials and legal proceedings (see no. 78, Scopist), many other trials, as well as various kinds of legal hearings such as arbitration negotiations, worker's compensation, and law-enforcement interrogations, use tape recorders and sound tapes that must later be transcribed. This job is done by a legal transcriptionist who, like a medical transcriptionist, frequently works at home using transcribers and computers to produce the documents that are used for record keeping and reference.

While technology has improved the way in which the work of legal transcription gets done, the basic work attorneys need to have done remains much as it has been for years. This ranges from transcribing one-on-one interviews recorded on tape to transcribing tapes dictated remotely into taping equipment in the legal transcriptionist's home office.

Legal transcription requires excellent typing ability and a devotion to accuracy and perfection. You will need to know the special vocabulary of law and the formatting conventions used in typing up legal motions, cross-examinations, summations, hearings, and other proceedings. Strong listening skills are critical, since you are transcribing from tape and must sometimes identify up to four voices—the judge, a witness, and two attorneys. Finally, you must also be able to work well under pressure, since some projects have short turnaround times.

Since it is the courts who hire most legal transcriptionists, to get started you can contact the state and federal courts in your area to find out about transcription needs and any certification requirements. Transcriptionists are usually paid on a per-page basis, and a diligent and accurate legal transcriptionist can generally type sixty to eighty or more pages a day. Average annual earnings range from $20,000 to $60,000 on a full-time basis, while on a part-time basis you can earn half this amount.

Software

SUMMATION LEGAL TECHNOLOGIES, (800) 735-7866/(415) 442-0404, *www. summation.com*

Training

MEDITEC.COM, (801) 593-0663, *www.meditec.com/*

Lifestyle and Hobby Resource Web Site

One of the great benefits of the Web is that it provides a way for participants of any lifestyle, hobby, or trend a way to find each other and exchange information, opinions, news, etc. From stamp collectors to gardeners, ballroom dancers to cigar devotees, and no matter where in the world, people with similar interests are connecting through the Web. Cyber entrepreneurs and enthusiasts have recognized the Web's unique strength and have created an income for themselves and helped the cause of their interest and passion. The Web provides exciting opportunities to pursue a passion and perhaps turn it into a viable business. The possibilities are virtually endless but should conform to the Web's unique strengths and characteristics: The more unique the content or subject, the better chance you will have of attracting online traffic. For example, a site that covers all aspects of jazz in America might not do as well as a site dedicated to American avant-garde jazz or the work of Charles Mingus.

The more interactive you make the site, the better. Include a "chat" room where visitors can interact with each other in real time and discussion groups where visitors can post messages for others to read and respond to.

Include audio and video content, if appropriate.

Include a well-thought-out page of links to other sites relevant to your content.

The more frequently you update your content, the better. Do it once a day, if possible. This gives visitors a reason to return frequently.

Unless you go into production of your resource site with a sponsor already in place, this enterprise may take awhile to generate income. We recommend that you start off on a part-time basis. A resource site works very well for Web-site designers, Web writers, Web consultants, and Web server hosts. Although the resource site might not create an instant revenue stream, it can help attract business to your main moneymaking activity. Once you have built a fairly high level of traffic on your site, there are several ways to generate income. You can sell advertising for a certain number of daily visitors that you can demonstrate visited your site. You can also approach potential sponsors such as equipment manufacturers or print magazines that cater to your visitors' interests or any company or organization that provides products or services of interest to your visitors.

Magazine

HotWired Online Magazine, www.hotwired.com

53

Local Area Network (LAN) / Intranet Consultant

Networking allows all the computers in an office, or throughout an entire company, the ability to share programs and allows users to work on the same document simultaneously and access the same data files. LANS (local area networks) can also be connected to the Internet, giving several computers access simultaneously. Although a great many small-business people recognize that networking their computers into a LAN would be of great benefit, most of them don't have the time or expertise to do it themselves, even though Windows has made this much easier to do.

Wireless networking is growing in acceptance, but inevitably problems arise. This creates a need for independent LAN consultants who are expert at configuring and maintaining local area networks.

Many LAN consultants focus their energies on serving larger and mid-sized businesses that have twenty-five or more computer users. We believe that there is a market for focusing on the home-based office and small-business market. Even if a home office has only two computers, efficiency of operations will greatly increase if those machines are networked. Most of the latest versions of the major word-processing, database, spreadsheet, and presentation graphics programs are all designed to accommodate net-worked situations. By helping home offices and small offices utilize the power of networking, you will help them take advantage of the power of the technology they already possess.

Lower-cost and less complicated networking software is designed specifically with the small office in mind. These are known as "peer to peer" networks. Peer-to-peer networks do not require a dedicated server and allow each machine in the network to communicate equally. In addition to the networking software, networks with more than two computers will require the installation of network cards..

As a LAN consultant for the home-office and small-business market, your potential clients are businesses that utilize two or more computers in their daily operations. You can find clients by networking, in person, that is, at your local chamber of commerce, business events, users' groups, and trade-organization events. If you can afford it, try running small advertisements in your local business journal that emphasize your focus on the home-office and small-office market. Rates can range from $60 to $100 per hour, depending on the complexity of the project and your level of experience and skill.

Books

SOHO Networking: A Guide to Installing a Small-Office/Home-Office Network, Peter Moulton, Prentice-Hall, ISBN: 0130473316.

Wireless Home Networking for Dummies, Danny Briere, Pat Hurley, Walter Bruce, For Dummies, ISBN: 0764539108.

The Wireless Networking Starter Kit, Adam Engst, Glenn Fleishman, Peachpit Press, ISBN: 032122468X.

Web Site

ZDNET.COM, source for many useful computer and networking magazines and products, *www.zdnet.com*

54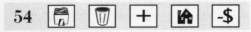

Mailing-List Service

A mailing-list service is a business that's relatively easy to enter and costs little to start up once you've purchased your computer and printer. It makes a good sideline business or an excellent add-on service for a wide variety of other businesses. It can also grow into a substantial full-time venture.

As a mailing-list service, you can put your computer to work providing a number of different services. For example:

List Creation: You probably won't be able to compete with the large mail-list companies that sell thousands of names in thousands of categories, but you can create lists tailored to your locality or your particular clients' needs. For example, you can contact new residents or businesses in your community, or make lists of solo practitioners such as doctors and dentists, or lists compiled from local associations, clubs, and groups. You can then sell these lists to companies in your area that seek sales leads and names for direct marketing or mail-order businesses. You can sell these specialized mailing lists that you develop or purchase from others.

List Maintenance: Maintaining mailing-list databases for clients, using their invoices or receipts of current customers. Since many businesses don't make use of their existing list of names, your job is to help them turn these names into a valuable mailing list, since it's always easier to get more business from existing customers than it is to find new customers.

Doing Mailings—Letter Shop Services: Since many companies don't have the expertise or equipment to do direct mail, you can design a campaign, using their list, a rented list, or your own list, and take charge of the printing, sorting, addressing, and mailing of the items to be sent out. Or consult with companies to help them do direct mail themselves.

List Brokering: Some services help clients to locate and choose mailing lists for specific objectives.

Teaching Clients to Handle Mailing Lists: Handling mailing lists may be complex enough for some clients that they want to engage the services of a tutor to teach them how to do their own mailings.

To get started as a mailing-list service, you will need a personal computer with a large-capacity hard drive, a high-quality laser printer that can handle mailing labels, and a database program, preferably a relational database program such as *Microsoft Access, Paradox,* or *FoxPro,* that allows you to store and sort through names and listings in many ways. You can purchase mailing-list software and bar-coding/sorting software. You need to learn about specific U.S. Postal regulations and rates, and about the automated services offered by the Postal Service. You may also wish to have your own folding and sorting equipment in the event that you manage direct mailings for companies. As for marketing your business, approaching owners of small local stores that are collecting customer names is the quickest route to getting maintenance or consulting business, and networking and advertising in the yellow pages are effective methods for selling lists you've compiled yourself.

Income potential for a full-time mailing-list service ranges from $40,000 to $100,000 a year. Depending on your services, you can charge monthly fees for database maintenance, set fees (usually per thousand names) to do mailings, or per-hour charges for professional consulting in direct-mail techniques. You can also increase your earnings by adding additional services such as pickup and delivery, twenty-four-hour turnaround time, high-quality printing, or folding-and-sorting capability.

While this business has few requirements, you will be most successful if you have some experience using database management systems that handle mail merge and relational sorting. You also should be familiar with all postal regulations regarding mass mailings and software such as *ArcList* and *AccuMail,* two of the best-selling products that are vital in the direct-marketing business for sorting addresses and applying zip+4 codes to addresses and bar coding of envelopes.

Organizations

MAILING AND FULFILLMENT SERVICES ASSOCIATION is the trade association for this industry but has few or no home-based members. Its *Forms Manual* may be of interest: (800) 333-6272/(703) 836-9200, *www.masa.org*.

NATIONAL POSTAL FORUM assists the United States Postal Service in building relationships with large mailers. Audiotapes of past conferences may provide you with useful information: *www.nationalpostalforum.org*.

Web Sites

ACT! CERTIFIED CONSULTANTS (ACCs) in your area can be located from the directory at *www.act.com/community*; Maximizer's at *www.maximizer.com/services*.

THE UNITED STATES POSTAL SERVICE'S site provides publications, business forms, mailing tips, and software tools: *www.usps.com/ncsc*.

55

Market-Mapping Service

Market mapping is a fast-growing and exciting field that helps companies track their customer demographics and dramatically improve their understanding of patterns such as sales potential and market penetration. The field merges sophisticated mapping software with database-management systems so that what was formerly difficult-to-decipher alphanumeric data and statistics can be turned into clear, captivating visual information in the form of maps. And now, thanks to low-cost but powerful PC-based mapping software, the field has become a viable desktop business that can be operated from home as easily as a desktop-publishing or word-processing service.

Market-mapping services can assist many kinds of clients. You might consult with a marketing director trying to decide the best location for a new franchise store or a restaurateur wanting to find the right spot for a new restaurant with the most foot traffic at lunch. Or you might work with a CEO needing to relocate the office but not wanting to disrupt employee drive patterns, or an advertising executive trying to decide where to place a billboard or in which newspapers a client should advertise. Even mail-order companies and small businesses can benefit from an analysis of their customers' location and purchasing habits.

Getting into this business does not require a special degree in geography or cartography, since the field focuses more on marketing concepts and the use and analysis of data. You do need a good understanding of market-mapping software and the applications it can perform, and a strong interest or background in marketing, sales, and data management. Besides typical computer hardware, you'll need a scanner, a digitizing tablet with pen or puck, and desktop mapping application software such as *ArcView* and *Atlas GIS* along with any various geographic-based maps you may need for your work.

Earnings in this field will vary depending on the volume and depth of your assignments. Given the professional nature of the work and the expertise you can bring a client your fees can range up to $100 per hour.

Software

ArcGIS product line, *www.esri.com*

Atlas GIS and Mapping Software, (909) 793-2853, *www.esri.com*

Book

Rand McNally 2004 Commercial Atlas & Marketing Guide (updated annually), Rand McNally, *www.randmcnally.com*

56

Medical Billing Service

While medical billing services have been around for many years, there are still opportunities in many parts of the country that are worth exploring if you have a sound knowledge of medical insurance and good computer and accounting skills. In recent years, the private health-insurance carriers have also recognized the value of electronic billing, which is a more efficient and preferred way of billing. A billing service prepares insurance claims using a personal computer and special medical billing software and then sends them electronically to the Medicare intermediaries and insurance companies for evaluation and payment. A medical billing service might also handle other related tasks in billing, such as following up on rejected claims, invoicing the patient for deductibles and co-payments (the portion that most health-insurance companies don't pay), and generally maintaining patient accounts.

A medical billing service isn't limited to serving medical doctors. Health professionals who also need billing services are medical specialists, chiropractors, commercial ambulance services, dentists, home nursing services, massage therapists, nurse practitioners, occupational therapists, optometrists, physical therapists, physician assistants, psychologists, as well as other counselors, respiratory therapists, speech therapists, and health-care providers who do third-party billing.

You do need specialized knowledge to succeed in this field. For example, you must know the rules and regulations for submitting electronic Medicare and private-insurance claims. CPAs, nurses, and people with experience as back-office personnel in medical offices or hospitals are good candidates for this business. If you don't have experience in the medical field, courses are offered at community colleges. You can also attend various Medicare-sponsored classes. Contact the Medicare office in your area for information about these classes. You will need to purchase a medical billing software package that allows for electronic bill submission.

The most effective way to market your medical billing business is to contact doctors' offices directly, as well as to do direct mail announcing your service. Since some doctors prefer to keep the billing in their control, you will need a strategy to convince them that you can do a better job than an in-house billing secretary could.

Books:

7 Steps to Getting into the Medical Billing Business, Rick Benzel, ClaimTek Software, 2004, *www.claimtek.com*

A Guide to Health Insurance Billing, Marie A. Moisio, Delmar Learning, 2000, ISBN: 0766812073.

Medical Billing, Claudia A. Yalden, CAY Medical Management, 1999, ISBN: 0739203614.

Medical Billing Marketing Success, Merlin B. Coslick, Electronic Medical Billing Network of America, Inc., 1998, ISBN: 189397801X. Coslick has other spiral-bound titles: *Setting Up Your Medical Billing Business*,

ISBN: 1893978052, and *Medical Billing Home-Based Business*, ISBN: 1893978044.

Start Your Own Medical Claims Billing Service, Rob Adams, Terry Adams, Entrepreneur Media, Inc., 2003, ISBN: 1891984802.

Associations Offering Training

ELECTRONIC MEDICAL BILLING NETWORK OF AMERICA, INC., (908) 470-4100, *www.medicalbillingnetwork.com*

NATIONAL ELECTRONIC BILLERS ALLIANCE (NEBA), (650) 359-4419, *www.nebazone.com*

Web Sites

CONSUMER CLAIMS OF MEDICAL BILLING SCAMS: *http:pub1.ezboard.com/bmedicalbillingscamwatch*

MEDICARE: Designed by the government for seniors, it has publications available for downloading, *www.medicare.gov.*

57

Medical Transcription Service

Medical transcription is a specialized field, in which much of the work is done by independent transcriptionists. Medical transcriptionists produce typed reports and documents from dictations that doctors, nurses, and other medical personnel have made regarding their patients. Medical transcriptions are required for many reasons: to create a record for other doctors who work with a patient to review; to serve as evidence in malpractice suits; and to obtain insurance reimbursement, since most insurance carriers require a report before they will pay for surgery and other hospital work.

To be a transcriptionist, you must train for a year or more learning the vocabularies of anatomy, pathology, pharmacology, and other related fields, as well as the format conventions for the various kinds of transcription reports. Many transcriptionists then specialize in only one or several medical specialties, such as orthopedics, neurology, or radiology. Transcriptionists can work for hospitals, private doctors and clinics, or for other transcription services that hire freelance subcontractors. However, many transcriptionists work in their homes as independent contractors or subcontractors, employed by large outsourced transcription agencies, or as home-based employees, or simply independently taking overload work from hospitals and other health-care providers.

Typically, doctors can call in their dictations to a computer where the dictation is stored digitally. The transcriptionists then download the information onto their computers and type up their reports from the digital file.

Use of voice-recognition software is emerging as well. Although it was originally thought that the capability of this software would eliminate the need for human transcriptionists, this has not proven to be true. Usually, text still needs editing either for spelling or grammar. So with voice recognition, the transcriptionists' work becomes editing the documents on screen.

Editing may range from minimal to extensive, depending on the quality of the speech-recognition software and the dictating habits of the originator.

To learn medical transcription, you can do one or a combination of things: take a home-study course or enroll in classroom training at a vocational or technical school, community college, or hospital. If you have a medical background, you can get an indication of your current proficiency by taking tests available on the Web at sites like *www.transcribeboston. com* and *www.cnctranscription.com.*

Because of the specialization required, it is difficult to get into the business without working first at a hospital or doctor's office for a few years, but with this experience, you can then start your own business.

Generally, transcriptionists charge by the line of type they produce. While it varies, the average is between twelve and sixteen cents per line. Often you will be required to provide a twenty-four-hour turnaround service. You can market your service by getting a listing in medical society publications and yellow pages or medical directories in your community. Directly contacting health-care providers or by checking out agencies that contract out this type of work is a good way to get business.

Books

The AAMT Book of Style for Medical Transcription, Peg Hughes, American Association for Medical Transcription (book and CD), 2002, ISBN: 0935229388.

How to Become a Medical Transcriptionist, Gordon Morton, Medical Language Development, 1998, ISBN: 0966347005.

The Independent Medical Transcriptionist, Donna Avila-Weil, Mary Glaccum, Rayve Productions, 2002, ISBN: 1877810525.

Medical Keyboarding, Typing, and Transcribing: Techniques and Procedures, Marcy Otis Diehl, Marilyn Takahashi Fordney, W. B. Saunders Company, 1997, ISBN: 0721668585.

The Medical Transcription Career Handbook, Keith A. Drake, Prentice-Hall, 1999, ISBN: 0130115401.

Association

AMERICAN ASSOCIATION FOR MEDICAL TRANSCRIPTION, (800) 982-2182, (209) 527-9620, *www.aamt.org*

Web Sites

ASSOCIATION FOR THE SENSIBLE METHOD OF ACQUIRING RATES FOR TRANSCRIPTION, *www.transcribing.com/asmart.*

MT DAILY, an online networking center: *www.mtdaily.com*

Training

Among the dozens of courses to choose from, the following are some of the better known ones:

AT-HOME PROFESSIONS, 2001 Lowe Street, Fort Collins, CO 80525, (800) 359-3455, *www.at-homeprofessions.com*

HEALTH PROFESSIONS INSTITUTE, (209) 551-2112. Offers the SUM program, *www.hpisum.com.*

MT MONTHLY newsletter has a training program, (800) 951-5559, (816) 628-3013, *www.mtmonthly.com.*

M-TEC EDUCATION CENTER, (877) 864-3307, (330) 670-9333, *www.mtecinc. com*

CAREER STEP has a special Canadian career center: (800) 246-7837, *www. canscribe.com.*

58

Mortgage-Auditing Service

Have you read any of the news stories over the past several years about lending institutions miscalculating the mortgage payments on adjustable-rate loans? How do such miscalculations occur? In a number of ways: improper rounding of a mortgage index, making the adjustment in the payment based on the wrong date, or using an index different from the one in the loan agreement (which may happen when a loan is sold to a bank in a different federal reserve district). These are among the ways buyers can pay their lender hundreds of dollars a year in undeserved loan costs. But a mistake in one year will make all subsequent calculations inaccurate as well, and with many loans going years back, the claims can be in the thousands of dollars.

The role of the mortgage-auditing service is to find these errors for the home buyer. If a miscalculation is found, the mortgage auditor supplies the clients with the information necessary to appeal the payment, or they represent the client in arguing the point with the bank. If a trial is necessary, they will appear as an expert witness.

Mortgage auditing can be a part-time business, or it might be an add-on service for financial planners or others providing financial services. It requires a solid understanding of mortgage tables. Software can be used to help calculate the correct payments. You might use a specialized program or set up your own formulas on a spreadsheet program like *Excel*. You can also use one of the many standard mortgage-calculation programs commercially available.

Mortgage-auditing services often charge an audit fee for checking a client's records, plus a percentage of the client's savings made from the discovery of errors. Others charge no up front fee but a higher contingent fee.

Software

LOANTECH'S *ARM Auditor,* (800) 888-6751, (301) 762-7700, *www.loantech. com/*

Multimedia Production

If you have an interest in education, training, communications, or marketing and a real love for advanced graphics and computing technology, you definitely want to explore the exploding field of multimedia services. Growing out of the advent of CD-ROM hardware and software, digitized sound boards, high-speed video cards, and linkages between PCs and video cameras, today's multimedia producer uses the PC as the central tool helping businesses and schools to create truly impressive multimedia presentations for almost any purpose.

No longer do audiences look at static overhead projections or sit in the dark lulled by slides that can put people to sleep. Technology allows you to create animation, three-dimensional graphics, sound, and motion to enhance any demonstration, tutorial, workshop, presentation, or training session. Your output may be a DVD that your client uses during the presentation or it may even be a kiosk that your client places in a convention center, hotel lobby, or airport for people to see. The Web is a major user of multimedia content and as broadband reaches into every home, its use will grow.

To be in this business, you must enjoy helping people organize information and figure out how best to present their message. You need to understand the various components of multimedia technology and be willing to stay continuously abreast of new developments that affect your business. You will also need good writing, visual, and graphic skills, since you will likely help your clients design and write their presentations on your equipment.

Starting a multimedia service will likely require an investment of leading-edge computer hardware, color scanner, laser printer, and graphic-design software such as *Photoshop* and *Illustrator* by Adobe, and an "authoring system" software program such *MacroMedia Director* that puts the whole thing together. (Note that there are certain standards that have been established by the Multimedia PC Marketing Council that you will want to make sure your equipment meets.)

Your clients can include companies or institutions of any kind that regularly have sales conferences, presentations, workshops, or training seminars. You market your services by advertising in the yellow pages, by sending out direct mail to companies, and by networking among trade and industry groups to make executives and training organizations aware of your capacities. Once you establish your business, word of mouth will bring you new clients if your presentations are unique and effective.

Fees for a multimedia service vary tremendously, but you can get $100 an hour or more for consulting and setting up a multimedia presentation for a business or association. This is one business that offers ground-floor opportunity for the creative, visually oriented person who can handle the technology involved.

Book

Making Money with Multimedia, Caryn Mladen, David Rosen, Reading, MA, Addison-Wesley, ISBN: 0201822830.

Newsletter Publishing

As information proliferates, more and more people realize that their best method of staying abreast of developments in their careers or personal hobbies is through one or more highly focused newsletters. As a result, the number of newsletters is growing. Just about any specialty you can name has a newsletter—innkeepers, coin collectors, medical billing services, users of XYZ software programs. And as the economy, technology, and world markets change, new markets for newsletters are created.

As newsletters increase in popularity, the distinction between newsletters, magazines, and newspapers is becoming somewhat blurred, but usually a newsletter refers to a publication that is two to eight pages in length, no larger than 8½ by 11 inches, and is not available on newsstands.

Anyone can start a newsletter or become the publisher for one that another person might write. There are, in fact, three ways you can use desktop-publishing software to earn an income in the newsletter business:

1. You can publish your own special-interest business or consumer newsletter, in which case you earn income from subscriptions and possibly from advertising. Prices for newsletters range from $25 to $45 a year for consumer-oriented ones to $100 to $1,000 for business/professional-oriented newsletters with highly specialized information. If you can get three hundred people to pay you $100 each, that's $30,000 for publishing information or news you gather! You can distribute your newsletter on CD or paper, by mail, or by fax.

2. You can write and produce newsletters for someone else, usually a company or association, who will use the newsletter to communicate with their employees or members or as a promotional tool to send to past, present, and potential clients. Associations range from professional and trade associations to interest groups and homeowners associations and PTAs.

3. You can write a template newsletter for a group of clients that you customize slightly for each one. For example, many accountants and lawyers are willing to pay to have a newsletter sent out with their name on it, so you write only one monthly newsletter and customize it with each professional's name on the masthead for his or her clients. Doctors and dentists are also prospects for newsletters. In this business, you can charge each of your customers several hundred dollars to create the newsletter and then a per-name fee.

Newsletter publishing can provide a full-time income, or it can be a sideline to another business you operate like association or private-practice management, or a bookkeeping or mailing-list service. To operate the business, you need to have a computer, desktop-publishing software, a laser printer, and a scanner. For qualifications, you need to be able to write good copy and headlines, have a good sense of layout and design, and have something to say.

The best ways to get your newsletter off the ground is to test-market one edition for free to a mailing list of potential subscribers. You can first check Newsletter Access (*www.newsletteraccess.com*), an online Web site, the largest online directory of newsletters covering business, investments, health, advertising, marketing, and every topic imaginable and then some to find out about competition.

A 1995 Northwestern University study found the industry average for starting a newsletter was $23,885. This is an average with some newsletters costing more, some less. At a minimum you can expect to spend from $4,000 and up sending out sample copies, purchasing mailing lists of potential subscribers, and advertising during the first year of publication. Once under way, continue sending sample issues to prospects. Some newsletter publishers have found it smart to sell a subscription of six issues instead of a year. That way they can begin publishing bimonthly and then move to monthly and obtain renewals.

Book

Starting & Running a Successful Newsletter or Magazine, Cheryl Woodard, Nolo Press, ISBN: 1413300839.

Training

THE NEWSLETTER FACTORY, online seminars, also available on video and audio, (770) 955-1600, *www.nlf.com*

Association

THE NEWSLETTER AND ELECTRONIC PUBLISHERS ASSOCIATION, (800) 356-9302, (703) 527-2333, *www.newsletters.org*

61

Online Product Sales

The Web has changed direct marketing. Direct marketing is loosely defined as any sale generated by a direct communication to a consumer. Prior to the Web, home-based businesses that directly marketed products primarily relied on mail and sometimes phone. The problem for such home-based businesses was the cost and the effort involved in direct mail and phone sales. It is incredibly expensive to produce a full-color catalog and mail it to enough people to realize a healthy-enough profit to justify such a large investment. With rising postage costs, a growing number of home-based mail-order companies that relied on catalog sales are switching to the Web exclusively. Even direct-selling/multilevel marketing companies like Amway have turned to the Web.

Thanks to the Web, the cost of presenting a line of products to a large number of people has been geometrically reduced. Now, a commercial Web site can reach more people than is possible through traditional targeted mailings. Web sites are an order of magnitude less expensive to produce than a standard catalog or mailing and can be infinitely updated to reflect new products, pricing, etc. Once a Web site is posted, it is available twenty-four hours a day, seven days a week to millions of Web users around the world. A well-designed site will encourage a viewer to browse or search through your listing of products, make their selections, fill out a simple order sheet with their credit card number, and submit it to you.

There are two models for businesses selling products on the Web: the online storefront and the online catalog. The online storefront is exactly what the name suggests, a Web site designed to suggest an actual store in which products can be bought. Online catalogs are also illustrative in their names; online viewers can browse through a site resembling a catalog and make selections. When structuring a business around either of these models, your chances of success will be greater if you gear it to the particulars of cyberspace. The Web thrives on uniqueness and niches. The more targeted your product line is (e.g., hot sauces, children's educational books, Eastern European folk music on 78rpm records, cigars, etc.) the greater your chances of being found by readers worldwide. Structure your virtual "storefront" or "catalog" to be as interactive as possible. Involve your viewers as much as possible; update your content frequently and be entertaining.

To get your business off the ground, we advise you to enlist the services of a top-flight Web-site designer who has experience in these kinds of sites and offers expert CGI (common gateway interface) programming capabilities (for online order forms). To build "traffic" on your site, the services of a Web promotions expert will provide you with many excellent options. You may also wish to hire an online publicist to ensure that your site receives the maximum exposure in the digital community. We also suggest that you spend a considerable amount of time online checking out what others are doing. You may also want to enroll in classes on online entrepreneurship.

Books

101 Ways to Promote Your Website, Susan Sweeney, Maximum Press, ISBN: 1885068905.

Net Words: Creating High-Impact Online Copy, Nick Usborne, McGraw-Hill, ISBN: 0071380396.

Permission Based E-mail Marketing, Kim MacPherson, Dearborn Trade, ISBN: 0793142954.

Selling Online, Jim Carroll, Rick Broadhead, Dearborn Trade, ISBN: 0793145171.

Starting an Online Business for Dummies, Greg Holden, For Dummies, ISBN: 0764516558.

Association

Direct Marketing Association, (212) 768-7277, *www.the-dma.org*

62

Payroll Preparation

If you are already doing bookkeeping, accounting, or any other kind of administration for a business, you might consider taking on the payroll-preparation function and earn some additional income. Although payroll modules for programs by Intuit or Peachtree make doing payroll for a small business much easier, many business owners still find the task tedious and difficult because of the frequent changes in federal and state tax rates, social security, and other deductions a company might need to make. Also, some business owners don't want employees to know what their co-workers earn, and by having the payroll preparation done on an outside contract, they can maintain secrecy.

Many large payroll-service companies compete in this business, but as a home business, you can win some jobs, you can win some business by offering personal attention, pickup and delivery, and a good price. You can also gain an edge by being willing to customize your service to the needs of your clients and by having a background in their field.

You'll most likely be able to underprice larger payroll services by charging less. In return, your clients will reduce the time they spend on payroll from hours each month to minutes. Be certain, however, to have a written contract with your clients that includes provisions that relieve you of liability for mistakes caused by the client.

Ways to get payroll clients are contacting small businesses in your area and networking in area organizations. Listings in the yellow page directories and on search engines like Yahoo Get Local and Google Local can work with your Web site, which should tell about your services and have testimonials.

Books

Essentials of Payroll: Management and Accounting, Steven M. Bragg, Wiley, ISBN: 0471264962.

Payroll Accounting, Frank C. Giove, Houghton Mifflin, ISBN: 0395959977.

The Payroll Toolkit: Nuts and Bolts Techniques to Help You Better Understand and Manage Your Payroll, Timothy F. Carse, Jeffrey Slater, Penn & Pearl Publishers, ISBN: 0970383800.

Software

QuickBooks Assisted Payroll, (650)944-6000, *www.payroll.com/assistedpayroll*

63

People-Tracing Service

Whether it's trying to locate an old buddy or sweetheart, track down a long-lost relative, obtain a private credit report, or find a person who has "skipped" out on a payment, the personal computer is changing the way missing-person and skip-tracing searches are done today. Technology such as online information databases and CD-ROM disks that contain phone books for the entire country allow access to massive amounts of data formerly available only to large companies, collection agencies, and private detectives. It is now relatively easy to obtain instant information on a person's address, phone number, credit reports, driver's record, and even bank balances.

As a result of the decreasing cost of technology, this entire field of investigative work is now open to home-based businesses. If you are interested in this field, however, first you must check to determine if tracing people is regulated by your state's laws. You may find, for example, that in some states you must be a licensed private investigator to provide tracing services. In other states you may need to obtain certification and be bonded. You should also be familiar with the various federal and state laws about privacy and the use of credit reports and financial information.

Beyond these important matters, you will need an up-to-date personal computer with an Internet connection and the ability to work professionally and creatively to find those people whom your clients are seeking. You should also be prepared to use the telephone as well as to search public documents at courthouses and city halls in order to complete searches that can't be found through your computer.

Marketing your business works best if you can serve both business and consumer markets, so advertising in the yellow pages under "Investigators" is useful. Again, check your state law before doing this because it may regulate how you can advertise such a listing. You may also wish to contact retail businesses that use investigative services, as well as make speeches to private clubs and associations to inspire people who might like to find old friends to use your services.

Fees for investigative searches can vary greatly, depending on the extent of the search and the cost of logging onto the databases you need. You will need to do some research in your local area to find out what the going rates are.

Books

Find Anyone Fast, Richard S. Johnson, Debra Johnson Knox, Independent Publishers Group, ISBN: 1877639850.

How to Locate Anyone Who Is or Has Been in the Military, Richard S. Johnson, Debra Johnson Knox, BRB Publications, ISBN: 1877639508.

Public Records Online, Michael L. Sankey, Peter J. Weber, Facts on Demand Press, ISBN: 1889150371.

You Can Find Anybody!, Joseph Culligan, Jodere Group, ISBN: 1588720004.

Personal Financial Management Services/ Daily Money Manager

If you enjoy working with numbers and are detail oriented you may be just the type of person who would be good at helping people manage their personal finances. As a personal financial manager (sometimes called a money manager) your business is to assist clients in establishing budgets, paying their bills, balancing their checkbooks, filing their records, etc. You need a working knowledge of a financial software package like *Quicken* or *Money.* This business will work well as on add-on to an existing financial-planning or bookkeeping service.

Your clientele will often be older adults whose adult children may live too far away or don't have the time to help their parents with day-to-day financial business. Also, people living on a fixed income who either may not have the time, the desire, or the health to take care of these tasks can be your clients. As a personal financial manager, you make out checks to pay your clients' bills on time and deal with any financial problems that arise.

For example, you may need to contact creditors about incorrect bills and, if appropriate, negotiate payment terms with creditors. If your client's problems require professional help, you then make the necessary referrals to lawyers, investment advisers, and tax professionals.

Some personal financial managers handle payroll records for tax reports needed for clients who have domestic help, although the actual filing of the tax reports may be done by the clients' accountant or tax professional. Some even become qualified as notaries.

Usually, bills are paid monthly, so once you establish a budget for your clients, you should be able to handle a typical customer's needs in about two hours a month.

Because of the level of trust involved, personal referrals will be your best route to finding clients. You might get referrals, for example, from your bank or your religious leader. Doctors, social workers, and mental-health professionals might be another source of referrals. Not surprisingly, those suffering from depression are often challenged by their personal finances. Also, the adult children of senior citizens might arrange for your services for their parents, so you might consider giving free seminars on financial issues involved in caring for aging parents. Networking with professional advisers like those who prepare tax returns or do financial planning is a good ways to obtain referrals to clients. Having a Web site that includes testimonials about your service helps out-of-town adult children conveniently learn about your services.

The average rate is $25 or $35 but can go as high as $60 an hour. Some personal financial planners charge a minimum monthly fee that is equivalent to two hours plus any expenses (postage, long-distance calls, mileage etc.).

Association

AMERICAN ASSOCIATION OF DAILY MONEY MANAGERS, INC., (301) 593-5462, *www.aadmm.com*

65

Professional-Practice Management Service

Managing a professional practice such as a medical or dental office requires an entirely different set of skills from the training that most practicing professionals receive. As a result, an increasing number of dentists, doctors, chiropractors, osteopaths, podiatrists, psychotherapists, and other professionals turn to professional consultants for help in managing the business and financial aspects of their practices.

Full-service private-practice consultants help their clients with virtually any aspect of running their offices. They may hire and fire personnel, train new staff, prepare payroll, handle billing and collections, manage the building, oversee investments and retirement programs, and select computer hardware and software when the business needs it. They may also use their organizational skills to improve productivity among the staff and the professionals themselves, by, for example, studying the scheduling of patients to help the professional increase business.

To succeed in this business, you need to have had some solid experience in office management and a background in or knowledge of the professional field in which you intend to work. Besides being competent in handling the business aspects of professional practices, you must be confident and have high self-esteem so that you can communicate your knowledge to the professionals you are dealing with. Practice-management consultants bill $75 to $125 per hour. Some work is "on retainer," which means they charge a monthly fee ranging from a few hundred to a few thousand dollars.

The best way to get business is through contacts in the field. Networking, building a referral base from your own professional clients, and speaking and writing about practice management are also effective methods.

Books

The Business of Medical Practice, Dr. David E. Marcinko, Springer, ISBN: 0826113117.

How to Join, Buy or Merge a Physician's Practice, Yvonne Mart Fox, Brett A. Levine, Mosby, ISBN: 0815128789.

Managing Your Medical Practice (annual), Charles R. Wold, Ahab Press, (800) 696-7090, *www.ahabpress.com*

Association

SOCIETY OF MEDICAL-DENTAL MANAGEMENT CONSULTANTS, (800) 826-2264, *www.smdmc.org*

66

Professional Reminder Service

We first heard of the concept of a reminder service twenty years ago, but despite its appeal, we haven't met many people who are actually doing it successfully. The problem seems to be that few people or companies are willing to pay to be reminded about birthdays, anniversaries, special occasions, and the like, especially in today's age of computers with calendars. Also, so many services are available both from Web and virtually any calendar program.

The most feasible idea for a reminder service, however, we think makes dollars and sense. Think for a moment about the doctor or dentist appointment you have. Don't you generally receive a call beforehand to remind you about the appointment, to be sure the doctor doesn't end up with a "no show" that costs him or her money? Veterinarians also make reminder calls. Well, herein lies the idea behind this business. Also consider wholesaling this service to a seller of gifts for them to offer free to their customers.

While many larger practices have a front-office staff to make these reminder calls each day, many solo practitioners, and there are three-quarters of a million of them, don't have sufficient help and probably suffer from a lack of time to make such calls themselves. But as many as 20 percent of patients don't keep appointments, so as a result, thousands of chiropractors, dentists, podiatrists, psychotherapists, massage therapists, estheticians, and other professionals are excellent candidates for a home-based "professional" reminder service. This business could take advantage of high technology in many ways, too. For example, the doctor could fax directly into your computer's fax/modem board or send you an e-mail of the list of appointments to be called for the next day, or allow you to use software like Norton *PCAnywhere* (Symantec) to log onto his or her computer each night and retrieve the list yourself. You could use autodialing programs to save on finger work, or even a voice-mail system to make the announcement automatically.

This business would make an add-on business for a virtual assistant or an answering/voice-mail service. It might also be a part-time business for a homebound person. It could also be a free service to stimulate business for a gift basket business. The requirements are few, with attention to detail and excellent communication habits topping the list. You could charge by the call or by the day. As to what you can charge, you'll have to do a little research on what the market will bear in your area. You could also target this service to other businesspeople who operate on appointments, e.g., hair stylists, service personnel, repair people, etc.

67 [ABC] [☾] [+] [⌂] [☼]

Proofreading Service

We know firsthand (boy, do we know!) that where there's writing, there are typos. Few things are more frustrating than sending out or posting to a Web site a report, prospectus, business plan, technical manual, or even a business letter and finding out later that a word was missing, or misspelled, or that something was punctuated incorrectly—or worse, the grammar itself was wrong. No matter how well written, thoroughly researched or professional appearing a document is, one little typographical error will greatly diminish its overall impact.

Large publication houses and newspapers have proofreaders on staff, but most midsized, smaller, and certainly sole-proprietor businesses do not. Yet all these businesses must communicate well and represent themselves as professionally as possible. We see a large demand for the services of independent proofreaders and copy editors.

If you enjoy language, have an eye for detail, and are knowledgeable about the rules of grammar, you may want to consider starting a home-based proofreading service. Almost every written communication these days is generated on a word processor, so the proofreading and editing documents can be greatly assisted by a number of software solutions. Most people are familiar with the spell-check features in their word processor, but few take the time to run the other feature common to most programs: the grammar check. You can choose to run the grammar check as starting point, or, better yet, you can opt to use your own skill in language and structure.

There are many secretarial and typing services who claim to offer proofreading and copyediting, but oftentimes their level of expertise in these areas falls short, as does the time they have available to devote to these highly specialized skills. By promoting yourself as an expert in proofreading, with a solid background in grammar, usage, style, and syntax, your perceived, and actual, value in the marketplace will be assured.

Proofreading is a candidate for a stand-alone business. It also will work well as an add-on to a word-processing, copywriting or technical-writing business. Potential clients run the gamut from small publishing houses to independent newsletter publishers, freelance writers, authors, Web writers, public-relations firms, and just about any other business or professional who relies on the published or printed word in their business. Networking online is a great way to get business. Find forums and discussion groups for any of the these businesses and let it be known what you do. It also might be worth your while to place small ads in local publications relevant to any of your target markets. In your communications with potential clients, emphasize your attention to detail and your depth of knowledge in grammar and syntax. This will differentiate you from many of the less specialized secretarial and word-processing services vying for the same business.

Books

Developing Proofreading and Editing Skills, Sue C. Camp, McGraw-Hill/Irwin, ISBN: 0028050029.

Handbook for Proofreading, by Laura Killen Anderson, McGraw-Hill/Contemporary Books, ISBN: 0844232661.

Go Ahead, Proof It!, K. D. Sullivan, Barron's Educational Series, ISBN: 0812097440.

Proofreading Plain and Simple, Debra Hart May, Delmar Publishers, ISBN: 1564142914.

Association

EDITORIAL FREELANCERS' ASSOCIATION, (866) 929-5400, *www.the-efa.org*

Web Sites

THE SLOT, *www.theslot.com*

LISTSERV DISCUSSION GROUP, *http:peach.ease.lsoft.com/archives/freelance.html*

68

Property-Management Service

Although real estate property management can be a rewarding business, it is not as simple as many people think. In addition to watching over properties, the professional manager maintains records on tenants, tracks income and expenses, audits and pays utility bills and taxes, contacts various personnel for repairs and inspections, and performs a host of other duties. The computer can help track all this information effectively, however, and therefore we've included real-estate property management as a home-based business for someone who knows how or is willing to learn how to work with spreadsheet and database programs or specialized software dedicated to property management.

Property management combines several managerial skills with a diversified day-to-day schedule. For example, the professional property manager who handles several buildings might spend the morning working on a rental lease for a new tenant, using a word-processor template and then developing an income projection using a spreadsheet program. During lunch hour, she might next show properties for rent, logging the prospective tenants' names and phone numbers into a database, and then make phone calls to various repairmen in the afternoon, finally collecting rents and updating the financials into an accounting program at night. As you can see, then, the more adept the property-management service is at using a full range of computer software, the more efficient and professional the business can be.

You do not need a real estate license to get into this business, but since you will be working for property owners who want to feel secure in their choice of management services, it helps to have some credentials in either office management, administration, or a field like accounting. Your office equipment needs to include an up-to-date computer and printer, a fax machine for quick correspondence with owners, and a good telephone system with two or three lines.

If you have not done property management before, the best methods for getting into the business include reviewing the classified section of your newspaper for want ads and making direct contact with landlords in your area. Once you establish your business, word of mouth is your best source of new business. A related business is managing condominium developments too large for volunteers to manage but not large enough to hire full-time staff.

Books

Property Management, Floyd M. Baird, Robert C. Kyle, Chicago, Real Estate Educators Association, ISBN: 0793131170.

Property Management for Dummies, Robert S. Griswold, For Dummies, ISBN: 0764553305.

Streetwise Landlording & Property Management, Mark B. Weiss, Dan Baldwin, Adams Media Corporation, ISBN: 1580627668.

Association

NATIONAL PROPERTY MANAGEMENT ASSOCIATION, (727) 736-3788, *www.npma.org*

69

Proposal and Grant Writer

The U.S. federal government annually contracts with thousands of companies based on competitive bids to supply products and provide services to its agencies. It also offers millions of dollars each year in special Small Business Innovative Research (SBIR) grants to companies that have ideas for new technology or products from which Americans can benefit. In addition to government grants, there are over forty thousand grant-making private foundations, double the number since 1980. Plus there are other publicly funded institutions that provide grants to individuals and nonprofit organizations for a myriad of civic, educational, and social-welfare purposes.

The challenge with nearly all these contracts and grants is, however, that anyone who wants one must traverse a lengthy, complex application process that begins with a special written proposal. Since most individuals and companies do not have the internal expertise to create this document, there is a growing need for freelance proposal and grant writers who guide individuals and companies through the process. These professionals write well and know the rules and regulations governing the creation and formatting of the proposal. Because of their backgrounds and personal experience, they frequently also advise their clients on how to improve upon the original product or service to ensure obtaining government or foundation approval.

Proposal and grant writers are sometimes generalists with a broad knowledge of diverse fields, but many are specialists in a single area such as agriculture, communications, energy, business, space exploration, or another advanced industry. Most proposal writers are also well versed in using spreadsheets, databases, and desktop-publishing software, since their job often includes producing the final document and corollary budget or bidding information for their clients. In addition to these qualifications, you must also have excellent communication skills since you will be working directly with CEOs and presidents of companies.

Proposal and grant writers usually obtain their clients through networking and sometimes through advertising or direct mail to companies that might be interested in government or foundation funding. Once established, they can then count on word of mouth since they have developed a reputation for successfully winning contracts or grants. Some proposals take only a few days to write, while others can take months, depending on the amount of research required. Successful writers can charge from $2000 to $10,000 per proposal, depending on length and complexity. Annual earnings for proposal writers range from $50,000 to over $150,000.

Making a living as a proposal and grant writer may require a few years of experience as you learn the ropes and develop contacts. However, if you have first-rate writing skills and enjoy working on a variety of projects, the opportunities are good.

Books

Catalog of Federal Domestic Assistance, Government Printing Office, http:12.46.245.173/cfda/cfda.html

Government Assistance Almanac, J. Robert Dumouchel, Detroit, Omnigraphics, Inc., ISBN: 0780806506.

The Only Grant Writing Book You'll Ever Need, Ellen Karsh, Arlen Sue Fox, Carroll & Graf, ISBN: 0786711752.

Proposal Planning and Writing, Lynn E. Miner, Jerry Griffith, Phoenix, Oryx Press, ISBN: 1573564982.

Winning Grants Step by Step, Mim Carlson, San Francisco, Jossey-Bass, ISBN: 078795876X.

Foundation Directory, The Foundation Center, New York, Russell Sage Foundation, annual publication, ISBN: 1931923515.

Training

THE GRANTMANSHIP CENTER, (213) 482-9860, *www.tgci.com*

H. SILVER AND ASSOCIATES, (310) 563-1240, *www.hsilver.com*

Public-Relations Specialist

Professional public-relations (PR) specialist involves anything from sending out media kits and press releases to being a vital part of the brain trust of an organization.

When corporations and organizations have to cut back on staffing, they increasingly turn to outside PR and marketing consultants who can do a top-quality job relating to their public in a cost-effective way.

Public-relations specialists help their clients establish a high profile in the public eye. Their goal is to obtain as much coverage as possible in the media, thereby alerting potential buyers to the existence and usefulness of the clients' products or services. To accomplish this, they produce written materials such as news releases, press kits, speeches, and brochures, and they develop contacts among radio and television producers and newspaper and magazine writers.

While many PR professionals work for many kinds of clients, others focus on a special niche such as corporate relations (e.g., preparing annual reports and investor newsletters or fostering employee and community communications), celebrity work (e.g., handling authors, television and movie stars), or certain kinds of businesses (e.g., restaurants, toy companies, or clothing manufacturers). Still others prefer to work for trade associations, nonprofit organizations, or political candidates and causes.

PR specialists need strong written and verbal-communication skills; they need to be creative and have an outgoing personality that can be both persuasive and assertive. PR professionals subscribe to directories, newsletters, and services that keep them up-to-date on media contacts. To make your operation run efficiently, broadband access and use-contact management software like *Act!* will enable you to work independently at home to produce the same quality of work as someone housed in a high-rise office.

While experience in a PR agency, publishing company, or corporate communications department is useful, you can enter the business as a solo practitioner through networking and personal contacts, taking on small projects and getting results for your clients, who can then refer you to new opportunities.

Many PR specialists charge monthly fees plus expenses, or they might charge per project depending on the the size of the client, the industry, and the regional market . Hourly rates vary widely and can be from $200 to $1,500 per day. An average daily rate for an experienced PR professional serving a large company is $1,000, while those working for a smaller organization might charge $600 per day. Those PR specialists who provide counseling services may charge $200 per hour or more.

Books

Effective Public Relations, Scott M. Cutlip, Allen H. Center, Glen M. Broom, Prentice-Hall, ISBN: 0135412110.

Public Relations: Strategies and Tactics, Philip H. Ault, Warren Kendall Agee, Glen T. Cameron, Dennis L. Wilcox, Allyn & Bacon, ISBN: 0205360734.

Public Relations Writing: The Essentials of Style and Format, Thomas H. Bivins, NTC Publishing Group, ISBN: 0844203513.

Public Relations Kit for Dummies, Eric Yaverbaum, Robert Bly, For Dummies, ISBN: 0764552775.

Winning with the News Media, Clarence Jones, Video Consultants, ISBN: 0961960353.

Newsletter

Inside PR, weekly e-mailed newsletter, *www.prcentral.com*

Associations

PUBLIC RELATIONS SOCIETY OF AMERICA, INC., (212) 460-1434, *www.prsa.org*

INTERNATIONAL ASSOCIATION OF BUSINESS COMMUNICATORS, (415) 544-4700, *www.iabc.com*

CANADIAN PUBLIC RELATIONS SOCIETY, (416) 239-7034, *www.cprs.ca*

Publishing Services

Publishing services produce books, catalogs, and directories for their clients who may be individuals, companies, and organizations. Projects might range from ghostwriting a book for an author who is under contract with a publisher to consulting with a company that wants to produce a mail-order catalog to editing a private directory for a local trade group or association to doing publication design.

Since the advent of desktop-publishing technology and with ready access to on-demand, short, and medium-run printers, home-based publishing services are also expanding into many additional areas that were once the preserve of small presses and vanity publishers. They may help an executive self-publish a showcase book that adds credibility to his or her name or work with a company or individual to write, produce, and market a how-to or nonfiction book through bookstores, direct mail, or mail order.

Although starting a publishing service does not require extensive experience in publishing per se, you must have strong writing and editing skills, as well as an excellent knowledge of how books and other publications are created from manuscripts to printed titles. Other important qualities are an eye for layout and graphic design and an ear for helping clients pick out book titles or rewrite material as needed. If you get involved in marketing matters, it is also important to understand the distribution options for books, guides, or directories.

The main tools needed by a publishing service are a computer with a large drive and one of the many powerful desktop-publishing programs that allow you to design a book, set type, and produce either camera-ready copy or files that can be used by a service bureau.

Publishing services may charge by the hour, by the day, or by the project, depending on the nature of the services they are providing. Their fees may range from $20 to $75 per hour for editorial consultations to several thousand dollars to edit and produce camera-ready copy for an entire book.

One of the best ways to begin a publishing service is by networking among graphic designers, printers, and even literary agents in your area, all of whom are often approached by people seeking assistance in developing a book or other publication. Other ways to get business include advertising in the yellow pages and online directory under "Publishing Consultant" or "Desktop Publishing" and working with your own professional contacts to locate people who have long thought about writing a book of some kind but who need help to actually do so.

Books

Guide to Self-Publishing, Tom and Marilyn Ross, Writer's Digest Books, ISBN: 1582970912.

How to Publish and Promote Online, M. J. Rose, Angela Adair-Hoy, St. Martin's Griffin, ISBN: 0312271913.

The Self-Publishing Manual, Dan Poynter, Para Publishing, ISBN: 1568600887.

Make Money Self-Publishing: Learn How from Fourteen Successful Small Publishers, Suzanne P. Thomas, Gemstone House Publishing, ISBN: 096646912.

Web Site

Dan Poynter's Web site and newsletter—*www.parapublishing.com*

Associations

EDITORIAL FREELANCERS' ASSOCIATION, (212) 677-3357, *www.the-efa.org*

PUBLISHERS MARKETING ASSOCIATION, *www.pma-online.org*

72

Real Estate Virtual Tours and Brochure Service

If you live in an active urban area where people frequently buy and sell housing, this business idea may appeal to you. The essential concept of the business is to help real estate agents and companies create effective sales materials that help them sell property. Such marketing devices also serve as good public relations for a company and often help to bring in new business as well.

In particular, many agents don't have the time to do as much marketing as they should and would be willing to pay a service to help them expand their opportunities to sell the houses they list. Your service is therefore to take high-quality digital movies for the Web and still shots for brochures of homes listed for sale. The brochures can be distributed to other agents or to prospective buyers. Agents can also use them to send as direct-mail pieces to entire neighborhoods to show potential clients the properties they have listed and sold. The equipment you need includes a good camera, tripod, and special software.

The tours can take less than an hour to get ready for a Web site and the brochures are easy to produce, quickly done, and inexpensive to print if you have the right equipment. This could also be an add-on business for a copywriter, desktop publishing service, or PR specialist.

Book

Real Estate Technology Guide, Saul D. Klein, John W. Reilly, Michael Barnett, Dearborn Real Estate Education, ISBN: 0793177324.

Virtual Tour Kits

REAL TOUR VISION, (866) 947-8687, *www.realtourvision.com*

VIRTUAL TOUR BUILDER KIT, (305) 803-3781, *www.rtvfla.com*

73

Referral Service

A referral service is based on the simple truth that most people today have little time to spend researching the many services or products they use. For example, you've probably seen or heard ads for services that offer referrals to lawyers, doctors, and dentists. This same idea can be applied to almost any area of importance to people: plumbers and contractors, appliance repair service people, tutors, caterers and party locations, wedding suppliers, child care, elder care, baby-sitters, house- or pet-sitters, auto repair, roommates, and dates.

Generally, a referral service works as follows. First, you put together a database of suppliers who pay you a flat fee, annual dues, or a percentage commission of their fee for each referral you bring them. Then, when people call your service, you ascertain their specific needs and refer them at no charge to one of the businesses registered with your service. Some referral services, however, such as a roommate-matching or dating service, will charge both parties for using the service, especially those that match people with people. Online referral services charge users on a pay-per-use basis or an annual subscription fee for a specified amount of research time.

The keys to a successful referral service are first the level and quality of the research you do in order to match people with the right service and, second, generating enough referrals to satisfy those who pay to list with your service. Your credibility depends on the accuracy of your information and the reliability of the businesses to which you refer your customers. It is therefore essential that you gather enough information so that you can refer with confidence or so that the consumer can make an informed decision. You'll also occasionally need to drop vendors from your referral list who don't meet your standards or about whom you get complaints that are not solved to the customer's satisfaction.

To start this type of service, you will need a computer and relational database management software such as *Access* (Microsoft) that allows you to create and search lists of vendors using many criteria: location, price, specialized services, guarantee or warranty policies, and so on. You will need to create attractive flyers that you can use in signing up vendors and for notifying potential customers about your service. Print as many flyers as you can afford and post them on bulletin boards such as those in stores. Distributing them widely throughout your market area is critical to your success. You may also wish to advertise on the radio (it's cheaper than you think!) and in local newspapers both to attract customers and to let vendors know you are making an investment in reaching people who want to be referred.

Earnings in this business will vary greatly. Some referral services charge vendors as much as $1,500 or $2,000 per year to be listed with them, and it's possible to make up to $100,000 per year. However, you may make only $3,000 or $4,000 in your first year.

Book

How to Start & Manage a Referral Services Business, Jerre G. Lewis, Leslie D. Renn, Lewis & Renn Associates, Inc, ISBN: 157916093X.

Business Opportunity

HOME OWNER REFERRAL NETWORK BUSINESS PACKAGE, (516) 374-8504, *www. homeownersreferral.com*

Repairing Computers

While most computers are now commodity priced and therefore readily replaceable, businesses and organizations can't afford to have downtime on their machines; and when their computers break down, they want them repaired immediately. Computer users also frequently prefer to upgrade rather than install new computers, which provides opportunities for selling and installing additional memory, drives, and other components.

Although there is plenty of competition from larger service companies, this is a perfect job to do as a home business because you can offer quicker, more personal service on site for a lower price.

Computer repair can be a part-time venture, a full-time career, or an add-on business for a computer consultant or trainer. While you don't need a degree in engineering or mechanical repair, you will need a good knowledge of computer hardware so you can provide your customers with total satisfaction on any job you do. You will probably want to have a contract that your clients sign, indicating your warranty policy and limits on liability.

Courses in computer repair are offered at community colleges and trade schools. The quality of such courses varies, but you should choose one that at least offers you a repair manual for most common OEM (original equipment manufacturer) boards and sources for high-quality replacement parts. Alternatively, since most PC repairs require simply swapping components, you can use the hands-on approach. You can buy a couple of old computers and several upgrade/repair books along with diagnostic software and a decent set of tools and dig in.

Fees for computer repair can range from $50 to $100 an hour, depending on your location and the type of service you offer. To increase your revenues, you might offer an annual contract to clients for a sizable fee, for which you will handle all maintenance and repair within forty-eight hours and/or provide backup computers, hard drives, printers, or whatever equipment they need. You might also expand by selling computer supplies or doing computer tutoring for your clients.

To build a computer-repair business, identify what type of computers you want to service and what industries or niches you wish to serve. You'll need less than a thousand dollars in parts. Then begin distributing flyers throughout the area you are willing to travel for work. Keep your travel area small because most people want and need prompt service. Distribute flyers at user groups, schools, and office buildings. Listings in the yellow page directories and on search engines like Yahoo Get Local and Google Local can work with your Web site, which should tell about your services and have testimonials.

Listing in the classified section of a local business or trade journal can provide another means of reaching prospective clients.

Books

Computer Repair with Diagnostic Flowcharts, Morris Rosenthal, Foner Books, ISBN: 0972380116.

Upgrading and Repairing PCs, Scott Mueller, Que, ISBN: 0789729741.

Upgrading and Repairing PCs Training Course, Prentice-Hall PTR, ISBN: 0130462713.

Upgrading and Repairing Laptop Computers, Scott Mueller, Que, ISBN: 0789728001.

Start Your Own Computer Business: Building a Successful PC Repair and Service Business, Foner Books, ISBN: 0972380108.

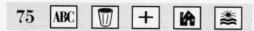

75 ABC

Résumé Service

It is now estimated that Americans change jobs seven times on the average over the course of their working lifetimes. Despite many books on the subject, job seekers don't all have the skill or confidence to create an effective résumé about their past careers or work and school experience. Growing numbers of people, in fact, head straight to the Web or the yellow pages to locate a professional service that can help them create clean, sharp-looking, and concise résumés. As a result, a growing industry of résumé writing services is mushrooming in every major city.

Today, it's not enough to just type up someone's credentials and work experience in a pleasing format. True résumé writers don't simply type up notes handed them by clients. They interview each client in order to select and develop the precise content for the résumé, write descriptions of the person's background, and lay out and design an impressive résumé that focuses the reader on the person's strengths and capabilities.

The growth of the Internet and the Web has changed the format and presentation of résumés as well. More and more job seekers are looking for jobs online. Jobs listed online ask that résumés be e-mailed to the prospective employer. Today's résumé service must be prepared not only to create effective printed résumés but also to prepare winning electronic versions. Some résumé services specialize in the type of clientele that they service: for example, legal, military, medical, or technical fields. For an extra fee most résumé writers offer add-on services such as developing a reference list, creating cover letters, thank-you notes, follow-up and/or acceptance letters, and so on.

To be in this business, you will need exceptional writing and interviewing skills, and some knowledge of how personnel directors and executives read résumés.

A high-quality word-processing or desktop-publishing software program with a good printer will enable you to produce attractive, well-designed professional résumés. Although template-based résumé-writing software is available, most of the packages are too limited for professional use except perhaps in writing a college student résumé.

There is a wide range in how résumé writers price their services. Some charge an hourly fee, some by the job, and others a combination of the two. Résumé prices range from about $50 for a one-page student résumé to over $300 for full curriculum vitae. Hourly rates range from $50 to $150 or more per hour. The price also depends on the typesetting and design requirements and the number of copies printed. Some résumé writers offer additional services to increase their fees, such as writing cover letters, handling the mailings, designing letterhead and stationery for the person, and offering post-office boxes.

Résumé services serve two primary groups of clients: university students and people in the business and professional community. As indicated above, listing on search engines like Yahoo Get Local and Google Local and yellow-pages advertising are among the best ways to market a résumé service. Also effective are networking in professional, trade, and civic organizations, both online and in person, and taking out classified ads under the "Employment Professional" sections in college or university newspapers or newspapers read by businesspeople and professionals. You also need a Web site that outlines your services along with testimonials from past clients.

Books

Books about résumés and interviewing number in the hundreds. Here are some representative titles.

How to Start a Resume Service, Teena Rose—emphasizes creating a nonlocal clientele, a downloadable book at *http:www.resumebiz.com.*

The Interview Rehearsal Book, Deb Gottesman, Buzz Mauro, Penguin Putnam; ISBN: 0425166864.

Resume Magic, Susan Britton Whitcomb, Jist Works, ASIN: 1563705222.

The Resume Handbook, Arthur D. Rosenberg, David V. Hizer, Adams Media Corporation, ASIN: 1558506160.

Winning Resumes, Robin Ryan, Wiley, ISBN: 047123656.

Associations Offering Certification

CAREER MASTERS INSTITUTE, (800) 881-9972, *www.cminstitute.com*

THE PROFESSIONAL ASSOCIATION OF RESUME WRITERS & CAREER COACHES, (800) 822-7279; (727) 821-2274, *www.parw.com*

NATIONAL RESUME WRITERS ASSOCIATION, *www.nrwa.com,* (888) NRWA-444

76

Reunion Planning

Literally thousands of milestone high-school and college reunions are held each year for classes that graduated from ten to thirty years ago. In fact, high-school reunions make up the majority of reunions planned. Even though nostalgia reigns and alums yearn to return to their youth, most people just don't have time to volunteer to organize their reunion, make phone calls, mail out information, and arrange for hotels, child care, catering, and the myriad other details that need to get done for a successful reunion.

Enter the professional reunion planner, a special category of event planner. The job of a reunion planner is to take charge of all aspects and every detail required to make the event successful, well attended, and fun. A reunion planner will locate missing class members, mail invitations, take reservations, hire bands, find food and beverage suppliers, and otherwise coordinate everything involved in the event. Much of this work is extremely time-consuming and requires good investigative abilities, since locating missing classmates may involve a lot of detective work. The biggest change in this business since the 1970s is that much of the investigative work can now be done electronically with databases rather than telephoning. Reunion-planning committees often choose to use a reunion-planning service because there is a charge to access to many databases. It's not feasible for individuals to purchase database access for one event, but a professional reunion planner spreads the cost among many clients. Due to the volume of research involved, reunion planners often start their work on a reunion more than a year in advance.

To do this business well, you have to take advantage of your computer and project-management/scheduling software, as well a personal information-management program to keep track of your phone numbers, contacts, conversations, and other data on the many companies you will deal with. It can also help to know how to do your own desktop publishing so that you can inexpensively produce your own invitations, brochures, announcements, and other printed materials you can include among your services.

Getting into the business is not difficult, but you should enjoy organizing events, working with people, and attending to details. Reunion planners typically receive a percentage of the registrations as their fee. Full-time professional planners can generate an annual income in the six-figure range if they handle multiple schools and reunions. In addition to high-school and college graduating classes, other types of groups that you can approach for business include military units and large families interested in planning family reunions. Reportedly, military reunions are now a growing source of new business for reunion planners.

Books

Planning Your High School Reunion, Rhonda Teel, Kimberly McElliott, Montage Publishing, ISBN: 0964633744.

So That's Who You Used to Be!, Patricia M. Bauer, ISBN: 0964615207.

The Reunion Planner, Neal Barnett, Linda Johnson Hoffman, Goodman Lauren Publishing, ISBN: 0963051695.

Association

NATIONAL ASSOCIATION OF REUNION MANAGERS, (800) 654-2776, *www.reunions.com*

Training

REUNION BUSINESS CONSULTANTS, *www.reunioncelebrations.com*

Web Sites

REUNION PLANNING MEETUP GROUPS, *http:reunion.meetup.com/*

YAHOO'S DIRECTORY lists reunion-planning groups and resources: *http:dir.yahoo.com/Business_and_Economy/Shopping_and_Services/ Gifts_and_Occasions/Parties_and_Events/Reunions/*.

77

Scanning Service

A scanning service could be a good add-on for many businesses where customers already come into your home, such as desktop publishing, word processing, graphic design, or bookkeeping services. You can turn what is now reasonably priced equipment into additional income. Using scanning software like *OmniPage* or *Paperport* and a flatbed scanner with automatic feed capability, you can take documents of any type and turn them into dozens of formats, including XML and PDF files for archiving.

Companies from law firms to publishers to database producers can use a scanning service. They may have old documents that need to be put into computer files but not want to invest the time or the expense to retype the entire document; they may have first editions of books or manuals that need to be updated but the old computer files are lost or damaged; or they may have artwork that needs to be placed into their document and not own a scanner that can handle the type of work they need to do.

No special skills are needed for this business, except the ability to manipulate the software to produce the output desired by your customers and enough familiarity with design and printing terms to know what they need. The best ways to get business are to advertise in the yellow pages and very small ads in local business newspapers or journals.

How to Do Everything with Your Scanner, Jill Gilbert, McGraw-Hill, ASIN: 0072191066.

Scanners for Dummies, Mark L. Chambers, For Dummies, ISBN: 0764507834.

The Scanning Workshop, Richard Romano, Que, ASIN: 0789725584.

78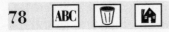

Scopist

Court reporters record testimony in courtrooms or lawyers' offices using a stenograph, a special machine that encodes words phonetically. In old movies you may see a stenograph spewing out narrow strips of paper, called stenotype; however, today's court reporters use computer-based writing machines that record their stenographic notes onto floppy disks or tapes. Once the information is recorded it must be converted into a fully written transcript—a time-consuming task. Court reporters often hire outside transcriptionists to produce the finished pages; these people are called note readers or scopists. The scopist reads the CAT (computer assisted transcription) version of each document, edits and correctly punctuates the material, researches or double-checks the spelling of technical terminology, medical words, and people's names, and proofreads the document.

Some court reporters may handle all the editing themselves, so before beginning in this field, check out how court reporting is being handled in your community.

Scopists are hired either directly by self-employed court-reporters or by court reporting agencies. In either case, they may do their work from home. Scopists are widely used and readily accepted in most parts of the country. However, in areas where court reporters have not yet used scopists, they must be educated to the scopist's ability to produce high-quality work and to enable the court reporter to earn more money.

As CAT software becomes more proficient at automatic translation of court reporters' notes, the nature of scoping may change. Most of this work can be transmitted electronically or via tape or disk sent by Priority Mail, so a scopist can work from any part of the country.

To be a successful scopist, you must be good at spelling, grammar, punctuation, and have an excellent command of English. The scopist profession requires some special training, including learning legal terminology and sometimes medical terminology, but much of this can be absorbed in a short time.

There are several main brands of CAT software that are not compatible with one another, so a scopist must either work with court reporters that use the same software or be able to use Rich Text Format (RTF), since most software today can translate into that format.

Most scopists work by the page. Rates vary geographically, but an average fee is $.75 to $1 per page. Beginners can usually scope between 100 and 150 pages per day, with experienced scopists reaching 200 to 300 per day. A first-year note reader–scopist typically earns between $10,000 and $12,000. Experienced scopists typically make around $42,500 annually and sometimes more.

Organization

NATIONAL COURT REPORTERS ASSOCIATION (NCRA), an association both for court reporters and scopists, (800) 272-6272, (703) 556-6272, *www.ncraonline.org*

Web Site

SCOPISTS.COM offers support and an e-book entitled *Scopistry*.

Training

Scopists may attend many of the four hundred court-reporter training programs offered throughout the U.S. Although the court-reporting program takes two years or more, scopists can finish in much less time. Several schools have specific short programs for scopists:

BEST SCOPING TECHNIQUES, (281) 277-3305, (239) 949-3145, *www.bestscoping techniques.com*

INTERNET SCOPING SCHOOL, (406) 273-2892, *www.scopeschool.com*

79

Self-Publishing

Each year, thousands of people publish their own books both printed on paper and in electronic formats—as e-books, on removable disks, and as sound files. They sell them at Web sites, through mail order, on Amazon, and in bookstores and specialty stores that relate to the subject of their book. Thousands of people each year no longer wait for commercial publishers to accept their book ideas or manuscripts.

Instead they learn how to publish and market something that they know interests them and will interest others as well. They write for smaller niche audiences than the hundreds of thousands of potential readers required by commercial publishers, producing everything from children's books and first novels to specialty cookbooks, guides, and how-to books. In fact, some people have been so successful at self-publishing that after their first successful book, they have gone on to establish their own publishing companies, expanding to publish other people's work.

Because of desktop-publishing software, the steps to self-publishing are easy today. In brief, you begin by developing your manuscript and focusing on your subject and your buyers. You then transform what you write into fully designed pages using programs like Adobe®, InDesign®, CS PageMaker®, or QuarkXpress.

If you want a printed book, you can use printers who do electronic "short runs" (printings of 100 to 1,500 copies) or if you want a book printed in ink, because of the setup costs you will need to print a minimum of 3,000 books.

You can decide to forgo print and go directly to an e-book, which enables you to provide your readers with color pictures and graphics, sound, moving pictures, and active hyperlinks within your book. You'll need to convert your books into a PDF file, or to make them available for portable readers, into the LIT format. E-book sales are growing at triple and quadruple annual rates and represent millions of dollars in sales. Of course, there's nothing quite as satisfying as a book in hand—unless it's money in your bank account.

Once your book is published, the next step is marketing it. You can potentially make the most money by selling the book yourself at speeches, workshops, and seminars or as an e-book on your own Web site or on Web sites like Cyclopsmedia, Booklocker, and Amazon.

Alternatively, you can seek a middleman—a distributor or wholesaler—to place the book in retail bookstores and other outlets such as museum and gift shops. However, then you will need to sell them at a rather steep discount—as much as 66 percent.

Whatever routes you take, the self-publishing process can be profitable if you hit upon a subject that taps into a trend or need. But don't count on print publishing to generate quick revenues, because it usually takes at least six months to a year before you see a return on your investment. Nevertheless, if you are a creative writer or believe you have special expertise to offer, this is a rewarding full- or part-time business. Of course, self-publishing can also be an add-on business for virtually anyone who wishes to package his or her expertise in published form.

Books

Guide to Self-Publishing, Tom and Marilyn Ross, Writer's Digest Books, ISBN: 1582970912.

How to Publish and Promote Online, M. J. Rose, Angela Adair-Hoy, St. Martin's Griffin, ISBN: 0312271913.

The Self-Publishing Manual, Dan Poynter, Para Publishing, ISBN: 1568600887.

Make Money Self-Publishing: Learn How from Fourteen Successful Small Publishers, Suzanne P. Thomas, Gemstone House Publishing, ISBN: 096646912.

Web Sites

DAN POYNTER'S Web site and newsletter—*www.parapublishing.com*

PRINT INDUSTRY EXCHANGE—printing quotes from commercial printing companies, *www.printindustry.com*

Organizations

THE SMALL PUBLISHERS ASSOCIATION OF NORTH AMERICA (SPAN), (719) 395-5761, *www.spannet.org*

SMALL PUBLISHERS, ARTISTS, AND WRITERS NETWORK, (818) 886-4281, *www.spawn.org*

80

Sign-Making Service

Signs, posters, and flyers of all kinds abound in virtually every area of our lives, from storefronts and office buildings to street banners and telephone poles. Most signs are pretty straightforward in delivering their information, but a good sign tells us more than the name of the business or individual doing the advertising; it also says a lot about the quality of the business behind the scenes and the attention they pay to their customers.

If you are someone who has a superior graphic sense and a feeling for writing and formatting words, you may be able to create a home-based sign business that stands out from the crowd. Maybe you've made signs as a hobby for volunteer events and received compliments or maybe you've worked in a sign shop. In addition to your graphic sense, you need to be able to understand your customers' needs and be able to translate those into signs.

The particular requirements for sign making are sign-making software, such as *SignLab*™, and a suitable printer. Because most custom signs are printed on vinyl, you will need a vinyl cutter/plotter. You may be able to reduce entry costs by buying your equipment on auction sites like eBay.

Customers for your business include new businesses; realtors; businesses needing signs for special promotions, exhibits, or trade shows; associations and groups that need signs or banners for meetings, banquets, and other affairs; private individuals who need signs or cards for parties, business, or special occasions; and even florist shops, gift stores, and craft stores, where you might be able to supply a special banner greeting or unique card to accompany a delivered gift. The best ways to market your business are advertising in the yellow pages ads and on local directory sites like Yahoo Get Local and SuperPages, approaching new businesses, offering promotions and special arrangements with other people in the gift business, using your existing clients for referrals, and seeking out owners of signs that need refurbishing.

The business can become full time or a good add-on business for a desktop publisher, marketing or PR specialist, copywriter, or graphic artist.

Books

Digital Imaging, Daniel A. Keegan, CD-ROM, Daniel A. Keegan, ISBN: 0971006318.

I Made That! How to Make Money Making Personalized Stuff, Cindy Brown, TLM Publishing House, ISBN: 0974882909.

Magazines

Sign Business, (303) 469-0424, *www.nbm.com*

SignCraft, (800) 204-0204, 939-0607, *www.signcraft.com*

Web Sites

SignIndustry.com. Free e-Newsletter, articles, links.

Sign Law—Informational American laws covering signs, billboards, and outdoor advertising, *www.signlaw.com*

Association

International Signs Association, *www.signs.org*

Software-Location Service

A software-locator service is a cross between a computer consultant and an information broker. Like computer consultants, people in this business help companies solve problems using software, but—and here is the twist—like information brokers, they search to locate software needed to meet their clients' special requirements.

The value of software locators is that they can save companies money. To illustrate how this is so, consider a typical scenario. XYZ Company realizes that their accounting department could improve profits by invoicing customers every two days instead of every two weeks. They are therefore considering hiring a programmer to come in and design a custom program that helps them automate the process. The programmer may charge $1,000 a day and expects the job to take three days. Do they need to go to this expense? Might there be a software program in existence already that would do the job for much less than that?

Such situations arise frequently, but many companies don't have the ability or the time to find out if software exists that will meet their needs. Before hiring the programmer, however, they could contact a software locator who will search his databases and might discover that, indeed, a program does exist that will do exactly what the business needs for much less than the cost of a programmer.

The software locator must first understand the client's needs and then identify software applications that will do the job. So to be in this business, you must be something of a software junkie and know the limitations of standard programs as well as a generalist who enjoys learning about many business operations so that you can grasp the nature of a client's special problem. You therefore need good communication skills and patience. For your research, you will need an up-to-date personal computer, database software, and an Internet connection for online searches.

Since this service is relatively unknown, your hardest task will be to educate your potential clients about what you can do and make companies aware of your existence. This means that you will need to do active networking among potential clients or advertise consistently in your local business newspapers and in computing magazines. Another way to get business is to make contacts with other consultants who can use your services when they need assistance in serving their clients. Fees for software locators can range from $35 to $75 per hour for searches and consultation.

Software location can be an add-on service for computer consultants and sales and service professionals.

Web Sites

SOFTWARE DIGEST RATINGS REPORT, NATIONAL SOFTWARE TESTING LABORATORIES, INC., (610) 832-8400, *www.nstl.com*

ZDNET. This site contains every software and product review from the family of Ziff-Davis publications. The search engine allows you find information by product name, company name, or type of product, *www. zdnet.com.*

Web search engines, such as Google (*www.google.com*) and Yahoo (*www.yahoo.com*)

82

Software Publishing

Names like Bill Gates, Marc Andreessen, and Peter Norton have become legends in this country and around the world, testaments to the fame and wealth that await the successful software publisher. It may not be as easy today to replicate what these entrepreneurs have done, but it is still possible to become a software publisher who can make money. In fact, more than a few top-selling software programs have taken off from a home-grown start; some have developed into full-blown software companies.

To become a software publisher, your first steps are to identify your audience and develop your program concept. You can decide to create add-on utilities for a hot new program from a major publisher, or maybe your expertise will lead you to develop a program for a specialized engineering or medical application; or perhaps you have an idea for a game with outstanding visual effects for home hobbyists or an educational program for students using virtual reality. Any of these ideas might fly, as long as the software is well designed, meets a need, and works on the hardware your audience owns.

After you've identified your audience and program concept, the next step is producing your software. You can either learn how to program yourself or you can strike a deal with an experienced programmer to handle the technical side for you. For this, you might either pay a flat fee or, better yet, you might offer a partnership agreement in which you do not pay the programmer any money up front but rather agree to share a royalty on any income earned.

After testing and retesting your finished software, the next step is to launch it into distribution. One of the most popular ways to do this today is through "shareware," a system in which publishers initially sell the software at a very low cost or even at no fee in order to build a clientele. The real money comes when people who like your software send in a registration card, along with a specified fee, which entitles them to the documentation and the right to get program updates and new versions.

The concept of shareware has caught on among millions of computer enthusiasts who like to experiment with new programs, or who simply balk at paying high prices for name brands when shareware companies frequently offer similar products for much less. The key to being successful as a shareware publisher is to distribute hundreds of free copies to computer bulletin-board systems, computer magazines, user groups, newsletter publishers, and others in order to get people talking about and using your product. Many shareware publishers also attend all the appropriate trade shows where vendors and users may be, and some arrange for consultants and other professionals in their area to resell the programs to their clients. Finally, you can also get your programs distributed through several middleman catalog companies that specialize in shareware, such as PC SIG.

It can take years to become successful in this business, so you shouldn't start out counting on a positive cash in-flow immediately. Typically fewer than 10 percent of users will register and pay you for your program, so if 10,000 people get your software, for example, and 500 pay you for it and you're charging $19.95, you'll make something under $10,000. However, shareware publishers do have several ways to encourage payment:

1. "Nagware," which are reminders built into the software until it's paid for when a code is provided by the seller.
2. Offering an incentive like an additional program or a printed manual when payment is received.
3. Selling through a retail site that specializes in shareware like Kagi, *www1.kagi.com.* Some shareware eventually finds its way to retail channels and larger distribution as well; however, if you are not interested in distributing your software as shareware, software companies do acquire the work of independent software writers.

Whether you distribute your software as shareware or through traditional distribution channels, you can create awareness of your products through some public-relations efforts by sending information about the new program and the availability of review copies to computer publications and broadcast media. You may do direct mail or advertise in specialty publications that target the people for whom you have written your software. Demonstrating your software at computer user groups is a key way of getting word-of-mouth recommendations under way. Even the most well-established software companies spend considerable resources catering to user groups, including sending their CEOs to speak to them. Likewise, including the online user groups on your PR list can help publicize your products.

Web Sites

www.zdnet.com, an excellent resource for IT professionals
www.jumbo.com, one of the Web's largest archives of shareware programs

Associations

ASSOCIATION OF SHAREWARE PROFESSIONALS, (765) 349-4740, *www.aspshareware.org*

SOFTWARE & INFORMATION INDUSTRY ASSOCIATION, (202)289-7442, *www.siia.net*

Sports League Statistics and Game Scheduling

Two things Americans love are sports and knowing where their favorite team or players rate. Keeping track of sports league statistics combines these American passions. Potential clients for someone making this a business include Little League teams, adult bowling leagues, country-club tournaments—any group who sponsors teams, leagues, or tournaments.

Using your computer and reasonably priced software, you can approach coaches, parents, or individual adults themselves and offer to provide them with a weekly tally of how they or their teams performed, complete with all the necessary running averages, win-loss records, and so on. You attend the games with your notebook or hire someone to keep paper records, which you later keyboard into your program. Then each week you print out in a nice chart format the various statistics that the league wants you to track, such as each player's batting average or bowling score, the team's history of play against other teams, and whatever other stats are useful to the coaches or parents.

Because many parents may not want their children to feel pressured by someone watching their performance, you might alter this idea by offering to keep records for Little League teams and publishing at the end of the season some kind of beautifully printed certificate of congratulations for each child or for the team to accompany the team photo. Each child's certificate would then include a positive statistic to help the child feel good about his or her experiences.

For your services, you might charge one fee such as $100 to track an entire team for the season, or you might charge each parent $10 to track their child including the certificate. If you are able to get the business for an entire league, your earnings from this business can range from a few hundred dollars to even a few thousand.

Software

All American SportsWare, (215) 860-8535, *www.allamericansportsware.com*

Bowling League Secretary; CDE Software, (206) 937-8069, *www.cdesoftware. com/bowling*

LeagueAnalyzer, www.analyzersoftware.com

Score-It, The Tucson Advantage, (520) 296-5893, *www.scoreit.com*

ScoreBook, *www.scorebook.com*

84

Technical Support

Are you one of those people who are called upon by friends and family to solve a computer problem? If so, working as a freelance technical-support person could be just the career for you. To be successful in this field you must have a technical aptitude and an understanding of underlying computer technology. You may be self-taught or bring skills learned while working for others. Either way, it is necessary to constantly upgrade your knowledge. One way of keeping up with changes is to network with other tech-oriented peers. Using sites on the Internet is another way of staying on the leading edge. For example, *www.slashdot.com* serves up a wealth of information.

Often a freelance technical-support person is a generalist who specializes in end-user support and may do anything from simple tasks such as installing software and hardware (like printers or scanners) to more complex tasks that involve troubleshooting. To many people computers are complex and intimidating. Very often all a client needs is "hand-holding" to guide him or her through a procedure.

You'll find that the types of clients best targeted for this business are home-computer owners and small businesses who cannot afford to keep technical-support personnel on staff. At first to attract business, you will need to advertise your services. Distributing business cards and flyers is a good way to start. Word of mouth and referrals from satisfied clients are the best ways of getting business. Having a Web site that describes your services can also help increase your clientele.

Technical-support workers charge for their services in different ways. You can establish a minimum charge for an on-site visit of one or two hours and then an hourly charge after that. Hourly rates range from $30 to $75 to more than $125. Others charge a flat monthly rate for phone and e-mail support.

Association

NETWORK AND SYSTEMS PROFESSIONALS ASSOCIATION (NASPA), *Technical Support* magazine, which has a "Consultants' Corner" section, is available on the site, *www.naspa.com*.

85

Technical Writing

Today technology is an integral part of our lives, and with every new product involving technology brochures, manuals, reference cards, instructional materials, reviews, and marketing materials are needed to communicate with the many people selling, servicing, and using the product. To succeed as a technical writer, it is crucial that you know how to communicate complex ideas in an understandable and easy-to-read manner. Different audiences create a need for different types of information, both in print and for the Web. For example, you can write and edit technical books and instructional materials. You may also write articles for trade magazines and create publicity materials and different types of business and consumer publications. Policies and procedures manuals are another example of technical writing that you might be contracted to do. Some technical writers also create online "help" files that are accessed from a software product either on CD or on the Web.

The technical writer must understand the publishing and design issues for whichever format is required and be able to use the technology and software to produce the document in the manner desired. Sometimes this requires only standard word-processing software like *Microsoft Word.* However, increasingly technical writers need to be skilled at using the latest in publishing software, for example, *Adobe Framemaker.* You should also have an understanding of or be able to learn quickly a variety of other software tools such as *QuarkXpress*, Adobe *Acrobat* (to create PDF's), *HTML*, *Powerpoint, Visio, Robohelp,* as well as others.

Potential clients more and more are asking technical writers to back up their skills with formal training, so it is advisable to take some training courses in this field. Both full-time and part-time courses are available at community colleges throughout the country.

To get work, make contact with the documentation departments and the marketing or research-and-development managers of companies who might use tech writers. Employment agencies that hire technical personnel often recruit technical writers. You can post your résumé on online job banks and search them for assignments. Participate in a visible way in trade associations and computer user groups. Create your own Web site and include testimonial letters and samples of your work.

The average rate for technical writers is between $40 and $60 an hour but can range from $25 to $90 an hour depending on the complexity of the project. It is not unusual to be asked to quote a total fee for a project.

Books

Documentation, Alan S. Pringle, Sarah S. O'Keefe, Scriptorium Pub Services, Inc., ISBN: 097047332X.

Handbook of Technical Writing, Alred Brusaw Oliu, Gerald J. Alred, Charles T. Brusaw, St. Martin's Press, ISBN: 0312393237.

How to Become a Technical Writer, Susan Bilheimer, Optimus Publishing Company, ISBN: 0970196415. Can be downloaded as an e-book from *www.writingcareer.com/sb001.shtml.*

The Complete Idiot's Guide to Technical Writing, Krista Van Laan, Catherine Julian, JoAnn Hackos, Alpha Books, ISBN: 0028641469.

Technical Writing 101: A Real-World Guide to Planning and Writing Technical Documentation, Alan S. Pringle, Sarah S. O'Keefe, Scriptoriuim Press, ISBN: 097047332X.

Associations

SOCIETY FOR TECHNICAL COMMUNICATION, (703) 522-4114, *www.stc.org*

AMERICAN MEDICAL WRITERS ASSOCIATION, (301) 294-5303, *www.amwa.org*

INTERNATIONAL SOCIETY FOR PERFORMANCE IMPROVEMENT, (301) 587-8570, *www.ispi.org*

Training

THE UNITED STATES DEPARTMENT OF AGRICULTURE GRADUATE SCHOOL offers courses in technical writing and writing skills at locations throughout the U.S.: (888) 744-GRAD, (202) 314-3300, *www.grad.usda.gov.*

Temporary-Help Service

Using temporary help has become a business reality in the United States. Companies frequently prefer to use temporary employees when they experience a peak in their businesses and for many other reasons. By specializing in an industry or in a particular type of worker, a home-based temp service can do very well and even out-compete the big firms with household names by serving a narrow niche market.

You can use your background and expertise to give you a leg up on other agencies by helping companies find qualified workers in a specialized field. For example, you might be able to offer a service in providing paralegals for attorneys and medical front-office staff or hospital social workers, escrow officers, pharmacists, short-order cooks, corporate pilots, or printing-press operators.

Companies use temporary-help services because it saves them the cost and time of looking for someone, training the person, and paying employee benefits. Temporary workers are hired for many reasons: temporary absences, vacations, sickness, seasonal workloads, special projects, and temporary skill shortages. And as many companies continue to experience the need to downsize, they will look increasingly to such services to provide them with temporary help because a regular temporary-help agency cannot provide them with the specialized workers they need.

To succeed in this business, you need to have knowledge of and contacts in the field you specialize in and you must create a database of reliable, skilled personnel. You will need an up-to-date computer, a printer and database, and word-processing and scheduling software. You will also need accounting software with a payroll module (unless you use an outside payroll service), because as a temporary-help service, you are the employer of the workers, and so you must pay their wages and taxes, Social Security, and unemployment insurance. This also means you will need to have a substantial amount of working capital to start this business, because you will have to pay the personnel you send out while you wait to receive payment from your clients. Income potential from this business could reach over $100,000 a year.

Association

AMERICAN STAFFING ASSOCIATION, (703) 253-2020, *www.staffingtoday.net*

T-Shirt and Novelty Design and Production Service

Computers have enabled home-based artists to use their skills to design and produce T-shirts, mugs, plaques, and other gift items, opening up creative and potentially profitable ways of expressing their talents. The technology combines scanners to bring in photos or other art, graphics programs that allow the photos or art to be edited, cropped, enhanced, and color balanced, and either laser printed using dye-transfer toners or thermal wax printed using special equipment. The final output image can then be placed on fabric, using a heat process that takes only minutes and completely eliminates silk-screening, or transferred to gift items of all kinds.

Creative graphic designers can customize art and text designs to a client's needs or produce unique eye-catching computer-generated art, cartoons, or type for logos, awards, gifts, and premiums. The savvy artist can therefore tap into many lucrative niche markets, including conventions, trade shows, museums, businesses, and private groups that purchase customized T-shirts or other novelty items for meetings, reunions, conferences, or fund-raisers.

Getting into this business requires graphic-design or artistic abilities, good marketing skills, and the creativity to discover a unique product or service. You may also need or want to purchase several pieces of specialized equipment in addition to your computer, including a scanner, a large-screen monitor drawing or illustration software such as *Adobe Illustrator*, and either the specialized laser toner cartridges that work in most standard laser printers or a thermal wax printer and various transfer equipment.

A trap for the home-based T-shirt maker is to try to compete in the traditional retail channels, where volume pricing and cash flow can be overriding obstacles. On the other hand, designing customized items for clients—e.g., sports leagues, reunions, associations, corporate events, art fairs, and fund-raisers—can be a more effective strategy. Or you might create a design for an attraction like a museum that presents the kind of information synonymous with the museum in a unique way. The museum then becomes your customer and resells your design. A successful design can be sold in this way for years.

Other methods of getting business include advertising in the yellow pages and in trade magazines or newsletters, telemarketing, and networking with meeting planners. Earnings for a T-shirt design business will vary considerably, depending on how many contracts you are able to obtain and the fees you charge for design and manufacturing.

Books

How to Print T-Shirts for Fun and Profit! Scott O. Fresener, St Books, ISBN: 0963947419.

I Made That! How to Make Money Making Personalized Stuff, Cindy Brown, TLM Publishing House, ISBN: 0974882909.

The t Shirt Book, Charlotte Brunel, Bruno Collin, Assouline, ISBN: 2843233461.

Supplier

RPL SUPPLIES, (201) 794-8400, (800) 524-0914, *www.rplsupplies.com*

88

Used-Computer Broker

A used computer or laser printer are like used cars, still serviceable after they are no longer the current model on the showroom floor. Used equipment is sought out by those who can't afford new machines or simply prefer to spend less for their equipment and by third-world countries seeking affordable equipment that is passed its prime in the United States. This demand has opened the way to opportunities in used-computer brokering.

Used-computer brokers can work in several ways. In some cases, they stockpile their own inventory by purchasing equipment from selling parties at one price and then finding buyers in due time to whom they can resell it at a higher price, with the difference being their profit. In other circumstances, they act as a third party who arranges a timely match between a buyer and a seller, fixes a fair price, and takes a commission from the sale. Brokers usually need to specialize, focusing on high-end engineering models, desktop-publishing equipment, or other specialty areas as lower-end computers have reached commodity prices.

In all cases, the main ingredient to a successful business is maintaining a large database of buyers, sellers, and equipment. This means that the used-computer broker must be constantly on the lookout for new suppliers and customers through advertising, telephone marketing, and word of mouth. Some businesses also network with other brokers to increase their chances of finding a piece of equipment needed by a customer, or a customer for a computer they already have.

While an aggressive broker can easily turn this into a full-time business, brokering can be a part-time business or add-on business as well. Earnings can vary and, depending on your ability to get desired merchandise and build a clientele, they can become significant.

Web Site

RECYCLER'S WORLD, a source for used computer and computer parts, (519) 767-2913, *www.recycle.net/computer/index.html*

89

Video Animator

Video animation is everywhere. Logos that fly into view before news broadcasts, sports scores and weather statistics. . . . Anytime you see a bit of programming that doesn't involve actors or landscapes, you're probably watching a video animation. Producing these sequences used to be solely in the realm of very high-priced, equipment-intensive specialty houses. This is no longer the case.

The increasing power of PCs, market demands, and the power of a new generation of software have changed the video animation, titling, and special-effects business forever.

Video animation can be a very well-paid full-time business. With artistic talent *and* computer graphics, multimedia-authoring or digital-video production experience you have the basic requirements to begin the process. Three-D video rendering and animation is not something you can learn overnight. You will need six months to a year or more before you are fully conversant with all the technology and skills involved. We recommend taking classes at your local college or doing an internship with an established business before setting out on your own.

Before purchasing equipment and software for your animation business, it would be helpful first to identify which market you wish to go after. If your aim is broadcast television and high-end corporate video, your investment in technology will be more substantial. Today there are a number of good software programs available such as Ulead's *COOL 3D™ Production*

Studio. If the higher-end market is a bit too daunting, there is a fairly large market in the middle-to-lower range. Many producers of CD-ROMs, local television commercials, cable commercials, and corporate training videos would love to include original animation and effects sequences into their productions but cannot afford the rates of higher-end studios. You can provide a dynamic and desirable product at a fraction of the cost of what a high-end studio would charge.

Prices vary considerably in video animation. High-end broadcast-quality animation is often charged for by the second. That adds up pretty quickly, but before you put a down payment on that Porsche, be aware that it takes about ten to fifteen hours to produce one second of top-quality animation. Many animators charge per project, as well. Check out what your local market can bear and structure your rates accordingly.

Books

3D Graphics & Animation, Mark Giambruno, New Riders Press, ISBN: 0735712433.

The Art of 3-D Computer Animation and Effects, Isaac Victor Kerlow, Wiley, ISBN: 0471430366.

Principles of Three-Dimensional Computer Animation, Michael O'Rourke., W. W. Norton & Company, ISBN: 039373083.

Magazine

AV Video Multimedia Producer Magazine, free, (847) 559-7314, *www. avvideo.com.*

Video and Audio Digitizing Service

For any video footage or recorded audio material to be used in any of the multimedia or Web applications, it must first be converted into a digital file format that can be read and played by a personal computer. The use of digital video and audio files has become more prevalent as multimedia content continues to make inroads on the Web. Many Web sites feature video and audio files, and more are being added every day. Multimedia and Web designers and developers often don't have the time required to digitize their own media and turn to video and audio digitizing services.

A video and audio digitizing service, or digitizing service, is similar in concept to a scanning service. As a matter of fact, the two businesses are quite complementary. Clients will come to you with existing video footage or recorded audio. Using your computer along with a video/sound digitizing board and special software, you will convert the material to the digital format your client specifies. This is a fairly straightforward business, but, unlike scanning two-dimensional images, the devil lies in the formats you will receive. You can reasonably expect video footage to come in a variety of formats such as VHS, S-VHS, 8mm, Hi-8mm, ¾ inch, and Beta SP, to name the main video formats. Audio may come to you on cassette tape, CD, long-playing LP (remember those!) ½-inch reel-to-reel, and DAT, again, to name only the more prevalent formats. Each one of these formats, both video and audio, requires its own playback machine. This can be costly. You can defray some of these costs by searching for used playback equipment.

In addition to playback equipment, you will need the computer equipment and software required for digitization. Start with an up-to-date computer as well as a special video/sound digitizing board and digitizing/editing software.

Your clients will include Web designers and developers, Webmasters, multimedia producers, and desktop video services. Networking, both online and directly with your potential clients, is the most effective way to get business. A simple Web site that outlines your service, the formats you handle, and your price structure is also helpful. Yellow pages and trade-journal ads have been proven effective for digitizing services as well.

A digitizing service can work as a stand-alone business, but we recommend it as on add-on to a desktop video business, scanning service, or other media-related venture.

Be aware that digitizing audio and video is time-consuming. If the original program material is fifteen minutes long, it will take fifteen minutes to actually digitize. It will also take additional time in the beginning to set the proper levels to ensure the highest quality, and will take even more time after the material is digitized in order for you to check it to make sure the entire program was completed without glitches or "dropout." Rates charged vary from region to region and market to market, so you should check locally what the going hourly rate is. You may prefer to charge on a per-project basis.

Web Site

INSTRUCTIONAL TECHNOLOGY CENTER provides a how-to paper on digitizing
video: *www.gsu.edu/□wwwitc/howto/temp.html*.

91

Virtual Assistant/Office Support

What is a virtual assistant? According to the Virtual Assistants Association (*www.ivaa.org*), a virtual assistant (VA) is "an independent entrepreneur providing administrative, creative and/or technical services." In other words, virtual assistants provide what used to be called secretarial services and more recently office-support services. This is a relatively new field that was born somewhere in the mid-1990s. As the name implies, VAs can be anywhere thanks to the growth of the Internet and the combined growth in telecommuting work and downsizing in the business world.

Virtual assistants work from home and perform a wide variety of tasks, including word processing, desktop publishing, transcription, editing and proofreading, business writing, office management and organization consultation, preparing spreadsheets or databases, maintaining contact-management programs, bookkeeping, billing, notary services, graphic design, multimedia presentations, answering services, mailing preparation, résumé writing, Web-site design, and Internet research.

A good candidate for this career is someone with good computer skills and a background in administrative services. As a generalist you can tailor the services you offer to what the office support needs are in your area, Or, if you have a background in a specific field—e.g., the legal or medical fields—you can specialize in that area. Typically most virtual assistants work for a variety of clients. New businesses, small businesses, and self-employed individuals who do not have full-time secretarial assistance are likely target markets. Your clients could be doctors, lawyers, real estate or insurance agents, or any business where the owner doesn't have the desire or time to do his or her own administrative work.

To be successful in this business you must be detailed oriented, work quickly, and produce top-quality work. You also need to be deadline oriented. You will be expected to create documents that your clients can't prepare themselves, so you need to be familiar with a variety of software packages from word processing and desktop publishing to graphic design, database, spreadsheet, and presentation software. You may want to consider obtaining Microsoft Office Suite (MOS) certification to add credibility to your skills.

Besides a computer with current software applications, other equipment you should have includes a scanner, a fax machine, and a photocopier.

To attract business it helps to network with local business groups and your local chamber of commerce. Having a Web site that includes a list of your services and testimonials can boost your business. Listing your business in the yellow pages and any business directories your community has will also increase your exposure.

Hourly rates range from about $20 to $50 an hour, with services like desktop publishing, graphic design, database and spreadsheet work, or editing commanding $75 per hour or even more. Some VAs charge a flat fee for ten to twenty hours a month, sometimes at a discounted hourly rate. Before deciding what to charge, determine what other virtual assistants in your area are charging.

Books

How to Start a Home-Based Secretarial Services Business, Jan Melnik, Globe Pequot, ISBN: 0762705159.

Industry Production Standards Guide, Office Business Centers Association International, (800) 237-4741, *www.officebusinesscenters.com*

Up Close & Virtual: A Practical Guide to Starting Your Own Virtual Assistant Business, Diana Ennen, Kelly Poelker, self-published, ISBN: 0974279021.

The Virtual Assistant's Guide to Marketing, Michelle Jamison, Word Association Publications, ISBN: 1932205675.

Training

ASSISTU offers a training program for virtual assistants, (866) 829-6757, *www.assistu.com*.

MICROSOFT OFFICE CERTIFICATION, *www.microsoft.com/learning*

WWW.ASSISTU.COM—twenty-week training from one of the founders of the field with high admission standards

International Virtual Assistants Association, *www.ivaa.org*

Virtual Assistance U (VAU), *www.virtualassistanceu.com*

Associations

International Virtual Assistants Association, (877) 440-2750, *www.ivaa.org*

International Association of Administrative Professionals, (816) 891-6600, *www.iaap-hq.org*

92

Web Content Writer

The unique combination of text and graphics is at the heart of what makes the Web such a powerful communications medium. Much attention has been given to the graphics side of the equation. The text side, however, is sometimes forgotten in the excitement over developments like the inclusion of animation, video, and sound into Web sites. Many Web sites today look great but leave something to be desired in the way of well-crafted, clear, and organized writing that enhances the unique characteristics of the Web's particular brand of communication.

Web designers, Webmasters, and other Internet communications professionals recognize the need for writing that communicates a site's message while conforming to stylistic and organizational conventions that the Web requires. Writing for the Web is different from writing for any other medium. We see a real need for writers who know how to write well for the Web and make this a specialty.

This is a great add-on business for copywriters, technical writers, freelance journalists, or anyone who enjoys writing, writes well, and can conform their style to the Web. Being able to write concisely and express ideas or concepts clearly and in an interesting way is vital for Web-site writers. Unlike technical documentation, where readers expect to take their time and consider a great deal of detailed information, people "browse" the Web, gleaning just the important facts. Copywriting, on the other extreme, tends to deal with short, catchy phrases that convey ideas or feelings about their subjects. This kind of writing doesn't work well on the Web as viewers expect a fair amount of substance from the site they browse. Finding your way between the copywriting and technical-writing models is your job as a Web writer.

Potential clients for Web-site writers are Web designers, Webmasters, and other communications professionals whose job it is to produce and maintain Web sites. Networking is your best bet for getting work from these prospects. Contact Web-site designers via phone or e-mail and introduce yourself. You might try browsing the Web and looking for sites that might need some help in the writing department. Then send an e-mail to the Webmaster with a well-written, Web-ready letter outlining your experience, skills, etc. If you have a technical or copywriting business already, try to migrate some of your clients over to the Web. Form an alliance with a site designer to help you do this.

Web-site writer rates are somewhere between copywriting and technical-writing fees, with the range being from about $25 to $60 per hour.

Books

Writing for the Web (Writers' Edition), Crawford Kilian, Self-Counsel Press, ISBN: 1551802074.

Hot Text: Web Writing That Works, Jonathan Price, Lisa Price, New Riders Publishing, ISBN: 0735711518.

Web Word Wizardry Net-Savvy Writing Guide, Rachel McAlpine, Ten Speed Press, ISBN: 1580082238.

Cyberwriting: How to Promote Your Product or Service Online (Without Being Flamed), Joe Vitale, New York, Amacom Book Division, ISBN: 0814479189.

Web Sites

www.useit.com/papers/webwriting—how users read on the Web
www.sun.com/980713/webwriting,—Sun Microsystems' take on writing and content strategies for the Web

93

Webmaster

Many companies outsource the day-to-day operations of their corporate web sites to independent contractors. Typically this job is known as a Webmaster. The job description of Webmaster varies a great deal and often depends on the needs of the individual company. This involves making sure the site's hardware and software are working properly, updating and creating Web pages, creating CGI and Perl scripts, keeping clients apprised of statistics, and replying to feedback. Many companies also require Internet programming languages such as Java, system administration in UNIX, Linux, and Windows environments, and knowledge of dedicated-line and dial-up communication protocols.

If you have many of these skills and experience requirements, you are a candidate for starting a home-based Webmaster service. If you have some Internet experience but cannot perform many of the skills listed in the previous paragraph, Webmastering doesn't preclude you. For any skill you don't know, such CGI scripting, Java, or communication protocols, you can find someone to subcontract to. The Web is increasing in complexity, and the ranks of specialists are growing. You do need a sound general knowledge of the Internet and the Web in particular, as well as good interpersonal communications skills, strong organization and project management skills, and an enjoyment of problem solving.

Your potential clients are new businesses and those just putting up their first Web sites, as well as any business that might be downsizing, streamlining, or restructuring. To find clients, we suggest that you team up with a Web designer or Internet consultant. That way, when they pitch a potential client to sell them a Web site, your service will be included in the package of services they can offer. Another way to find clients is to search the literally hundreds of online job listings. Look for Webmaster listings, then contact the companies and convince them to outsource the job rather than hire someone to do it in-house. You might also try writing and publishing an article on the benefits of outsourcing Webmaster duties. If you are currently employed as a Webmaster or Web-site developer, turn your employer into your first client.

Books

The Corporate Intranet: Create and Manage an Internal Web for Your Organization, Ryan Bernard, New York, Wiley, ISBN: 0471149292.

Planning, Developing and Marketing Successful Websites, M. Miletsky, Course Technology, ISBN: 0619035633.

Designing Network Security, Merike Kaeo, Cisco Press, ISBN: 1587051176.

Magazines

Information Today's Online, *www.infotoday.com.*

Webmaster Magazine, *www.webmasterzine.com/webmastermagazine,* has articles for freelance Webmasters.

Associations

WEBPRO INTERNATIONAL, a professional association, (704) 814-7277, *www.webpro.org*

WORLD ORGANIZATION OF WEBMASTERS, (916)608-1597, *www.joinwow.org*

94

Web-Site Design

E very passing day fewer businesses think they can do without a Web site. The Web has become a standard tool for communication and commerce for businesses of all sizes. And to stay competitive, businesses must continually update or redesign their sites.

While easy-to-use programs like FrontPage enable most people to design their own Web sites and free templates for Web sites are widely available (*www.templatesbox.com, www.freelayouts.com,* and *www.webzonetemplates.com* to name a few), many if not most corporate and institutional owners realize that for their Web sites to be effective, the expertise of a professional Web-site designer is required.

Randy Caruso, a top Web designer, observes, "For the average site owner, the reality is that it's too much." Indeed even for professionals, Web sites have become quite complex, and it can be a challenge to keep up with the ever-changing technologies.

There are two types of Web-site designers: those who work on the "front end" design, which is the interface you see when you visit a site, and those who work on the "back end," specializing in such site functions as e-commerce, chat rooms, database integration, dynamic site elements, CGI programming, PERL scripting, Active Server Pages (ASP), Java Scripts, and Java.

Caruso points out, "While there are many specialists who are kept very busy, the generalist's role is critical. A generalist will be your point person:

this is the definition of a relationship worth fighting for. . . . Most important is the understanding of communications through the lenses of graphic and information design. These two primary skills take much longer to hone than it does to learn a design program."

Most clients prefer to have a complete solution designed by one Web-site design company. This means there will always be a role for generalists, but it also means that solo Web designers either have to expand their skills to meet their clients' needs or partner with specialists so they can work together to provide the necessary services for each other's clients.

To be a competitive Web-site designer, a background in graphic design or a related field with a firm understanding of basic marketing concepts is important. Good-looking, effective sites are still created from the same basic principles that govern top-flight graphic design.

Besides the usual computer equipment, you will need software such as Macromedia *Freehand* or Adobe *Illustrator* to mock up a design; and Adobe *Photoshop* with add-ons, Adobe *ImageReady* or Macromedia *Fireworks* for photo manipulation. For designing sites for Windows you'll need a high-end program like Macromedia's *Dreamweaver.* For the actual site design on the Macintosh you'll need programs such as Adobe *PageMill,* and for high-end work, *CyberStudio Pro* by Golive. New versions of software are constantly being introduced, so you'll need to stay current.

A good source of clients for your Web-site design business is local Internet service providers (ISPs). ISPs often offer Web-site design and hosting to their customers, and they often farm out the design work. Another good way to find clients is networking through local and national users' groups. And, of course, using the Internet itself is an ideal way to network as well as demonstrate your capabilities.

Billing structures for Web-site designers are by no means universal. Web-site designers typically charge from $60 to $170 per hour, while others charge by the project. Yearly earnings range from $25,000 up to $100,000 and more.

Books

How to Start a Home-Based Web Design Business, Jim Smith, Globe Pequot, ISBN: 0762727896.

How to Be a Successful Internet Consultant, Jessica Keyes, American Management Association, ISBN: 0814471390.

Secrets of Successful Websites: Project Management on the Web, David S. Siegel, Hayden Books, ISBN:1568303823.

The Real Business of Web Design, John Waters, Allworth Press, ISBN: 1581153163.

A well-regarded line of technical books and journals for back-end work is published by Tim O'Reilly, (800) 998-9938, *www.oreilly.com.*

Magazines

Internet World, Mecklermedia, (203) 559-2849, *www.iw.com.*

Web Developer, www.webdeveloper.com

Training

WEBMONKEY—daily tutorials, *www.webmonkey.com*

95

Web-Site Publicist

Building a Web site is the easy part for most companies and organizations. The hard part is getting people to visit it. A Web site, like most things in business, needs good promotion to be successful. As cyberspace becomes more crowded, and therefore more competitive, we believe that most companies who rely on the Web as an integral part of their marketing plan will turn to experts in Web-site and Internet promotion to help them stay ahead of the game. Many already are.

Commercial Web sites are used by companies as part of their overall marketing approach. Their Web sites are as targeted to their specific markets as are their advertisements, catalogs, brochures, etc. But unlike print ads and direct mail, once a Web site is completed, the right people need to know it's there. This is where a Web-site publicity expert comes in. As a site publicity expert, you will need to understand the intricacies of the Internet and the Web. You will also need to identify your client's target audience and reach it effectively. Techniques for this include submitting the site in just the right way to the most relevant search engines. Other techniques currently used by top Internet promoters include e-mail marketing, link exchanges, submissions to newsgroups, and cross-advertising on related sites. Good publicity also includes e-mail and written press releases sent to print and online media.

To do Web-site promotion, it is helpful if you have a background in PR or marketing, as well as a good understanding of the Internet and the Web. This can easily be a full-time business. Web publicity can also be a synergistic add-on business for Web writers, electronic publicists, Webmasters, and public-relations companies. Unless your eventual aim is to promote on a full-time basis, you may wish to limit the number of promotions clients you take on, as publicity campaigns do require a great deal of time and creative energy. Campaigns can also help fledgling Web designers get started by offering additional income, but once a Web-design business gets going, the activities involved are too divergent and time-consuming, and you probably won't be able to perform either function effectively. You should focus on one or the other.

The best way to get clients is to demonstrate your promotional skills in your approach to marketing your own business. By this we mean use the same techniques you would use to promote a client's site to promote your services. First construct a simple, high-impact Web site that outlines your services and then submit it to the popular search engines. Networking is a key to landing business, such as with Web designers, Web writers, Webmasters, and other Internet and Web professionals. Convince them that your service would be valuable to their clients. Have them refer business directly to you, or have them offer publicity as part of their menu of services and outsource the promotions to you.

Good online publicity is usually a targeted campaign that encompasses a range of services. Therefore, most Web promotions specialists set their prices in terms of packages. Here's an example of an average promotional package:

1. Review of site data for keywords, description, etc.
2. Site URL and description submitted to the top five hundred search engines and promotional sites
3. Write and submit a press release to five hundred press sources, including newspapers, television networks, radio stations, and Internet publications.
4. Seek out fifty sites of similar interest and place a targeted link.

Your menu of services, packages, and costs will be unique to your business. Check your competition to find out what they're charging and set your prices accordingly. It is best not to charge lower than all your competition, nor is it effective to be the most expensive. In general, we believe start-up businesses do the best by charging rates somewhere in the middle.

Books

101 Ways to Promote Your Web Site, Susan Sweeney, Maximum Press, ISBN: 1885068905.

Complete Guide to Internet Publicity, Steve O'Keefe, Wiley, ISBN: 0471105805.

Magazine

BtoB, The Magazine for Marketing Strategists, www.btobonline.com

Press Release Service

EWORLDWIRE, an example of a press release service, (973) 252-6800, (973) 252-0999, *www.eworldwire.com*
Also check the resources for "Web-Site Promotions Specialist"

96

Web-Site Promotions Specialist

As the Web develops and matures, businesses and organizations are beginning to expect more in terms of bottom-line results from their Web sites. Marketers on the Web realize that not only can their site bring their company to the market, but the market can give them valuable information about itself. Exciting new ideas and technologies are now available to help any company with a Web site find out detailed information about each person who browses their site. Ethically, the people who are browsing should volunteer this information themselves. One way to get them to do this is a clever promotion programmed into the Web site itself. For example, Stu Heinecke, Inc. (*www.cartoonlink.com*), offers personalized Web cartoons that can be programmed into any Web site. The cartoon is the first thing a browser sees when logging onto a site. This is fun for the visitor and at the same time provides a detailed demographic profile that is automatically stored in a database. Making your job researching the kinds of promotions available, and perhaps designing a few of them yourself, we see potential for a new kind of online marketing consultant: Web-site promotions specialist.

By recommending promotional solutions such as Web cartoons, you can provide a much-needed service to online marketing managers, Webmasters, and site designers. These professionals have a difficult-enough time keeping up with the developments in their fields of expertise and generally do not have the time to stay abreast of the developments in Web-site promotions. By making this your area of expertise, you can offer a one-stop source for a number of different promotion options that will help your clients get the most out of their online marketing efforts. The more deeply you research what's available, the more you will know about the latest techniques and technologies, and the more valuable you will be.

Web promotions include, but are certainly not limited to:

1. Search-engine optimization
2. Free downloadable software
3. Free downloadable screen savers
4. Newsletters offering useful information
5. Giveaways and contests
6. Interactive "guest book" type applets
7. Special online events such as interviews with experts or well-known personalities

As a Web-site promotions specialist, you can market your services to any business or organization whose Web site forms an integral part of their overall marketing plan. The best way to find clients is to contact them directly by e-mail through their Web sites. Keep your marketing efforts targeted to specific industries. Search the Web to find a list of sites in an industry. Look through the site and then send a short, personal e-mail to the Webmaster describing how your service will help attract visitors to his or her site. Also explain that you can provide ways to obtain important marketing and demographic information from each visitor. Choose mid-to-larger companies to target as they will have the resources, and the need, to actually institute the promotions you suggest.

Because this is a relatively new business idea, fees or price guidelines are not clearly established. The promotional technologies you represent will no doubt cost you a specific amount. You will, of course, need to add a markup in cost to cover your time and expertise. We recommend that you start out as an add-on service to a more established business, such as a PR agency, Web publicist business, or a Web-site-design or Web-site-hosting service.

Books

Getting the Search Engine Ranking Your Website Deserves (e-book), Transformata Publishing LLC, ISBN: B00008Wl71.

Search Engine Optimization for Dummies, Peter Kent, For Dummies, ISBN: 0764567586.

The Super Affiliate Handbook, Rosalind Gardner, Webvista, Inc., ISBN: 0973328703.

Web Sites

ClickZNetwork, a commercial site that tracks Web statistics and advertising trends, *www.clickz.com/stats*

SearchEngineWatch, a leading source of developments for search-engine marketing, *www.searchenginewatch.com*

Web Digest for Marketers, *www.wdfm.com*, a free weekly e-mail marketing newsletter from Chase Online Marketing Strategies, (212)619-4780, *www.wdfm.com*

97

Web-Site Reviewer

There are millions of Web sites in the electronic universe out there. The majority are either business or education related. Taken as a whole, these Web sites offer an impressive range of information useful to a vast number of people, but they have to know it's there in the first place, and they have to know where to find it. Search engines are helpful, but many people find the most useful sites on the Web by either reading about them in online and traditionally published publications or through on-site links.

The need to list and review Web sites is creating a new kind of editorial product—Web-site reviews—that publishers hope will draw advertisers and viewers to their online and print publications. Most of the Web-site reviewing is currently being performed by independent and freelance writers. As publications, both online and printed, devote more of their column space to the Web, the need for experienced, fast, and dependable Web-site reviewers will increase as well.

Web-site reviews are usually 100 words or less, although publishers sometimes ask for lengthier reviews. Within the review, you should sum up the informative value of the site, define its usefulness, and spell out which audience it will be useful for. Unless specifically asked by a publisher, never include your own opinion in the review; simply sum up what you see (and maybe hear) on the site.

Web-site reviewing only is probably not a good candidate for a full-time business, but it can be used as add-on business for copywriters, technical writers, Web writers, and even Web-site designers. In addition to bringing in extra income, reviewing sites will bring you in contact with a wide range of businesses, designers, Webmasters, publishers, and editors. It will give you a greater overview of what's going on out there in cyberspace. If you are given a byline, it will also help to publicize your name and help establish your credibility as a Web expert or journalist.

Potential clients are any online publication or printed magazine that devotes space to the Web itself. Draft a query letter, in which you briefly outline your experience and describe what makes you qualified to review sites on the Web. If you have any specialized experience, such as a concentration in one of the sciences, be sure to mention it. Then, send the query directly to the publisher of each publication. If you don't hear back in a week's time, call the publisher and inquire about the status of your query. It helps if you research each publication before you submit query letters. If the publication has a specific angle or focus area, let the publisher know you have taken the time and done your research by mentioning it in your query. Another approach is to search the many online employment listings for "Web-Site Reviewers Wanted." Contact the employers and try to convince them to outsource their Web reviewing rather than hiring someone for an in-house position.

Books

Online Markets for Writers: How to Make Money by Selling Your Writing on the Internet, Anthony Tedesco, Paul Tedesco, Owl Books, ASIN: 0805062262.

Writer's Online Marketplace, Debbie Ridpath Ohi, Writer's Digest Books, ISBN: 1582970165.

Writing.Com, Moira Anderson Allen, Watson-Guptill, ISBN: 1581152701.

Writer's Market (annual), Writer's Digest Books, Cincinnati, OH, ISBN: 1582971897, *www.writersmarket.com*

Web Site

The Business Researcher's Interests, *www.brint.com/interest.html.* This Meta site is packed with literally thousands of links to business-related information. Of interest to Web-site reviewers is the extensive listing of online and printed magazines, journals, and other publications.

Use any search engine for "Magazines," "Online Magazines," or "Internet Magazines" and you will receive enough listings to keep you busy sending query letters for months.

98

Web Specialty Programmer: CGI Programming

Specialization continues to grow with the expansion of the Web. Web sites are becoming more sophisticated, and their component parts are becoming more complex and involved. Web designers have a difficult time keeping current with the latest developments and technologies. More and more they are turning to Web specialty programmers and service providers. One hot area of specialization is CGI programming.

Have you ever filled out an order form or survey while accessing a Web site? Have you ever searched through a site using a search engine that's incorporated right into the site? If you have, then you've seen the power of CGI programming. CGI is an acronym for Common Gateway Interface. CGI is a special language that creates interactive forms, guest books, and Web-site search engines that work with databases and clickable image maps. CGI is more complex than HTML, but not nearly as difficult to learn as traditional programming languages like C++.

We see the need for CGI programming on the increase. Many Web designers who want to stay competitive outsource their CGI programming to specialists. Potential clients for CGI programmers are independent Web designers, Webmasters for companies and organizations, design companies or agencies, and even Internet service providers. The best way to find clients is to directly contact any of the above mentioned and tell them about your service. Two or three busy designers can give you more than enough work to keep you going. As a word of caution, do not rely solely on just a few sources for your livelihood. Even if you have solid, ongoing relationships with a core of clients, losing just one could be devastating. Always network to develop additional potential sources of work.

You have a choice of billing hourly or by project. Hourly rates vary by region. You can check rates in your area by calling the competition and pricing your services accordingly.

Books

CGI Programming 101, Jacqueline D. Hamilton, *CGI101.com*, 2000, ISBN: 0966942604.

Perl and CGI for the Web, Elizabeth Castro, Peachpit Press, ISBN: 0201735687.

Writing CGI Applications with Perl, Kevin Meltzer, Brent Michalski, Addison-Wesley Professional, ISBN: 0201710145.

Web Site

PROGRAMMERS HEAVEN.COM, *www.programmersheaven.com*

99

Web Specialty Programmer: Java

Java is a programming language that grew out of more traditional programming languages like C++. Its main function, in terms of cyberspace, is to allow a Web page and its embedded features, such as spreadsheets or calculators, to run on any computer, such as IBM, Mac, Unix work station, etc. Java allows a developer to actually write independent programs, called applets, and embed them into Web pages. Other uses for Java applets include the scrolling marquees you see on Web sites, animation, moving background, sounds, or music.

Java is a bit trickier to learn than HTML or CGI but is much easier than C++ and other computer languages. We know many people without previous programming experience who have successfully taught themselves how to program in Java in less than a month. It simply takes solid computer experience, logical abilities, and some practice. There are many helpful books available on learning Java. Java information on the Web is very helpful, and comprehensive to the point of overload. Many community colleges and extension programs teach courses in Java as well.

Web designers and Webmasters are fully aware of the power of Java, and Java programming, like CGI, is often outsourced by smaller organizations.

As a Java programmer, your best sources for work are Web designers, Webmasters, online publications, Internet service providers, and Website hosting organizations. The best ways to approach potential clients include networking, direct contact (calling them up and introducing yourself), and very targeted mailings. To find the names of organizations, decision makers, and independent designers, start with the Web itself. Search for "Web Designers" in your geographic region. Consult the various online employment listings and search for "Java Programmers Wanted." Contact the organizations and ask them if they would consider outsourcing their Java programming instead of hiring full-time positions. You can network in online user groups.

Like other specialty Web programming businesses, you may find that just one or two clients give you more than enough work to keep busy. This can be a problem, however. If you lose one of these clients, you can find yourself in trouble. Always keep up your networking so that you can replace major clients without too much trouble. You may also want to limit how much work you accept from clients so you can maintain a diverse client base where no one client represents a sizable bulk of your business.

As an expert Java programmer you can easily charge from $40 to $100 per hour or even more, depending on your market, direct competition, and level of experience. You may be asked to bill your services on a per-project basis. In this case, estimate the amount of time you think it will take, and then add an additional 20 percent to cover any unforeseen problems. On per-project jobs, you should also include specific language in your quotations that specifies the time period in which the job will run and includes price contingencies should the job run overtime.

Books

Beginning Programming with Java for Dummies, Barry Burd, For Dummies, ISBN: 0764526464.

Java(tm)2: A Beginner's Guide, Herbert Schildt, Osborne/McGraw-Hill, ISBN: 0072225882.

Java & XML for Dummies, Barry Burd, For Dummies, ISBN: 0764516582.

Learn to Program with Java, John Smiley, McGraw-Hill Osborne Media, ISBN: 0072131896.

Web Sites

JAVAWORLD ONLINE magazine, *www.javaworld.com*

SUN MICROSYSTEMS, the official Web site for the latest Java software, a resource for everything Java, *www.developers.sun.com*

Web Audio or Video Program

One of the most exciting aspects of the online digital revolution is the democratization of content distribution. Never before has mass distribution of creative content, such as prose, video, and audio, been available to more people. For a long time now, it has been very easy to download and play back high-quality audio and video files from the Internet.

These days, anybody with a video camcorder and a PC manufactured in the past few years can create high-quality video productions. You don't need a radio tower and millions of dollars in equipment to broadcast an audio program or a television station and an international broadcast network to get a video program into the homes of people *around the world.* With your computer you can also produce and distribute (sometimes called *netcast*) a weekly video-based program. And like broadcast television and radio, you can attract sponsors for your Web program and potentially earn a comfortable income.

The equipment required to record audio or video, digitize the content, and then distribute it over the Web is surprisingly low cost. Getting started is pretty easy. First, you'll need a reasonably good quality consumer camcorder. You install a capture board, hook up your VCR or camera, start your software for doing captures, and you're ready.

With "video stream" software, you can broadcast "live" right over the Internet. If you wish to edit video footage and broadcast a finished program from tape, you will need some sort of editing equipment. You can edit your programs with analog equipment (a number of manufacturers offer excellent, low-cost editing equipment). You'll have to research this on your own. Space limitations prevent us from going in-depth). If you wish to use your computer to edit, please see the "Desktop Video" listing on page 54 of this book. For audio, any of the sixteen-bit stereo digitizing boards will work well. You will also need your own Web site from which to broadcast. When looking for a server for your site, make sure that the Web-hosting company you use knows that you intend to use your site to broadcast (or netcast) an audio or video program. This takes up far more bandwidth than nonmultimedia sites, and some servers are not set up to handle the extra load.

Once you have the equipment and the Web site secured, you're ready to start. In terms of content, you're on your own. To create and build an audience for your program you may wish to hire the services of a Web publicist and/or a site content promotions specialist or public-relations firm. The bigger the audience you can attract to your program, the more you can charge potential sponsors for advertising. Once you can demonstrate a sizable, consistent audience for your site, you can approach specialty ad agencies that will sell space on your site during program times. They will keep a percentage of the fees charged to each of your sponsors.

Like everything related to the Internet, ad rates for high-traffic sites vary and can change quickly, so you will need to investigate this yourself; but we feel the earning potential is quite high.

Books

Digital Video for Dummies, Keith Underdahl, For Dummies, ISBN: 0764541145.

Editing Digital Video, Robert M. Goodman, Patrick McGrath, McGraw-Hill/TAB Electronics,ISBN: 0071406352.

Mastering Internet Video, Damien Stolarz, Addison-Wesley Professional, ISBN: 0321122461.

PC Magazine Guide to Digital Video, Jan Ozer, Wiley, ISBN: 0764543601.

Producing Great Sound for Digital Video, Jay Rose, CMP Books, ISBN: 1578202086.

Associations

THE DIGITAL VIDEO PROFESSIONALS ASSOCIATION, (888) 339-3872, *www.dvpa.com*

WORLD DIGITAL VIDEO ASSOCIATION, (925) 989-9107, *www.wdva.org*

101

Web Publication

Content is king on the Web. Industry pundits are almost unanimous (a rare occurrence where the Web is concerned) in saying that the most powerful sites are the ones that consistently offer viewers high-quality information they can use or entertainment they can enjoy. Combine this with the Web's unique and powerful distribution possibilities and you have the recipe for a fulfilling and potentially profitable business: producing a Web-based publication.

Producing a publication for the Web is less expensive than producing one for print. There are no prepress and printing costs, no paper costs, and no mailing costs. Design and creative services such as article writing and photography are much the same as producing a printed publication, but if you do the majority of them yourself, these expenses can be greatly reduced. When the publication is ready, you simply post it on the Web. Any corrections or updates can be made instantly.

The content of your publication is up to you. Any idea suitable to a print magazine can certainly become a viable Web publication. In fact, major magazines and television networks also have Web-based publications. For example, *HotWired* publishes online and in print (*www.hotwired.com*). The popular Home and Garden Television Network (HGTV) produces and broadcasts TV programming and maintains a complementary Web site (*www.hgtv.com*). Many Web publications take full advantage of the Web's multimedia capabilities, such as *IUMA*, where viewers can read text, see illustrations and photos, hear music, and watch video.

To produce a Web-based publication, you will need the same basic equipment and software as a Web designer. If your interest lies more in the editorial aspect of the publication, you will certainly need to team up with a Web designer. If you're visually oriented you may want to team up with a wordsmith. Between the two of you, with some creativity and innovation, you have the potential of putting together a high-impact, cutting-edge publication that can realistically compete with those produced by much larger publishing entities.

A Web publication, like a Web audio or video program, will require some time to get started and build up an audience. Even then, of course, there are no guarantees of success. If you are able to attract a large, loyal readership, you can sell advertising and sign up sponsors. Advertising and sponsorship rates on the Web change frequently. Advertisers usually pay based on the number of readers of your publication. For banner ads rates are usually in specified increments, for example, $75 for every 1,000 viewers. Rates are ever changing, so for current information you will want to check into this when you are ready to publish. When your readership is up, you may wish to secure the services of an agency that specializes in selling ad space in cyberspace. You may also pitch larger entities to form strategic partnerships with others.

A Web-based publication is a synergistic side venture for Web-site designers, Web writers, and other creative Web professionals, such as specialty programmers. Although perhaps not initially profitable, a publication will give you good exposure in the Web community and establish your reputation as an expert. It is also a great way to generate business for your main money-making enterprise.

Books

Hot Text: Web Writing That Works, Jonathan Price, Lisa Price, New Riders Publishing, ISBN: 0735711518.

Secrets of a Freelance Writer: How to Make Eighty-five Thousand Dollars a Year, Robert W. Bly, Henry Holt and Company, ISBN: 0805047603.

Web Word Wizardry Net-Savvy Writing Guide, Rachel McAlpine, Ten Speed Press, ISBN: 1580082238.

Writing for the Web (Writers' Edition), Crawford Kilian, Self-Counsel Press, ISBN: 1551802074.

Web Sites

ONLINE PUBLISHING NEWS, *www.onlinepublishingnews.com*

FREELANCE ONLINE, *www.freelanceonline.com*

HOTWIRED, covers cyberspace and cyber culture, *www.hotwired.com*

RESOURCE CENTRAL, *www.resourcehelp.com*

USEIT.COM: Jakob Nielsen's tips and resources for writing for the Web, *www.useit.com*

WRITERS WEEKLY, *www.writersmarkets.com*

Association

ONLINE PUBLISHERS ASSOCIATION, association of content providers, (646) 698-8071, *www.online-publishers.org*

PART II

47 Questions You Need
to Answer to Start

Making Money
with Your
Computer

*A goal is a dream
with a deadline.*

BRIAN TRACY,
The Psychology of Success

If you have read through the profiles in Part 1, you have probably selected a few businesses of interest to you and are already beginning to think about the next steps you will need to take. We have, therefore, devised this portion of the book as a guide through the most important personal, financial, and legal issues that you will need to address to actually set yourself up making money in a computer-based business. Answering the following forty-seven questions will take you through a logical sequence of decision making that will essentially become your business plan for success. When you finish answering these forty-seven questions, you will have the equivalent of a comprehensive business plan for your home business.

Note: You may wish to open up a document file in your computer or get a notebook at this time so that you can do the various exercises that follow.

1. Why do you want to make money with your computer?

How you answer this question will help you answer many of the other key questions below, from which business you will actually want to select to how you will market and price your products or services—even to what you will tell people when they ask what you do and why.

Additionally, in our experience, we've found that "why" people set out to make money on their own influences how long they will persist and how much difficulty they will put up with. So what's your motivation for starting a business? Is it to

____ be home with your children or other family members?

____ do something more interesting than what an employer will pay you to do?

____ fulfill your dream to become your own boss?

____ get paid for something you have a talent or skill for?

____ provide additional income?

____ offer a product or service you think people need and will pay for?

_____ pay for a hobby or a special purchase or expense?

_____ pursue something you passionately like doing?

_____ supplement a retirement income?

_____ some other reason: _____

Having a clear reason to succeed will make you more likely to achieve your goals than someone who, for example, simply purchases a business opportunity on a whim. In short, your answer to this question can serve as a guiding principle for your entire venture and can help you get past the large and small annoyances you will encounter along the way.

2. Do you want to derive a full-time or part-time income from your computer-based business? Do you intend to work full or part time?

Some businesses are more or less likely to produce a full-time income than others. For example, keeping sports-league statistics, doing astrology charts, or data conversion are less apt to generate a regular and sufficient income to serve as the sole source of earnings for a family. They can, however, bring in extra money, supplement a retirement income, or become an add-on to an existing business.

Some businesses, like a specialized temporary-help service or a computer-repair service, are more difficult to operate as sideline businesses. Others, like bookkeeping, Web-site design, or data conversion, can be done either full time or on the side.

3. Do you want to continue working in the same field doing the same or similar work?

There's apt to be a way for you to make money with your computer in a field in which you've worked or are currently working. There are several advantages to sticking with a type of work you've had some experience in or at least to staying in the same field. As we mentioned earlier, you'll find getting started will be easier and quicker. Presumably you are already skilled at the work you do, so you won't have to go through a learning curve before you can do a good job for your clients and customers. Also, when you start out familiar with what you're doing, you're able to complete your work more quickly and therefore will be able to take on more clients or customers in the same period of time.

More important, by staying in your existing field, you may be able to capitalize on whatever reputation you've already built. Hopefully you have contacts in the field who can become invaluable sources of referrals or even potential clients. (If you don't have such contacts outside your company, you can begin making them now before you start your business.) And you know the "territory," so to speak. You know who's who, what's what, the lingo, the taboos, the needs, the problems, and the current issues. Otherwise, in order to avoid costly mistakes in entering a new field, you would have to take time and spend whatever money is needed to acquire such "insider" information.

However, if you don't enjoy doing the type of work you've been doing or you're "burned out" from it, even with these considerable advantages we don't advise trying to "stick it out" in the same line of work just because it would be easier. To really make money on your own full or part time, most people need to enjoy what they do, at least enough to look forward to getting up (or staying up) to do it. This is particularly true if you are starting a sideline business and must put in additional hours after coming home from a tiring day on your job. So if you're burned out or bummed out from your current line of work, we urge you to investigate other possibilities you would enjoy more.

The following four questions are designed to help you decide if you can make money full or part time on your own doing the type of work you've been doing. If you are certain you do not want to continue in your existing line of work, skip to Question #4.

3a. Are there other people doing something similar to what you would do on a freelance, consulting, or independent basis?

If there are already self-employed individuals doing something similar to what you do, this could be a good sign that there will be a market for your services if you go out on your own. You will need to ascertain, however, if there is enough business for one more—particularly if it's a business in which you serve local customers. If not, what could you offer that would be sufficiently better or different to compete successfully against your competition? To explore the possibilities further, talk with as many people already in the business (or who have been in the business) as possible. We'll discuss this further in Question #6.

3b. Can your current employer become your first customer?

Would you be a difficult employee to replace? Is what you do integral to the success of your company? If so, you may be able to turn your employer into your first client.

A survey of home-based businesses found that 49 percent of the respondents said they were doing or had done work for their former employers. The best time to approach your boss about such an arrangement is when doing so would clearly benefit the company. Listen and watch for any indication of imminent cutbacks. Be alert to impending layoffs, early-retirement offers, or other cost-saving measures. Companies today are looking for ways to get more for less, so one of the surest ways to transition into self-employment is to make a proposal your company cannot refuse. Demonstrate how much money you can save them (but don't shortchange yourself) and how much work you can produce working as an outside consultant, freelancer, or subcontractor for a specified number of hours each week or month.

☞ **ALERT** ☜

If you are able to turn your ex-boss into your first client or customer, do not be lulled into the trap of relying on that one source of income. Most important, if you work for only one client, even if you are working under a contract as an independent contractor, you run the risk of the IRS ruling that you are still technically an employee—even if you don't get the fringe benefits you formerly received. If that happens, you will not be able to claim your business expenses as tax deductions. Getting neither the tax benefits of being self-employed nor the fringe benefits of being an employee will certainly lower your income, even if you bring in about the same money. So make sure you work with multiple clients.

3c. Could any of the people or companies you currently work with on your job ethically become your clients or customers as well? How many?

For many people, their plans to go out on their own begin when someone they're working with says, "If you ever go out on your own, let me know." When you can do that ethically (that is, without a legal or ethical conflict with your employer's interest), you need not wait until such a person approaches you. You can approach him, tell him of your intentions, and get his reaction. Clearly, the more commitments you can get, the better the indication that there will be work awaiting you.

3d. Are there other clients for whom you could do your current job on a freelance, consultant, or subcontract arrangement?

Remember, it's important not to put all your eggs in one basket. You should never rely on the income from only one client, because if that client decides to discontinue your contract, you're out of business, at least temporarily. And since it can take one or more months to sign up new clients, even if one contract is keeping you busy, when that contract runs out, unless you have been actively marketing yourself, you will have no business in the pipeline. So always invest some time lining up new clients no matter how busy you may be with one major one.

If you want to stay in your own field, explore these other sources of possible clients or customers:

Large corporations. Many companies are cutting back staff and yet they still need to have work done. As a result, they are choosing to contract out whole job functions that were once done by in-house staff. They're "outsourcing," that is, hiring outside consultants, small-business people, freelancers, or independent contractors for everything from marketing and billing to purchasing and technical writing, though a hunk of this work is also being offshored. Even this sometimes opens up opportunities if you speak the language of the country where the work is being outsourced, in which case you play the role in setting up, training, managing, overseeing, or troubleshooting outsourced activities.

Smaller companies. While large businesses are cutting back, the number of small businesses is growing, but often they're not large enough to hire full-time employees to do specialized tasks they need to have done. Instead, they're contracting out for many services like bookkeeping, public relations, security, training, and graphic design.

New fields or industries. Even if there is no market for your services in your own field or industry, another industry or an emerging field may have a need for what you offer. For example, while realty companies or banks may be cutting back on using computer consultants in a tight market, collection agencies and loan brokers may be expanding and therefore have a growing need for such services. Or while advertising agencies may be using fewer freelance graphic designers, specialty magazine and Web-site editors and producers may need freelance designers to design Web-based magazine layouts.

Information services or products. Even when the work you've been doing cannot be done outside a large organization, you may be able to successfully turn your expertise from the line of work you've done into a source of income by providing information about it to others. For example, if you are a customer service representative or bank teller, you probably won't be able to do your work on a freelance basis, but you could become a consultant or trainer and use your expertise to help other companies set up and train similar employees. In fact, there are at least sixteen ways you may be able to package the knowledge you have into profitable information products.

If you are now certain you want to continue doing the type of work you have been doing, skip to Question #5.

4. If you don't want to, or cannot, do the same type of work you've been doing, what other things do you do well and enjoy doing?

Make a list of your skills, talents, abilities, interests, contacts, and hobbies.

As you can see from the profiles in Part 1, there are at least 101 ways you can make money using a personal computer. So there is no need for you to feel limited to the type of work that you've been doing. You can use your computer to turn a talent, skill, passion, hobby, bright idea, interest, pastime, or mission into a business. Identifying what you do well and enjoy doing is actually the ideal way to start finding the best way to make money with a computer.

In fact, we strongly advise against picking a particular computer-based business simply because it's popular or has high-income potential. No matter how promising a particular business is, if you aren't especially good at it or don't particularly enjoy it, you jeopardize your chances of success. You would not want to find yourself in the same predicament as Gary Mc-Clelland, who came to a seminar we gave, "How to Make Money with Your Computer."

In introducing himself, McClelland told the class that he had run a highly successful home-based medical-transcription business for the past three years. Everyone was immediately curious about why he had come to this course if he was already making money in one of the best computer-based home businesses. His answer was simple: "I had heard that I could earn a good living at this and I do, but I sit at my desk all day transcribing tapes, and actually I hate it. So now I'm looking for something I can do that I'll enjoy."

The 101 businesses we've profiled are ones many people can do, and they should suggest a variety of new avenues for you to explore for matching your talents, skills, interests, ideas, and goals to an income-producing activity. But in addition to these 101, you can use a computer to make money in many other ways that only you can identify because they cap-

---

SIXTEEN WAYS TO TURN WHAT YOU KNOW INTO INFORMATION PRODUCTS

1. Write a book on the subject. E-book sales are growing.

2. Host an online discussion group on the topic.

3. Publish a Web site on the topic.

4. Speak on the topic.

5. Create educational DVDs.

6. Create audio CD programs.

7. Write articles or a column for magazines, newspapers, or trade publications.

8. Publish and sell a newsletter.

9. Train or conduct seminars.

10. Provide consulting services.

11. Produce prepackaged e-learning training programs.

12. Develop a product.

13. Design a computer-assisted instructional software program.

14. Create a television show.

15. Originate a radio program. Internet radio is growing.

16. Sell your knowledge as a database through a Web site on the public or private Web.

---

italize specifically on your unique background, skills, contacts, and interests.

It's easy to overlook the income potential of the things we enjoy and do well. We tend to take these abilities and interests for granted or assume everyone can do them. We may even think that if we really enjoy doing something, no one would pay us to do it. Not true. Here are just a few examples of ingenious ways people are using their computers to provide products or services based on their unique combinations of skills, talents, interests, hobbies, and abilities.

Michael Cahlin turned his love for chocolate into Chocolate Software, a line of computer programs filled with chocolate recipes. Cartoonist Stu Heinecke developed the idea for personalized cartoons and uses his computer to create direct-mail cartoon advertising campaigns for some of the largest advertisers in the world. In addition, he has recruited other top cartoonists in the country and created the Personal Promotion Kit, a desktop micro-ad campaign that puts the power of the personalized cartoon at the fingertips of anyone with a PC.

Rita Tateel turned her interest in celebrities into a database business called Celebrity Source. She matches charity events with celebrities who will attend and endorse their causes. A public-relations specialist in Detroit was a tennis pro earlier in her career and still teaches tennis in her spare time. She uses her computer to provide a tennis scholarship–matching service.

Ted Artz went from art school into designing custom interiors and furniture, where he got in on the PC revolution early by being among the first in his industry to use a CAD system in his work. His love of computers has now brought him closer to his original career vision: The company he began at home as Amalgamation Haus produces top-notch video-animation sequences for broadcast and industrial video productions. Samantha Greenberg had pounded a keyboard for twenty-five years as a bookkeeper and accountant when she took a particularly demanding job entering medical data. This new job required that she work long days without breaks. Within months she developed a repetitive-strain illness and ended up unemployed. Even after surgery she was unable to pick up anything heavier than a paperback book. After researching her disability to learn as much about it as she could, Greenberg started a database business called Computer Injury Network, providing information on the resources available to the 185,000 similarly injured workers who are reported nationwide each year. She also conducts seminars for businesses on VDT-related afflictions.

Here are a few other examples: Jinjee and Storm Talifero started *TheGardenDiet.com,* a Web site selling e-books, CDs, and coaching and following a raw-food diet.

Dee Louzginov has always been a home-based graphic designer. Taking advantage of developments in the multimedia field, Dee combined her design experience with her expertise in new media and created her latest home-based business. Eclectica Mediaworks was one of the first companies to create interactive, multimedia high-school yearbooks on CD.

Because his passion is boating, Will Milan has developed software for first-time boat buyers. As a professional planner, Wayne Serville was aware of the complexities citizens face when serving on local planning boards, so he has created a business for himself producing a newsletter for lay planners. Susan Pinsky and David Starkman love 3-D photography. They use their computer to run Reel 3-D, a mail-order company selling items of interest to 3-D photographers.

Here is a worksheet to help you discover the gateway to turning your particular talents, skills, passions, hobbies, ideas, interests, and desires into a viable income with your computer:

WORK SHEET: FOUR GATEWAYS TO CREATING YOUR OWN JOB

There are four gateways to identifying and turning what you do well and most enjoy into a profitable computer-related business. Answer the following questions to find the best ones for you.

1. Harvesting Your Gifts

Is there anything people readily and spontaneously compliment you on or appreciate you for? It may be a talent, hobby, skill, or interest. It may be something that goes back to your childhood, or it may be something you developed later in life. Such compliments may take the form of someone asking you to do something for them because you do it so well or it may be a more direct comment like "You sure are good at this. People would pay you for this!" Someone might have even said something like "You ought to start a business doing that."

If you've had such compliments and you enjoy doing this activity, why not turn your talent, gift, or skill into a source of income for yourself? About one in four self-employed individuals use this strategy as their gateway to self-employment.

This approach has many advantages. First, you already know people appreciate and admire your skill in doing it. Second, you can approach the very people who encouraged you to see if they might become your first clients, customers, or referral sources. Third, since you're already a "master" at this type of work, you'll be able to produce positive results right away for your clients or customers.

If your answer to this question is "yes," describe your talent or skill here and indicate on a scale of 1 to 10 how interested you would be in developing this gift into a business:

My gift is:

Not Very Interested   *Somewhat Interested*   *Very Interested*
1   2   3   4   5   6   7   8   9   10

2. Profiting from Your Passion

What do you feel particularly passionate about doing? About one in every six people who work for themselves have found a way to turn their passion into a profitable line of work. Some people describe this as having a "fire in the belly." These are the people who say about their work: "I'd do this even if I weren't being paid." Is there anything you feel that strongly about?

Even if your passion is something you'd never think that you could make money doing, don't automatically write it off. Go ahead and describe those things about which you are most enthusiastic. We've seen businesses arise from a love of golf, tennis, pets, model railroading, art, cross-dressing, writing family histories, comedy, matchmaking, music, and even going to parties. One advantage of turning your passion into a living is that your work will often feel like play. You'll get paid for doing what you'd otherwise do for free. And, of course, you'll rarely have problems motivating yourself to get to work.

Some people want to keep work and play separate, so if your answer to this question is yes, describe your passion here and indicate on a scale of 1 to 10 how interested you would be in developing this passion into a business:

My passion is:

Not Very Interested   *Somewhat Interested*   *Very Interested*
1   2   3   4   5   6   7   8   9   10

3. Earning Your Living from a Mission

Are you the sort of person who is motivated by "wanting to make a difference in the world"? Have you been wishing you could find a way to do more meaningful work than past jobs have provided? Do you have an idea for a new business product, service, or invention that you think could help change the world? Do you want to spend your working life solving a problem or taking on a cause?

Solving problems or turning a "great" idea into a reality can serve as the source for a livelihood. About one in five people who go out on their own have turned such an idea, problem, cause, or mission into a business.

The problems or ideas you want to develop may be of a personal nature, affecting a small percentage of the population, or they may be related to larger social ills that affect many. Write down the your idea or problem here and indicate on a scale of 1 to 10 how interested you would be in earning your living pursuing this idea, mission, or cause:

The problem I'd like to help solve is:

The idea I have to solve it is:

Not Very Interested				Somewhat Interested			Very Interested		
1	2	3	4	5	6	7	8	9	10

4. Choosing an Opportunity

Are you seeking something to do on your own primarily to earn enough money so you can do something else that's important to you? Are you simply wanting to find some way to earn a better full- or part-time income? Are you primarily wanting to be at home more, have greater control of your time, be with your children? Are you developing a career as an artist or entertainer and need a flexible way to support yourself until you break in?

Nearly half of the people going out on their own don't have any particular gift, passion, or mission they want to use their computer to pursue. For them, a business is a means to an end, not an end in itself. They are looking for an income opportunity, and their task becomes choosing a financially viable option that they can do successfully. Sometimes they buy a business opportunity or franchise. Sometimes they become active in a multilevel sales organization. Most often, those who succeed either decide to continue in the same line of work if their job ends or they simply CHOOSE something they can earn money at that already has a proven track record of success.

If this scenario best describes your situation, use Part 1 of this book as a checklist to make your choice, focusing on businesses that are among the easiest to start and have a strong existing demand. Since you will not be highly motivated by the work itself, the other reasons you have for going out on your own will need to keep you motivated. So write down the other goals that making money will help you achieve and indicate on a scale of 1 to 10 how important it is to you to find a way to pursue them:

> **My other goals are:**
>
> *Not Very Interested*   *Somewhat Interested*   *Very Interested*
>
> 1   2   3   4   5   6   7   8   9   10

Two of our other books will be helpful if you need to do more probing into identifying a career path that's right for you: *Finding Your Perfect Work* (2003) and *Best Home Businesses for the 21ˢᵗ Century* (1999). *Profiles from Best Home Businesses* are available at *www.funcareers.com.* You can download excerpts from both these books at our *workingfromhome.com* Web site. The current edition of *Cool Careers for Dummies with Marty Nemko* (2001) has some minimal material on self-employment.

Whichever pathway you choose to earn a living on your own, there are three alternatives for packaging your gift, idea, passion, mission, or choice into a viable product or service. Consider each of these possibilities:

1. You can sell what you **KNOW** in that area as a consultant, teacher, speaker, seminar leader, or coach.
2. You can **CREATE** an information product or a tangible product related to your gift, idea, passion, mission, or business choice—e.g., books, DVDs, novelty, e-learning course.
3. You can **DO** whatever it is you aspire to do as a service for others— e.g., programming, training, financial planning.

5. Who needs the kind of products or services you could offer? Make a list of all the types of people or companies that need them.

Whether you are doing the same kind of work or changing fields, no matter how good you are at what you want to do or how great an idea you have for a product or service, unless there are people who need and are willing to pay for it, it will forever remain a "good idea." We call this the WPWPF Principle—What People Will Pay For. The more precisely you identify what people need and will pay for, the better. If, when you visualize who your prospective customers are, you get no clear picture or your image includes everyone, that's a signal that you have not sufficiently defined your business concept. In today's economy, even large companies are becoming niche marketers.

To determine if your products or services will meet the WPWPF Principle, start by listing all the possible groups of people and companies that you THINK might need and will pay to use them. Then you will need to determine to the extent possible if, in fact, they WILL and start narrowing down those you are uniquely or most advantageously positioned to serve.

The following five questions, #6 through #10, should help you find out if, in fact, you have selected a viable service or product and narrow down your list of prospective customers to a "target" or niche group you can specialize in serving. Also for help in defining your niche, see our book *Getting Business to Come to You*. You can download excerpts from this book at our *www.workingfromhome.com* Web site.

6. Who is your competition? Is anyone else providing similar services or products?

If other people are now providing the products or services you wish to offer, this is a good sign that they are things that people will pay for. It's an especially good sign if you determine that your competition has been in business for some time and is doing well. Don't assume, however, that there is room for one more. You'll need to find out if there is enough unsatisfied demand for you to thrive.

You can locate people doing what you want to do by searching the Web, reviewing trade and professional-association directories on organization Web sites, checking yellow-pages listings, asking your business and personal contacts and members of networking groups, and by talking with likely customers about others they have bought from or used.

Should you find a considerable number of people are doing what you do, it's important to determine if this is an indication that there's a large demand for such work or whether it means that the market is saturated.

If you discover that no one else is doing what you do on an independent basis, you will need to investigate whether that's because there's not a sufficient need for it or enough profit in it or whether you are simply the first to consider providing these services independently. The best way to determine this is to identify how many people or businesses could use your services and begin talking with some of these potential clients personally.

If you discover that the area in which you live or the niche you have selected is not large enough to provide full-time support, you may need to branch out by offering related products or services. For example, if there are not enough clients in your community or niche to support a copywriting service, you might broaden your business as Robert Cooper did to include writing of other kinds. Cooper breaks his services down among copywriting, freelance magazine writing, and writing newsletters for law firms.

7. How is your competition doing? Are they busy? Are they turning away business they could refer to you?

Once you identify your competition, find out as much as you can about what they do, whom they do it for, how they do it, and how long they have been doing it. With a service business, your "competition" can become a source of business. You may be able to specialize in handling work they don't provide or want to do. You may be able to do overload for them when they're too busy. You may be able to serve customers or clients whom they are unqualified or unwilling to serve.

One of the best ways to find out about your potential competition and how they're doing is to talk with them personally. Tell them about the products or services you're planning to offer and then listen carefully to their reaction. If they generally are closemouthed or negative about the field, this is not a good sign. If, however, they generally respond positively to your plans, this is an indication that their business is doing well, and they may even become a source of referral business for you. In fact, do offer to set up an overload exchange with them; you can do backup for them, and they can back you up when the day comes that you need help with extra business. Likewise, determine what their specialties are as well as whom they don't serve.

8. What specialty or "niche" can you carve out for yourself?

Unless you are one of very few people who do what you do or you live in a very small community, you will probably do best to specialize in a "niche," a target group of clients you will serve. The more specialized or "niched" your business is, the easier and more cost-effective it will be to market yourself. When you specialize, you can focus your marketing activities on the specific groups of people you want to reach. Also, having a niche makes it more likely that people will refer to you because they will be able to more easily remember who you are and what you do.

Here are several ideas about how to find your special niche:

Specialize in one industry that you have unique knowledge of or contacts in. For example, a woman from one of our seminars decided to specialize in providing a billing service for anesthesiologists because her husband was an anesthesiologist. He became her first client and served as a source of referrals to other doctors. As part of his job in the media-services department of a major orthopedic teaching hospital, Chris Richter developed an extensive Web site for the facility. So many orthopedic surgeons from all over the country e-mailed him asking for Web sites that Chris developed an independent add-on business designing Web sites.

Offer a service no one else is providing. For example, we mentioned that when systems engineer Wil Milan decided to develop his own software company, he chose to specialize in software for people who, like himself, want to own a boat. He could find no software for prospective or new boat owners so this became his niche. His first package helps perspective boaters estimate the cost of owning their own boat.

Provide a product or service to a group that has yet to be served. Can you identify a group of people for whom no product or service currently exists? For example, Steve Dworman had been consulting in the infomercial industry and recognized that this was a growing industry with as yet little information or support available for companies producing them. So Dworman decided to offer a newsletter called *Steven Dworman's Infomercial Marketing Report.* He produced the first eight-page issue and sent out a sample with an order form. His thorough knowledge of this industry had earned him the confidence of his potential subscribers and has led to collaborations with *Ad-Week* and a book, *$12 Billion of Inside Marketing Secrets Discovered Through Direct Response Television Sales* (ISBN: 097264380X).

9. How will you identify people or companies that need what you can offer? If you are not already aware of many possible people or companies that need your services, or if the customary pools of clients are well saturated, here are several ways to match up what you enjoy and do well with what people will pay for.

Listen for who's complaining. Complaints are clues to problems people will spend money to solve. Ask yourself: Who is or could be having a problem that my product or service could solve?

- Use the Web by checking sites that register complaints like *TheSqueaky Wheel.com* and *Thecomplaintstation.com;* message boards; and bidder histories on *elance.com* and *guru.com.*

- Attend meetings and other gatherings of the type of customers you wish to serve and listen for their "ain't-it-awful"s, the things they're bitching about.
- Read feature articles and letters to the editor in newspapers, magazines, and trade publications and look for problems, concerns, and issues you might address.

You may read, for example, about college graduates complaining about not being able to find jobs. New graduates are not just in a struggle with each other for jobs; they are also competing with some of last year's graduates who are still job-hunting and with many people who are still being laid off from their jobs each year. This ongoing problem creates new clients for résumé-writing services, graphic designers, image consultants, job-placement and referral services, and so forth.

Follow trends. Trends suggest possibilities for new groups of customers or clients you could serve. To identify trends that could mean business for you, read and listen for who's doing what? What's coming in? What's going out? Who's moving in? Who's moving away? Who's expanding? And, most important, how could you help them?

OTHER WAYS TO CARVE OUT A NICHE

Here are a few of the ways you can slice up your market and find your niche:

Market Slice	Examples
Corporate function	Finance, sales, personnel, training, purchasing
Demographics	Age, sex, marital status, lifestyle, income
Geography	West Side, East Side, MacArthur Park, statewide
Hobbies	Animals, cars, collecting, cooking, gardening, music
Industry	Medicine, construction, law, real estate, banking, insurance
Life events	Birth, marriage, divorce, death, retirement
Price sensitivities	Premium quality, best value, bargain basement
Problem	Collections, turnover, cash flow, drug abuse
Size of company	Fortune 1000, under $50,000,000, five to ten employees
Special interests	Antiques, history, sports, self-improvement, travel

---

Within the next fifteen years, nearly seven million people will be over eighty-five years old. Older people have special needs and interests. Lynne Farrell foresaw this trend and used her computer to create a referral service to help senior citizens with their housing needs.

Here's another example of a trend that is creating a demand for computer-based business services: As companies downsize, they must turn to outside consultants and freelancers to help them on an as-needed basis. But how do they locate such experts? Bill Vick and Ron Ternosky established the Phoenix List (*www.thephoenixlink.com*) to connect experienced executives and technologists with interim and full-time positions. Their site is an example of "Expert Referral or Brokering Service," the subject of a profile in Part 1.

Managing projects using such "contingent" workers also calls for special project-management skills. Philip Dyer of Atlanta fills this need by providing consulting and training for larger companies on how to accomplish their work on a project-management basis. And if the number of expert service brokers or project-management consultants continues to grow, they may well need a Web site, a professional association, or a newsletter tailored to their industry—other computer-based business possibilities found in Part 1.

The popularity of scuba diving is another example of the business potential that's embedded in popular trends. Scuba diving may be on its way to becoming the next fitness craze. Between 1966 and 1980, the Professional Association of Diving Instructors certified only one million scuba divers. By 1980, it had grown to four million and by 2000 to 8.5 million. Scuba diving attracts new diving devotees in the market for a wide array of information and services related to their passion. How about providing a Web site for scuba divers with special needs or interests? For example, Linda Kennedy at the age of fifty began making waterproof fanny packs for divers. She patented her design, and it's become the basis for her company, Watchful Eye Designs, LLC.

Do-it-yourself home-improvement projects is another trend rich with business possibilities. With the popularity of cable channel HGTV, *Extreme Makeovers,* and other such shows about home improvement, interest in this area keeps growing. Even in sluggish economic years, Home Depot and Lowe's sales keep growing. So if you're thinking about starting some type of referral service with your computer, you might tap into this home-repair trend by creating a home repair/home improvement hot line to refer callers to tradespeople who will go into people's homes or offices not to do the work themselves but to teach their customers how to do it or help their customers through a job they're stuck on. For more about this business idea, see p. 43.

Here's another trend that could mean business. Ambulatory-care health and surgery clinics provide an increasing amount of primary care. If you're providing a business service like public relations, copywriting, or mailing-list management, you might want to specialize in serving these clinics. Find out which other kinds of services or information you could provide to the patients who use these facilities. Use this kind of analytic thinking whenever you hear about a new trend.

Find applications for new technology. New technology also opens doors to groups of customers and clients not being served by others. New technology provides the opportunity to offer more to your clients by enabling you

---

How to Spot a Trend

- **Watch for statistics** in news and features stories in both print and Web publications. If you get *USA Today,* make a habit of checking the "factoid" boxes.

- **Read articles and watch TV news** segments for signs of "what's in and what's out."

- **Watch for "hot" new businesses** or older businesses gaining new popularity.

- **Make links between seemingly unrelated phenomena,** e.g., more older people equals new rules on processing medical claims; traffic on the rise equals more people who have a computer and modem at home; corporations are cutting back staff equals an increased demand for customer service.

- **Pay attention to news segments** about populations that have special problems and new laws being passed on their behalf.

- **Read publications that track trends** such as *American Demographics* and *The Futurist* and articles and books by futurist authors such as Marvin Citron, Faith Popcorn, and Gerald Celente. If you prefer listening to reading, check out *Trends* magazine's monthly reports on business trends in an audio format: (800) 776-1910, *www.crucial trends.com.*

---

to do what you do better in less time than competitors who are still using older technology, like earlier versions of software that don't recognize current formats of the same program.

For example, if you're operating a mobile business or are a consultant, having the technology that's emerging to maintain a constant Internet connection even when traveling from state to state or from nation to nation can mean being able to serve clients with your full services from virtually anywhere. Sometimes new technology also makes it possible to provide new services to clients or to reach whole new groups of clients.

Capitalize on new legislation. The passage of new legislation creates an immediate demand for professionals who can educate and train others in how to comply with the new regulations. It creates a new specialization for consulting opportunities. Materials and manuals instructing how to comply must be designed and prepared. Procedures must be established and documented for managing inquiries from various parties—customers, other businesses, and the public. Newsletters may spring up filling people in on the implications of the legislation, etc.

New occupations may come into being like geriatric care managers; existing ones may expand. For example, The No Child Left Behind law has provided opportunities for tutors.

10. What can you offer that your competition does not offer? Could you do what they do better in some way?

In order to get clients and customers, you will not only need to be able to tell them what you do; you will also need to be able to tell them why they should use you in a way that meets their requirements better than others who offer the same or similar products or services. This is sometimes referred to as your "unique selling advantage."

At first glance you may not think that you have anything special to offer. But if you pay attention to what prospective clients and customers need, listening carefully to what they complain about, chances are you will uncover many ideas for how you can make what you offer better. If you become sufficiently familiar with your competition, you will begin to notice how what you do is, or can be, different. You may be more experienced, for example, with a particular type of client. You may be able to do what you do faster, for less cost, or more thoroughly. You may be able to offer a more personalized service. Perhaps you can pick up and deliver or provide twenty-four-hour turnaround.

11. How will you let your potential customers and clients know about what you will offer?

At this point, you have focused in on your product and service and considered to whom you can sell it. Now you must let them know about it. No matter how great an idea you have or how good you are at providing a product or service with your computer, unless people know about what you're doing and how they can contact you, you won't have any business. So once you know who needs your products and services and the niche that you wish to carve out for yourself, your next task becomes to identify how you could spread the word about your products and services to those people.

Consider these questions as you build a list of at least twelve ways you can inform them about what you do.

- When prospective customers or clients use the Web to search for what you offer, what words or phrases do they use? Two sites that can help you determine this are *www.WordTracker.com* and Overture's Search Term Suggestion Tool at *http:inventory.overture.com*.
- When prospective customers use the print yellow pages or directories like *switchboard.com* and *anywho.com*, what listings do they choose? For example, will it be for "Virtual Assistant," "Word Processing," "Secretarial Services", or "Typing"?
- Where do your prospective clients or customers gather? Could you put materials about what you do in these places? Could you give a speech or presentation?
- What other services do they use? Could you get referrals from those other sources?
- What do they read? Could you write articles for these publications or take out a small ad?
- How could you get a list of their names, addresses, and telephone numbers so you could send them materials or call them?

List ten ways in which you could inform your potential clients about what you offer:

1._____	4._____
2._____	5._____
3._____	6._____

7._____	9._____
8._____	10._____

However many hours you plan to work each week (and we recommend that you put in *at least* eight hours a week even in a part-time business), you should plan to spend every one of those hours when you are not doing paid work in marketing yourself through such activities. It can take anywhere from thirty days to several months to obtain a new customer, so you should plan to set aside up to 40 percent of your time for marketing, even after you have ample business.

Fortunately, getting the word out about your computer business need not be expensive. In fact, the majority of the most effective ways very small businesses get business—such as networking, direct solicitation, referrals, and public relations—are not that costly. Largely from our book *Getting Business to Come to You*, written with marketing consultant Laura Clampitt Douglas, we list thirty-nine ways people can successfully get the word out about what they do on pages 199–200.

12. Do you know anyone or any company that needs what you offer right now? How many such potential clients do you know?

The more people you know right now who need and will pay for what you have to offer, the better off you are. Some of the most successful computer-based businesses have started almost by spontaneous combustion. In other words, people they knew signed up to do business with them right away.

When Bill Osborne started his newsletter *Only Good News*, for example, ten out of ten of the companies he had worked with in the past as a marketing consultant wanted to take out ads in his new newsletter. When Bruce Pea started his mail-order catalog of sales-training books and tapes, his first clients were all salesmen he already knew. From those initial contacts, he developed a large and loyal national mailing list. Dental hygienist Gayle Lawrence transitioned from "teeth to travel" and created Journeys of Discovery—Mind, Body, Spiritual Adventures for Women, *www.ajourneyofdiscovery.com*, in a corner of her kitchen. She takes women on trips all over the planet.

To get your enterprise under way, begin with the people you know. Create a list of every possible personal or business contact you can think of who might need what you are offering and call or e-mail them personally to let them know what you're doing. With most business communication being done through e-mail today—and a great deal of it being screened

1. Principal Promotional Methods

1. Word of mouth
2. Networking
3. Web sites, online forums, and discussion groups
4. Mentors and gatekeepers
5. Volunteerism
6. Sponsorships
7. Charitable donations
8. Referrals
9. Business name
10. Letterhead and business card
11. Product packaging
12. Point-of-sale display

2. Public Relations

13. Writing articles for e-zines, printed magazines, and Web sites
14. Letters to the editor
15. News releases: printed and electronic
16. Speeches and seminars
17. Publicity:
Newspaper
Magazine
Radio and TV
Business and trade publications
World Wide Web

3. Direct Marketing

18. Sampling
19. Incentives
20. Discount Pricing
21. Contests and giveaways
22. Newsletters
23. Circulars and flyers
24. Trade shows and exhibits
25. Sales seminars
26. Demonstrations

27. Direct mail
28. Promotions on a Web site

4. Inventive Advertising

29. Web site
30. Listings on Yahoo Get Local, Google Local, and SuperPages
31. Yellow-page advertising
32. Business directories, such as those found in *dmoz.org*'s listing of business directories
33. Classified ads
34. Bulletin boards with tear pads
35. Your own radio show, increasingly possible because of Internet Radio
36. Your own TV show
37. Social networking in Web forums and on social-networking sites like Ryze and Tribe
38. Direct-response ads
39. Card decks

out with filters—you're apt to get a better response with a personal phone call. You don't have to consider your initial contact as a "sales" call. Think of it as an "information" call. You're simply calling to let people you've had contact with in the past know what you're doing and that you will be glad to serve them when they need you.

Listen carefully when you call, however, for any clue that they would be in the market for your product or service now. Such clues are "buying signals." Here are several examples:

- Complaints or horror stories about previous experiences
- Comments like "I've been thinking about something like that" or "We could sure use something like that"
- Explanations of why they don't have or are already using a product or service like yours
- Even comments like "Ummm, that's interesting" can be a sign that someone is already starting to imagine herself using your service

Take such buying signals as cues to ask if they would like more information, and either set up an appointment or agree to send them material. If you make your first contact by mail, make a date on your calendar for when you will follow up with a phone call to see if they got the material and find out if they have further questions and if they're interested in doing business.

Put the names of everyone you contact who might use your products or services at any time in the future into a computer "contact management" database (see Part 3.4) and make periodic contact by phone or mail with your entire list. Continue building this contact list by adding the names of new people you meet. Soon you will have a top-quality mailing list to whom you can send a newsletter or direct-mail pieces via e-mail or land mail.

13. Do you know people in other fields who work regularly with the people or companies that need what you have to offer? Such people can become your "gatekeepers."

Gatekeepers are people who in the course of what they do come into regular contact with people who need what you are offering. They can be an invaluable source of ongoing business for you. Here's an example of just how helpful they can be.

One January day, a weapons designer was beginning to realize that his position might be eliminated, when he heard us talking about self-employment on KGO radio in San Francisco. After listening to the show, he got a copy of our book *The Best Home Businesses for the 21st Century* and, realizing he was a competent writer, decided to start a business from home helping others write business plans. This business is featured in that book as well as in Part 2 of this book. Once he decided to become a business-plan writer, he began thinking about who would be in a position to put him in contact with people who need to have business plans. Loan officers seemed like a logical answer and, indeed, loan officers have become his gatekeepers. They send him all the business he needs. In fact, only four months after hearing us on the show he became so busy that he had to hire two people to work with him, and he's making more money than he did as an engineer designing weapons.

To identify who your gatekeepers might be, create a "Gatekeepers' Network" as follows. Take a sheet of paper (or if you'd prefer, diagram it with software such as is available from Word's Insert menu) and draw a circle in the center. Write the type of customers or clients to whom you are planning to sell your products and services in the center of the circle. Then draw a spoke off the center circle for each other type of business or service these people might use.

Now begin making contact with and collecting names of people who represent each spoke on your gatekeepers' network. Introduce yourself and your product or service to these gatekeepers, then develop a relationship with as many of them as you can. To let them know you're interested in them, ask them questions about their business like "What kind of customers do you like to get?" "How do you like to get referrals?" "Do you have a particular specialty?" Then, after you've established a relationship, maintain a high profile with these individuals so they will think of you whenever one of their clients or customers needs what you have to offer. To keep your name fresh in their minds, create a database of the gatekeepers you identify so you can keep in regular contact with them by e-mail or phone.

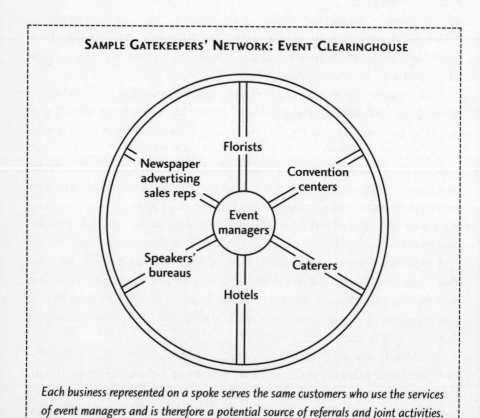

SAMPLE GATEKEEPERS' NETWORK: EVENT CLEARINGHOUSE

Each business represented on a spoke serves the same customers who use the services of event managers and is therefore a potential source of referrals and joint activities.

14. How much money do you need to have coming in each month?

To determine how much money you need to have coming in, calculate three things:

- Living expenses—How much do you need to make to live on? This is the "salary" you will need to produce to support yourself and your family. Be sure to include taxes and fringe benefits such as health insurance and money for retirement formerly covered by your employer.
- Direct costs—How much will it cost you to actually produce your product or deliver your service? This includes the cost of all the travel, communication charges, materials, and supplies used in serving a specific client or customer.
- Overhead—How much will it cost you to run your business? This includes all the other costs of being in business like your marketing, utilities, office furniture, and equipment.

Determining Your Salary

To calculate how much your earnings need to be, first identify three income figures. What you need:

- To survive _____
- To be comfortable _____
- To thrive _____

It's important to know these three figures because all products or services you might choose do not have the same income potential. Also, knowing what you need and want to earn will help you set goals, price your services, and determine how many hours you will need to bill out each week.

For example, unless you're looking for a way to pay for a hobby, we don't think you should even consider undertaking a business that will not enable you to at least achieve your survival income. That's why in Part 1 we classify some of the businesses as merely part-time or add-on businesses rather than full-time ventures.

Also, while you might be willing to live at the survival level for a while, over time you probably won't be happy putting in long hours for an income that barely keeps you afloat. So you should also project how what you offer can provide you with what you consider to be a comfortable income within a reasonable period of time. And if the business you're considering can never produce what you'd need to thrive, even after several years of working at it, you may burn out in that business within a short time. So make sure that the business you choose has at least the potential to achieve all three of your income targets.

Identifying Direct Costs

Direct costs—those that are directly billable to your clients or customers or that you must spend up front to produce a product—are quite low for many of the businesses you can start with a computer, like résumé writing or computer consulting. Even such businesses as these, however, have some direct costs like the high-quality paper used to print out the finished résumé or the cost of driving to meet with consulting clients, so don't minimize them.

Businesses such as computer-designed T-shirts and novelties, online information research, or producing a newsletter have higher direct costs. You have to pay for the manufacturing of novelties, for example, or the costs of getting online to do the research, which can be expensive. In such cases, you will need to pass these costs along to your clients by making sure you set your prices high enough to cover these costs or in some cases by billing separately for them.

At times, you may need to pay for these costs before you get paid by your clients, so calculating these costs carefully will help you manage your cash flow. Calculating your direct costs enables you to know and plan for the cash you need to have on hand between the time you do your work and when you actually get paid.

Including Overhead

By working from home you will either avoid or reduce overhead costs by nearly 40 percent of the typical expenses required for storefront or office-based businesses. You will, nonetheless, have some overhead costs, which people working from home often fail to build into their fees. Then they wonder why they always seem to be living on less than they expected.

We discovered one reason for this common oversight in the process of interviewing home-business owners for our *Best Home Businesses* books. We learned that very few operators of home businesses know what their overhead is. But by using money-management software like *Quickbooks, Quicken,* or *Microsoft Money,* you can quickly and easily track your overhead and therefore make sure your prices account for these costs.

The following work sheet includes standard home business overhead items you can use in making your initial calculations.

How Much You Need to Make Each Month

Calculating Your Income Needs

Estimate how much you would need to spend each month on each item for the three income targets you project.

	Survival	Comfortable	Ideal
Auto expenses	_____	_____	_____
Clothing	_____	_____	_____
Food	_____	_____	_____
Health insurance	_____	_____	_____
Home maintenance	_____	_____	_____
Entertainment	_____	_____	_____
Education	_____	_____	_____
Medical and dental care	_____	_____	_____
Personal care	_____	_____	_____
Rent or mortgage	_____	_____	_____
Taxes (federal, state, self-employment)	_____	_____	_____
Utilities	_____	_____	_____
Other living expenses	_____	_____	_____
	_____	_____	_____
Total Living Expenses	$_____	$_____	$_____

Calculating Direct Costs of Producing Your Product or Service

Estimate what each item/service you provide will cost you.

Cost of materials	_____
Travel to and from customer sites	_____
Cost of labor (employees or subcontract services)	_____
Supplies	_____
Other	_____
Total Direct Costs:	$_____

Calculating Overhead Costs for Monthly Operating Expenses

Estimate what each item will cost per month

	Survival	Comfortable	Ideal
Communications:	_____	_____	_____
Internet access	_____	_____	_____
Phone (cell, land, VoIP)	_____	_____	_____
Insurance	_____	_____	_____
Interest or loan payments	_____	_____	_____
Marketing costs (e.g., advertising, Internet, publicity)	_____	_____	_____
Maintenance	_____	_____	_____
Office supplies	_____	_____	_____
Postage/shipping	_____	_____	_____
Professional fees (e.g., accounting, legal, Web design)	_____	_____	_____
Repairs and maintenance	_____	_____	_____
Telephone and fax	_____	_____	_____
Utilities (above household usage)	_____	_____	_____
Web-site hosting and maintenance	_____	_____	_____
Other	_____	_____	_____
Total Overhead:	$_____	$_____	$_____

15. How much will you need to charge and how many hours or days will you need to bill for in order to produce the monthly income you need? Is this fee within the range people will pay you?

Once you know your three income targets and have estimated your operating expenses, you are in a position to sit down and calculate the following:

- How much would you have to charge to cover those costs and have enough left over to meet your income goals?
- At that rate, how many hours would you have to work (or how many products would you have to sell) and how many clients or customers

would you need to work with per day, per week, or per month to achieve those goals?

Once you have made the calculations necessary to know what you would have to charge, then you must determine if you will actually be able to charge the fees you need to in order to hit your target income. To do this, begin by comparing what you would need to charge with what successful existing competition is charging. Here are several ways to find out what others are charging:

- Some national trade and professional associations and trade publications do periodic surveys of what members or subscribers are charging.
- If there is a local chapter of a trade or professional association for your field, call the chapter president and ask for the range of fees people are charging in your community.
- Check prices for services on sites like *elance.com* and *guru.com* and for products on auction sites like *eBay*.
- Conduct your own study by checking Web sites of people in your business or directly contacting people in the field.

From what you learn, you can determine the "going rate," that is, what most people charge. The "going rate" is not likely to raise any eyebrows, but if you find that you would need to charge more, then you need to figure out what you can do that will add sufficient value to justify pricing above the going rate. If you are more qualified or can do what you offer faster, better, or more conveniently, then you may be able to charge more and get a premium price.

Pricing is always an experiment, however, so ultimately you will need to test the price to find out what people will actually pay. Of course, the most direct way to test your price is simply to ask potential clients what they would expect to pay for what you offer. For example, here's how Bill Garnet found out just how much he could charge when he began offering his Mississippi-based legal research service. Garnet called potential clients and asked them what they were used to paying and what they would like to pay. Based on this feedback, he began charging a lower fee than they expected and then began raising his prices until he started getting complaints. At that point, he backed his prices down somewhat to set the optimum fee.

If what you are offering is something that can be sold by mail or over

It is better to be conservative in calculating how many hours you can actually bill out each week, month, or year. One of the common mistakes people make is to assume they will be able to bill out a forty-hour week, week after week, as if they were employed. They calculate, for example, that if they say, are doing desktop publishing, they work forty hours a week and charge $40 per hour, they will be earning $1,600 a week. All they need to do is bill out at forty hours per week and they will have a gross income of $80,000 a year and have two weeks' vacation.

However, in most home-based and self-employment businesses you will be spending a portion of each week marketing, performing administrative tasks, and doing other work for which you can't bill your clients. For example, the typical full-time desktop publishers we interviewed were billing an average of four hours a day. So working full time, they were grossing an average of $800 per week or $40,000 a year.

In like fashion, the typical computer tutor was billing an average of three days of training a week. Information brokers were billing from ten to twenty hours a week. Some successful consultants find they have weeks when they have no billable work. At the other extreme, however, some medical transcriptionists we interviewed were billing thirty hours a week and some computer programmers over forty hours per week. It is the rare business, however, that can bill out a forty-hour week. Even after the business is up and running successfully, many people find they need to spend as much as 40 percent of the week marketing their business and carrying out administrative tasks.

A common mistake people make in a part-time enterprise is to overestimate how many hours each week they will be able to work on their business. They tend to overlook how tired they will be when they get home from their salaried jobs and are overly optimistic about how many weekend hours they will actually be able to put in.

So whether you will be working full or part time, be realistic about your schedule and realize you will only be able to bill out a percentage of the hours you will need to work. Then make your income projections accordingly.

---

the Internet, another way to test your prices is to do a series of mailings or e-mail releases to separate lists of potential buyers offering several different price levels, and then see which price draws the most responses.

Another approach might be to exhibit at a trade show where you can watch and listen for how your prospective buyers respond to your price.

Make sure, however, that you know in advance of exhibiting that the people attending the show will, in fact, be the type of people you plan to serve. You can use similar methods to help identify the feasibility of various prices when you're offering something that no one else is providing. In this case, it's also important to identify what potential buyers are comparing your product or service to, because even if it is not actually similar, if they think it is, their perceptions will influence how much they are willing to pay for it.

Should you find that people simply will not pay enough for what you offer so that you can meet your income needs, then you will need to choose another business or rethink the business you have chosen to make it profitable.

16. How can you support yourself until you have enough business coming in?

As you can see from having calculated the income you will need, your largest expense is not the cost of starting or running the business venture itself. Assuming your business does not required specialized equipment like what is required for medical transcription, the major costs of getting your business under way will be for your marketing and for covering your living expenses while you build up your business income. Unless you have plenty of business lined up before leaving your job, you should have an entry plan for supporting yourself and your business for three to twelve months while you build your clientele. Here are eight entry plans.

EIGHT ENTRY PLANS FOR STARTING OUT ON YOUR OWN

1. **The Moonlighting Plan.** Keep your full-time job and develop your business as a sideline. When it takes off, you can go full time.

2. **The Part-Time Plan.** Work at a part-time job to provide a base income while you're building up the business. When your business equals the base income, drop the part-time job.

3. **The Spin-off Plan.** Turn your previous employer into your first major customer or, when ethically possible, take a major client with you from your previous job.

4. **The Cushion Plan.** Find a financial resource to support yourself with while you start your business. Your cushion should be large enough to cover your base expenses for at least six to twelve months.

---

5. **The Piggyback Plan.** If you have a working spouse or partner, cut back your expenses so you can live on one salary until your business gets going.

6. **Do Temporary Work.** Work through a temporary agency or job shop while you build your business. Most such agencies offer enough flexibility that you can take on some "temp" jobs while building your business income.

7. **The Have-Your-Clients-Finance-You Plan.** If you have sufficient stature in your field, you might obtain retainer contracts with clients for the first year that provide you with assured revenue in exchange for offering them services at 25 percent less than the billing rate you establish.

8. **The Gofer Plan.** While keeping your existing income, hire or have someone as a gofer to do the legwork and research needed to lay the groundwork for a successful start-up. Look for someone who charges less than you earn.

17. What start-up costs will you have?

You've now estimated your income needs and cash flow. There are, however, undoubtedly one-time start-up costs that you must arrange for in order to get under way. By working from home, your start-up costs will be considerably lower than setting yourself up in an outside office or storefront. The Small Business Administration has found the average small business is started with under $5,000. Of course, start-up expenses vary from business to business. In calculating your start-up costs, plan to include funds to cover the following:

- Communications, such as phones and the Internet
- Printed collateral such as business cards, stationery, brochures
- Decorating expenses to adapt space for your home office
- Dues of organizations and cost of attending meetings
- Office equipment, such as computer and printer, software
- Office furniture
- Professional fees, such as legal and accounting
- Special requirements of a particular business
- Supplies

- Travel for research, etc.
- Web site

Of course, if you already have the equipment you need, you will be that much further ahead. Use the following chart to estimate your start-up costs. Add more money if you know or think you will need any of the other equipment on the list below. Also, add in an account for cash you will need to cover initial operating expenses until you receive your first income.

Calculating Start-up Costs

Estimate how much you will need to spend on each item for the three levels of income you project:

	Survival	Comfortable	Ideal
Auto expenses	_____	_____	_____
Business licenses, permits, and other fees	_____	_____	_____
Consulting and training fees	_____	_____	_____
Initial inventory (if any)	_____	_____	_____
Initial marketing costs (Web site, memberships, business cards and collateral materials)	_____	_____	_____
Installation (phone, Internet access)	_____	_____	_____
Office equipment (computer, printer, etc.)	_____	_____	_____
Office furnishings (desk, chair, storage, etc.)	_____	_____	_____
Professional fees (legal, accounting)	_____	_____	_____
Redecorating/remodeling for home office (if needed)	_____	_____	_____
Software:			
Office suite	_____	_____	_____
Specialized	_____	_____	_____
Specialized equipment for your business	_____	_____	_____

Other start-up expenses specific to your business	_____	_____	_____
	_____	_____	_____
Total Start-up Costs	$_____	$_____	$_____

18. How will you finance the start-up costs involved to adequately set up, equip, supply, and market your business?

While increasing numbers of banks are now offering loans to home-based businesses, usually you will need to have been in operation for several years before you can qualify for such loans. But, in actuality, you will probably not need a loan to get started. Whereas Jeffrey Seglin, author of *Financing Your Small Business*, claims few traditional small businesses are able to finance their business start-ups themselves, this is not true of full- and part-time home businesses. Because start-up costs are usually so low, most people self-finance, or "bootstrap," their ventures themselves, using personal income, savings, or profits in order to get under way. When necessary, they turn to a variety of less conventional means to cover start-up costs.

Here are several of the more commonly used sources of start-up funds:

SOURCES OF START-UP FUNDS	
Earnings from job	Life-insurance policies
Savings	A line of credit through a home-equity loan
Credit cards	Loans from relatives or friends
Cash settlements	Loans from suppliers or colleagues
Inheritances	Microloan programs
Retirement funds	Selling assets like a boat, an RV, a second home
Credit unions	

A basic adage of making money on your own is that first you must support your business; then it will support you. Starting a business, no matter how small, is like raising a child; you have to invest in it before it can stand on its own. (Fortunately most businesses become self-sufficient much more quickly than the average child does!) But do plan to invest in your business at first. Do it in a way that won't set you back financially. Here are several rules of thumb for financing your start-up costs safely:

1. Be prepared to start and grow your business from funds you have on hand, from your existing income, credit, contacts, or the initial business you generate. If your funds are limited, begin with your "survival"-level projections and expand as your business expands.

If you are employed, one way you can finance a sideline business is to reduce the amount of your salary withheld for federal income tax purposes and use the extra income you take home in each paycheck to finance your business startup. As long as you spend this extra money on tax-deductible business expenses, you do not risk owing additional taxes by reducing your withholding. Check with an experienced tax professional or accountant about how you can best take advantage of the tax benefits that open up to you when you start a business.

2. If you must borrow, borrow the smallest amounts possible to finance one-time purchases that will pay for themselves or that can be paid for from work already in progress. Unless you have a considerable amount of work already under contract when you start or you are someone who performs best under financial pressure, you don't want to burden yourself with the added overhead of having to make large loan payments. Borrow only an amount that you can project specifically how you will be able to repay within a year or less.

Your best source of loans is from relatives, friends, colleagues, or suppliers who are impressed by your character, capabilities, and business prospects and who will benefit either personally or professionally from your success.

You may be able to qualify for a microloan funded by the Small Business Administration. Currently microloans may go up to $35,000. To locate this and other SBA lending programs, like the 7a, you can call the Small Business Administration or Small Business Development Center nearest you or check the SBA's Web site at *www.sbaonline.sba.gov*. A book that helps applicants understand applying for an SBA loan is *The SBA Loan Book*, Charles H. Green, Adams Media Corporation, 1999, ISBN: 158062202X.

3. Borrow little or no money to cover your living or operating expenses. Instead make sure you have an entry plan like those described under Question 16 to cover as much of these costs as possible.

Admittedly, the drawback of such a "bootstrap" strategy is that your growth will be limited by the business you generate. But we believe this is a far safer and more reliable way to proceed. In fact, we've seen too many cases where having a lot of money for starting a computer-based venture actually was more of a drawback than an asset. In such cases, people overspent their once-ample funds on unnecessary equipment, untested ideas, or marketing methods and lost it all.

By "bootstrapping" your business, however, your growth will be limited only by your results. And, of course, if you suddenly find yourself with signed purchase orders or contracts in hand for more work than you have the cash to produce, then it's time to consider a loan strategy such as those outlined in *Where to Go When the Bank Says No*, David R. Evanson, Bloomberg Press, 1998, ISBN: 1576600173.

19. Do you have a good credit rating?

Clear up your credit if possible before going out on your own. Here's why. Since you will have some start-up costs and direct expenses before you have any money coming in, you may want to delay payment for these cash outlays for thirty days or more. One way to do this is to pay for such expenses by credit card. But, of course, you can't get a credit card unless you have a reasonably good credit rating. Also, vendors will sometimes bill or even finance your purchases, but only if they can determine that you have a good credit rating. Otherwise, you'll have to pay cash up front for services or materials.

Sometimes a good credit rating can also help you get business. Depending on the business you've selected, some clients will check into your credit rating before hiring you for a major project.

Don't assume, however, that you're out in the cold if your credit record is less than perfect. You can begin now to repair it. For example, to gain a share of the market, some credit card-companies are overlooking the minor credit problems of applicants. They are making credit cards available at favorable rates even to people with slightly blemished credit reports. Getting such a card and using it wisely are good ways to start rebuilding a good credit history.

Another route to building your credit rating is to obtain a secured credit card, which allows you to borrow a minimum amount secured by funds in your savings account. After you use and pay off purchases over a period of time, you may then be able to obtain a regular credit card.

20. Do you have two credit cards: one for business, one for personal expenses?

For small and home-based businesses, credit cards can be among the only sources of ongoing credit. Federal Reserve data indicate credit cards are the source of 39 percent of small-business loans. Keep in mind, however, that credit cards are one of the most expensive forms of borrowing.

Nevertheless it's a reality that many home-based business owners—28 percent of small businesses, according to an SBA study—use at least one business credit card to help finance marketing and other costs of business expansion. So if you don't have a credit card, get one. In fact, get two—one that you designate for personal expenses and one for business expenses. A business credit card will allow you to finance initial costs like printing, supplies, equipment, etc. The card you designate for personal use can help you handle unexpected costs you didn't include in your salary projections like having to pay for a costly and unexpected auto repair, a dental emergency, or a roof that springs a leak.

Unlike interest paid on personal expenses charged to a credit card, the interest on business expenses is deductible, but since interest on credit cards is high, make sure you don't end up draining your chances for success by having to pay off large credit-card balances month after month. Here are several guidelines for keeping credit-card costs down.

KEEPING CREDIT-CARD COSTS DOWN

1.   The best credit-card policy is to pay off your balance each month. The most cost-effective use of your cards is to use them to help your cash flow, so you can "delay" payment until you have collected for work you have in progress. Of course, you may not always get the expenses you bill out for paid within thirty days, so here are several additional ideas.

2.   Resist the temptation to run up your credit-card balance with desirable, but unnecessary, charges. Use your business card to finance purchases that you know realistically will pay for themselves (hopefully within six to twelve months) in increased productivity or additional business. This is not an unreasonable goal for many computer-based service businesses when you consider that sometimes just one client will more than pay for a piece of software or equipment

---

that enabled you to produce the Web site that got you the client in the first place.

3. Get the best rates. Shop around for the best credit-card interest rates. CardTrack provides comprehensive information on credit card borrowing at *www.cardtrak.com.* CardTrack can also be contacted at Box 1700, Frederick, MD 21702. Be careful of credit-card deals that require you take a cash advance when you get the card. Sometimes the interest rate on such credit cards is low, but the rate on the cash advance is much higher, and you will be forced to pay it immediately since you accepted the cash advance. Also, watch out for low introductory interest rates that change to much higher rates six months or one year later.

4. Make sure finance charges on your card are calculated by the average daily balance (ADB). Low credit-card rates won't save you much money if the issuer uses the "two-cycle method" to calculate your interest payment. Most issuers compute their financial charges based on the ADB in the prior month. But some issuers are charging interest based on your average balance over the last two months, so if you pay only the minimum balance each month you could end up paying twice on the same charge. Card issuers must disclose their computation method on applications, cardholder agreements, and monthly statements. So check out your existing cards and any future ones you consider and change cards if need be.

5. Pay more than the minimum balance whenever possible. Minimum-balance payments cost you the most. For example, if you charge $500 on your card and pay only the minimum each month, at 18 percent interest, the item will actually cost you almost $800 and take six years to pay off. If you pay $50 a month, you'll save almost $250 in interest and be debt-free in only eleven months!

21. How committed are you to proceeding with your venture?

Now that you've had a chance to ponder your business opportunities, think about how and where you might sell your service or product, and examine the financial side of getting your computer-based business under way, are you still committed to doing it? Indicate on a scale of 0 to 10 how important it is to you to proceed with your plans.

_____ 0 It's better than nothing, but I can take it or leave it.

_____ 3 I need money, but I'd really rather make it on a job, or at least a better-paying one.

_____ 5 I'd like to give it a try; it sounds like a good idea.

_____ 8 I've been wanting to do this for a long time, or I realize I'm ready for this; it's the next step for me.

_____10 I want to do this more than anything else right now.

Your chances of success go up the closer you are to a score of 10. Being highly motivated is the number-one most important variable we've found in those who are able to make money on their own. It's more important than how much money you have to invest in your business, how much experience you've had, even how good you are at what you do. Those who are truly motivated learn what they need to learn, do what they need to do, and persist until they do it.

So if you score 0 to 3, we'd advise that you skip the idea of making money with your computer at this time until it becomes a higher priority.

If you scored 3 to 6 on this scale, we would suggest that you consider starting a part-time venture, almost as if it were a hobby, so you can determine if you like it sufficiently to invest the time, money, and energy involved to become successful.

If you score a 7 or above, you are probably sufficiently motivated to proceed with a full-time venture.

22. Do you have a separate area in your home where you can work productively?

Fortunately most computer-related businesses can be operated just as easily from home as from anywhere. However, we recommend, if at all possible, having a separate area in which to set up your home office. In addition to the considerable savings on overhead it affords you, setting up and operating from a home office offers you a variety of tax benefits. If you set up your home office to meet Internal Revenue Service qualifications, you can take the home-office deduction that entitles you to deduct part of your rent, your mortgage, and other household costs in proportion to the percentage of your home you use for business purposes.

To qualify for these valuable deductions, your home office must be used exclusively, on a regular basis, as your principal place of business.

The space you use for your home office need not be a separate room. It can be a portion of a room such as your bedroom, but the portion of that room that you designate for your business must be used only for business. So if you don't have a separate room, we suggest that you clearly demark the portion of the room you use for work space with a divider, screen drape, or furniture arrangement. This is not only useful for tax purposes; it also will help you get to work, stick to business, and keep you from feeling as if you don't have a private life.

Our book *Working from Home* includes additional information on how to claim home-business tax deductions.

POSSIBLE DEDUCTIBLE HOME-OFFICE EXPENSES

- Cleaning a home office
- Depreciation on office space in home
- Household furniture converted for use in the home office
- Household supplies used in business space
- Interest on mortgage attributable to business use of home *
- Internet expenses related to business
- Real estate taxes attributable to business use of home *
- Rent paid for office portion if you rent or lease
- Repair and maintenance of office portion of home
- Telephone, except the base local service for the first line into your home
- Trash collection
- Utilities attributable to business use of home (electricity, gas, water)

*Deducted before calculating Social Security.

---

23. Do you have the support of your family and friends?

Making money on your own, whether you'll be doing it full or part time, will be much easier if you have the support of family and friends. Family and loved ones need to be aware and supportive of the changes that starting your business venture will make in all of your lives.

For example, if you plan to earn money part time as a sideline to your job, those in your life will need to adjust to the fact that you won't be available for personal activities at certain times during evenings or weekends. If you'll be working on your own full time, you may have to put in longer hours initially than you had been in a previous job. And your income may dip at first while you get your business under way. Once you are working from home, those you live with may also have to adapt to having business calls or even clients and customers coming into your home.

So alert your family and loved ones to all the changes you expect and to the fact that there may be other changes you can't predict. Then make sure your plans take into account their concerns and reactions to these changes. To learn about how parents and grandparents have accommodated family needs, see the "A Day in the Life" descriptions in the book we and Lisa Roberts wrote, *The Entrepreneurial Parent*.

24. Have you checked the zoning regulations and homeowner-association restrictions to see if you can legally operate a moneymaking venture from your home?

Every local community has its own ordinances governing what kind of commercial activity can and cannot be done in residential neighborhoods. Unfortunately, some local zoning ordinances still have not been updated since the industrial era, when communities wanted to protect residential neighborhoods from the noise, pollution, danger, and congestion of factories and storefronts. Therefore, you need to find out exactly what you can and cannot do from your home and make your plans accordingly. To check your zoning situation, contact the zoning department at your city hall or county courthouse.

If zoning prohibits you from working from home, you can usually rent a postal address or use an executive suite as an official address while doing your actual work quietly at home.

If you're among the fifty million Americans now living in a location with a homeowners' association, you also need to check the restrictions contained in the Covenants, Codes and Restrictions (CC&Rs). Unlike zoning ordinances with mechanisms like conditional use permits and variances, the only appeal in a homeowners' association is to a board of directors, which tends not to be lenient, and CC&Rs are difficult to change.

25. Will your neighbors have any objection to your doing the type of work you plan to do from your home?

Neighbor complaints can cause zoning and homeowner-association problems. Therefore, you want to make sure that whatever you do from home in no way interferes with the residential nature of your neighborhood. Fortunately, most computer-related businesses can be virtually invisible, but it's nonetheless important to consider and respect neighbors' rights and concerns.

The kinds of things that tend to bother neighbors include noisy equipment, parking problems caused by too many people coming to your home office, inventory filling your garage, leaving your cars parked on the street overnight, deliveries, people coming to your home early in the morning, and large amounts of mail clogging communal mailbox areas.

Ironically, neighbors and people in condo associations that limit work from home may be unaware of the many advantages and the few drawbacks of having people on the premises who do work from home. They may be unaware, for example, that crime goes down in areas where people work from home. They may not have considered that when tenants work from home, there's someone to respond to emergencies like broken pipes, fires, or flooding. These benefits are especially important now that both men and women in most households often work outside the home. So if limitations exist where you live, take steps in concert with others who are already working quietly at home to have the regulations changed to prohibit only those activities that actually interfere with the residential character of the area.

26. Does what you intend to do require any special state license?

Licensing regulations vary significantly from state to state, and some states license certain computer-related businesses like financial planning, business brokering, skip searching, and tax preparation. You can probably determine if you need a professional license by using the links provided at the Council on Licensure, Enforcement and Regulation (CLEAR)'s site, *www.clearhq.org/boards.htm*. But it's wise to call or visit your state agency to verify what you find and what you need to do.

27. Have you obtained a local business license?

Most communities require a business license to operate an income-earning enterprise of any size. Going to the trouble to take out a business license says that you take your business seriously. Fortunately, it's becoming a whole lot easier. As of this writing, you can apply for a business license on twelve states' Web sites.

While many home-based businesses operate without a business license, consider that it makes a statement that you want to make your venture official. It reflects a desire to pay attention to details, to dot the i's and cross the t's, to do the homework that will not only get the business off to a good start but also be reflected in other aspects of how you run the business. So we advise making your business official by getting your business license.

28. Will you be required to charge sales tax on what you offer?

If you're providing a taxable product or service to customers in your own state, you will need to obtain a sales permit and find out how to pay the tax. Keep in mind that different states have different laws and rulings on what is taxable and what is not. And if you live in Oregon, New Hampshire, or Delaware, you don't need to worry about collecting and paying sales tax.

In general, the requirement to pay sales tax depends on where the buyer is located, not the seller. So if you are a computer consultant and sell components like memory to your clients, you will need to collect sales tax on the sales you make to the end user. However, if you sell these same items to a wholesaler or retailer who will in turn sell them to the end user, you do not need to charge sales tax. Instead, you will need to make sure that your buyer has what is variously called a "seller's permit," "certificate of authority," or "resale certificate" from the state. Keep verification of this on file with their account.

The answer to this question is a whole lot more complicated if your business involves the Web as a means of commerce. Some states have determined that Web services, such as designing Web sites, uploading Web

☞ **ALERT** ☜

Be aware that when you apply for a business license your zoning may be checked, so it's important to find out your zoning situation first and take the steps that will enable you to be licensed.

sites, maintaining Web sites, and updating Web sites, are not taxable; but if part of a transaction is the transfer of tangible personal property or prewritten software, it may make all or part of the transaction taxable.

When it comes to products, the Internet Tax Freedom Act has placed a moratorium on new sales or other taxes applied to Internet purchases. Thus if you're selling products on *eBay*, you're not required to collect sales taxes on sales made to out-of-state buyers. However, the obligation to collect and pay tax on sales to in-state buyers is not a new one and is taxable.

Depending on the kind of business you're in, the answer to whether you collect sales tax may get murky, so contact the agency in your state that handles sales taxes to determine if any aspects of what you offer are taxable. If you are unclear or confused by the response you get, consult an attorney.

29. Will you sell your product or service yourself or will you sell it through someone else?

The traditional avenues for selling products or services (direct sales, wholesalers or brokers, and retailers) have been multiplied and added to by the Web. In addition to selling from your own Web site, on auction sites, and in Web shopping malls, yet another avenue is sales you get from referrals. The best route for selling your products or services will depend on a variety of factors such as the nature of your business, your personality, your contacts, the needs of your clients and customers, and the community in which you live. Many businesses sell through multiple channels, usually with one being use of the Web. Here are some ideas for utilizing each route.

Five Choices for How to Sell Your Products or Services: How to Make the Most of Each

1. Selling on the Web

To sell from the Web you'll need fast online access via wireless, cable, DSL or satellite, a digital camera with some lights, and a backdrop for photographing your products.

Among the ways to sell what you produce from the Web are:

- Adding e-commerce ability to your Web site. This is becoming increasingly popular and less expensive to do. PayPal offers an easy way for customers to pay for even small retailers and service providers.

Tips on making effective use of PayPal can be found in *PayPal Hacks*, Shannon Sofield, Dave Neilson, and Dave Burchell, O'Reilly, 2004. Offering direct payment by credit cards will attract additional sales, but your overhead will increase $10 to $60 a month.

- Auction Sites. *eBay* is the home to hundreds of thousands of home-based sellers and one of the top names on the Web. But *eBay* is not the only auction venue. Among other auctions sites are *Bidville.com* and *Ubid.com,* and the auction sections of Amazon, Yahoo, and Overstock.com. By selling at auction sites, you do not have to maintain a Web site, though having a Web site where you can support what you sell can be helpful. Because you'll be able to feed traffic to your Web site from your auction listings, you'll be able to sell products other than ones currently listed for auction. Among the many resources available to provide guidance on auction selling are several e-newsletters such as Auction Bytes, *www.Auctionbytes.com,* and Auction Seller News, *www.auction-sellers-news.com. eBay* has scores of Seller and PowerSeller groups you can join.

- Creating an electronic storefront. Yahoo! Small Business Merchant Solutions (*http:smallbusiness.yahoo.com/merchant/*) has proven to be a solution for both small merchants as well as large ones. A basic site/storefront costs only $40 a month.

Here are several tips for selling on the Web:

Be quite specific in describing what you are selling. This includes a good photograph. If you are selling something used, candidly describe any flaws or blemishes.

Keep in contact with past customers. Notify them of sales and promotions and special newsletters.

If you are selling from your own Web site:

- Do what you need to do to be sure your site has a high rank on search engines vital. You can keep up-to-date on search-engine developments on *www.searchenginewatch.com.*
- Getting and keeping a high ranking varies from search engine to search engine and changes frequently. However, one truism is to keep your site stocked with frequently updated relevant, good-quality, and unique content.

- To keep traffic coming, consider paying for hits by using search engines like Google and Overture that sell this service.
- You also boost your sales by having an affiliate program with other Web sites in which you pay site owners a commission on any sales they send your way.

If you are auctioning goods:

- Set a low initial bid and don't use a reserve, which requires a buyer to meet or exceed a minimum price. Reserves discourage bids.
- Make sure your auctions cover weekends when traffic is highest.

2. Direct Sales

Direct selling involves you or your representative contacting prospective customers or clients directly. It includes "cold calling" by phone or in person as well as other methods of reaching those you serve directly such as networking, advertising, selling by seminar, or using direct mail.

In writing our book *Getting Business to Come to You,* we surveyed home-based businesses to determine what they find to be the most effective marketing methods. We found direct solicitation to be the fastest, although most personally time-consuming, way to get business. To make the most of direct sales:

Find out as much as you can about the needs and problems of your clients so your sales calls, presentations, ads, and mail pieces can speak "their language."

Warm up your cold calls or mail by using public relations to increase your visibility. If prospective clients recognize your name, they'll be more likely to take your calls and keep your direct-mail pieces. Design and maintain a Web site that not only promotes your business but also offers information that's valuable to your customer base and industry. Become an active participant in online forums and Internet newsgroups that are relevant to your customers. Speak at trade and professional conferences in your field. Write a column for the professional and trade publications. Have your own newsletter that educates prospective clients about how you can help them.

Appearing on local television and radio provides visibility so people will recognize you or your Web site when you make personal contact or do a mailing. You can have your own cable show in communities where the local government has negotiated public access into the franchise agreement with the cable company. Public-access, or community, TV provides low-cost (sometimes free!) access to broadcast-quality video-production resources as well as an outlet for your show. Access shows are not allowed to be outright commercials, or infomercials, for your business, but, if your enterprise revolves around providing a service, you can frame this information in the form of a how-to show that people can actually learn from. For example, Steve Grody, a martial-arts instructor in Los Angeles, augmented his business selling instruction video through the mail and over the Internet by producing a self-defense cable-access show. A list of communities with public access can be found at *videouniversity.com*. To find out more about cable access in your community, click the link from the list or contact the Access Department of your local cable provider.

Whether talking about what you do or writing for your Web site, don't focus on your background, training, or the features of your product or service. Talk about how what you do solves the problems or avoids the disasters your clients and customers know about only too well. Give examples of how you've actually helped those you serve solve problems or achieve goals.

For example, don't say something like "I'm a business plan writer. I worked for ten years in the loan department of Savings Bank, where I was a loan officer and ultimately headed up the department. Now I'm helping owners of small businesses write viable business plans." This information may be factual and even impressive, but you want to sell—not just inform or impress. You'll get a much better response if you say something like this: "You know how difficult it is for a small business to get bank loans, especially now with the economy being so tight? Well, I've been a loan officer for many years, and I know what bankers are looking for—what turns them on and what turns them off. I can show a small business how to develop a business plan that will get past a banker's resistance so you'll get the capital you need."

To learn how to talk and write about your business in these terms, check out *Getting Business to Come to You* and resources by Ron Richards on his ResultsLab Web site at *www.resultslab.com*.

3. Wholesalers or Brokers

Wholesalers or brokers are like middlemen (or -women) who represent your products and services. Traditionally, a wholesaler is someone who would purchase a product from you at a discount and sell it to retailers. The concept of wholesaling, however, is now applicable to selling services as well as products. Many self-employed individuals are able to sell their services through brokers, referral services, registries, agents, or bureaus—who are, in essence, wholesalers. Such representatives are also "middlemen" between you and your clients. They market your services and mark up your price to provide their fee.

Using wholesalers or brokers of some kind can be a good idea for several reasons. First, using a wholesaler frees you from selling so you can spend your time actually delivering your product or service or developing new marketable skills. Also, wholesalers are ideal when you are homebound or don't have the personality to sell. Finally using a wholesaler or broker takes advantage of what we call using OPE—Other People's Energy!

Wholesalers have been slower than others to embrace the Web. So to locate a wholesaler, it's best to work through referrals and personal contacts. A site that seeks to use the power of the Web to help with this process is *www.Wholesalerhub.com*.

Here are three tips for increasing your chances of selling through wholesalers or brokers:

Demonstrate a demand. Wholesalers or brokers are usually interested in products and services that already have a track record of success and a high demand, so to get a good wholesaler you will need to demonstrate that people do or will buy what you offer.

Develop a line of products or services. Wholesalers also often prefer representing a line of products, not just one. So consider developing a range or variety of products or services you can offer, e.g., consulting services, e-learning courses, DVDs.

Build a partnership. Make sure the wholesaler or broker you select believes in and will take a personal interest in your product or service. Remember: out of sight, out of mind. Develop a personal relationship with your wholesaler or broker and keep in regular contact with him or her. Also, don't leave everything to him or her. Use public relations to build your visibility so that when the wholesaler or broker mentions you and what you offer, buyers will have heard about it—or better yet, will have had people asking for it.

4. Brick-and-Mortar and Online Retail Stores

Placing your products or your materials in the right retail stores is one way to make sure the people who need what you offer will find it. Here are several tips even service businesses can use to make sales through retailers:

Make tie-ins with retailers. Don't overlook working with retailers just because you have a service business. Think of where your clients and customers shop. For example, a desktop publisher might tie in with a printer. An organizer could affiliate with a closet store, a Web-site designer with an Web-hosting service, or a computer-repair service with a computer retailer.

Be willing to pay for such retailer arrangements. You can arrange to pay referral fees or you can let the customer pay the retailer directly and then pay you a percentage. Be sure, though, to set your "wholesale" fees high enough to cover your costs and still have a profit.

Don't undercut your retailers. If you want to develop good relationships with retailers, the ultimate customers should not be able to buy directly from you for a better price. For example, if you have a computer-repair service, you should establish one fee for your services, not one fee if the customer goes through the computer store and a lower fee if she or he contacts you directly.

5. Sales from Referrals

Some of the most effective selling strategies for home-based businesses are sales you get from referrals. Here are a few examples:

- Develop a program to build referrals from existing clients. Referrals usually don't happen automatically. Let clients and customers know that their referrals are important to you and have a method through which they can make them. For example, you might give your clients gift certificates for a free initial consultation they can give away to friends or associates, or you might give them discount coupons to use or give away.
- Make reciprocal referral arrangements with your competition. Let them know you will do overload work for them, and send your overload their way. Offer to work with customers who have specialized needs. If appropriate, offer to pay them a referral fee.
- Identify and build relationships with gatekeepers. As we indicated above, gatekeepers are those people who have ready access to your potential customers. A convention bureau is a gatekeeper for an event planner, for example. An event planner is a gatekeeper for a reunion planner. A commercial real estate agent is a gatekeeper for any number of business services because he or she knows about new businesses that will be opening soon. You can make reciprocal referral agreements with such gatekeepers and/or arrange to pay referral fees. Our book *Teaming Up: The Small-Business Guide to Collaborating* discusses how to create these and other useful strategic alliances.

ADVANTAGES AND DISADVANTAGES OF DIFFERENT FORMS OF BUSINESS

	Advantages	Disadvantages
Sole proprietorship	Inexpensive to start, maintain, and end	Not considered as prestigious
	Few legal restrictions	Outside financing more difficult

	You have complete control	You take all responsibility and risk and are personally liable
	You keep all profits	Limited to your lifetime
Partnership	Pooling of time, talent and energy	*Finding good partners difficult*
	Partners share risk	Liability for partner's actions
	Teamwork and support	Disagreements between/ among partners common
	Minimal governmental control	Breakups often messy
	Sharing of expenses	Profits split
Limited-Liability Company	Limits liability	*Most states require more than one person*
	Taxed like a partnership	Dissolves on death of a principal
	Less paperwork than a corporation	More cost than sole proprietorship
Corporation	Best business image	*Most expensive to start and operate*
	Limits liability	Many regulations to meet with extensive record-keeping
	Business can survive owners	Tax benefits often negligible
	Easier to sell	Difficult to change
	Raising capital easier	Double taxed in some states
	Easier for large corporations to contract with you than if you work solo	Insurance may be more expensive

30. Under which form of business do you wish to operate?

One of the decisions you need to make is the legal form you will pursue your business as. Your choices are:

____ Sole proprietorship: a business owned and operated by one person

____ Partnership: when two or more individuals operate a business as joint owners

____ Limited-liability company (LLC): the newest kind of business entity offering tax advantages and limited liability

____ Corporation (for profit or nonprofit): an association of individuals who form a legal entity that is independent of the individual members

31. Have you selected a name for your enterprise?

The name you select for your business activity can be one of your most important marketing decisions. The right name will get you business; the wrong name will cost you business. The right name, for example, will attract attention to you in the yellow pages. The right name can be enough to make sure someone keeps your card. The right name helps people remember you even when they didn't get or keep your card.

Today businesses, particularly ones based on using a computer, need to take into account whether a business name will also work as a domain name for your Web site. How much the Web is influencing business naming is evidenced by driving down a street and noticing the businesses whose names end with ".com." Today one's business's name is often either first a domain name or an existing business name that was changed to add

---

☼ TIP ☼

If you are going into business with anyone other than a spouse, either organize your business as a limited-liability company or incorporate. This applies even when working with a spouse if your business is one that could subject you to legal liability or the liability insurance you can get does not protect you sufficiently, also consider this. Nolo Press (*www.nolo.com*, [510] 549-1976) offers numerous do-it-yourself books and software products for organizing a business. Once you've created your documents, it's a good idea to have a small-business attorney review them.

---

the dot-com moniker. You'll also see dot-com business names on the signage of trucks and cars.

What works for picking a domain name can be somewhat different from what works in traditional business usage. Let's consider an example of a business like computer consulting that gets most of its work from local customers. Let's say you choose a long business name like "Any Hour of the Day Computer Consulting." With hyphens or dashes in the name (*Any-Hour-of-the-Day-Computer-Consulting.com*), it will be easier to recognize and may rank higher in search engines than if it appears as *"AnyHouroftheDay-ComputerConsulting.com."* But most people won't know to put hyphens in when looking up your name after hearing about it at a religious service or when trying to recall it from a sign on your vehicle. Our view is that you pick a name for the spoken word. Why? Because most very small businesses still get their customers or clients from word of mouth. But if you get most of your business from links on the Web, having a hyphenated name makes sense.

Here are some of our candidates as examples of winning names:

COMPLETE BILLING SERVICES with the accompanying domain name *www.CompleteBillingServices.com*

GROWING SPACES with the domain name *www.GrowingSpaces.com/*

REEL 3-D with the domain name *www.Reel 3-D.com*

WORDS ARE MY BUSINESS with the domain name *www.wordsaremybusiness.com*

Consider these four rules of thumb in selecting a business name that will mean business:

1. Only use your own name as a business name if you are so well known in your field that your name will be immediately recognized and respected (or if you are willing to spend the time and money it will take to make your name readily recognizable). Then make sure to use a tag line on your materials that tells what you do; e.g., "Rick Baily, Network Installation."

2. Make sure the name you select is easy to pronounce, understand, spell, and remember. Strange or unusual names may be interesting or clever, but if people can't pronounce them, understand them, spell them, or remember them, you'll miss business that otherwise could be yours. Yahoo, Google, and Amazon when they

---

were new seemed strange, but they were easy to pronounce, understand, spell, and remember.

3. Avoid names that don't convey what you do. Unless you plan to become or appear to be a large conglomerate like ITT or Textron or are going to launch a massive initial marketing campaign, the more precisely your name relates to your service, the more of an asset your name will be. Instead think about what your customers will be looking for or will appeal to them.

4. Include a benefit in your name. If your name not only tells what you do but what's special about the way you do it, it becomes a miniadvertisement, reminding everyone who sees or hears it just how wise they would be to use your products or services.

32. Have you opened a separate bank account and installed a separate business phone line?

For tax purposes and for financial planning, it's useful to have a separate bank account for your business, into which you deposit all the business income and from which you pay all your business expenses, including your salary. A separate business bank account is important even if your business is only part time. For one thing, with a separate business account, if your business should be audited by the IRS, the audit won't necessarily need to involve your personal tax return.

In order to open a business bank account if you are using a name other than your own, your bank will usually need a copy of your fictitious name registration (commonly referred to as your DBA, "Doing Business As") or registration papers for another form of business organization.

A separate telephone line for your business is desirable because a business line will get you listed as a business in the business yellow page listings. This makes it possible for potential clients and customers to find you when they look for you in the business listings in Web directories like switchboard.com, *anywho.com,* and *smartpages.com* or call information to get your telephone number.

A separate line also helps you manage your business from home more effectively. For example, with a separate line you can make sure you answer your business line with a suitable business greeting. You can also have an appropriate voice mail/answering machine message on the line you don't

CHECKING WHETHER A BUSINESS NAME IS AVAILABLE TO USE

To find out whether someone else is already using the name you are considering, check:

1. Local phone books; call information for recent listings.

2. Web-based directories like *www.switchboard.com*, *www.anywho.com*, *superpages.com*, and *www.theultimates.com*. For Canada, *www. canada411 .ca*

3. Whether the name has already been registered as a domain name on a domain registrar like *www.godaddy.com* or a service like *www.betterwhois.com*, which is a shared domain registry. Even if the ".com" is taken, other extensions may be available, but if someone in the same business has the dot com, you're apt to be sending business to their site, because dot com is the equivalent of a default in most people's minds.

4. Local courthouse and the state office that registers fictitious name registrations, also referred to as "DBA's"— "doing business as." (Check to see if your county and state place these records on the Web.)

5. Your state office that handles corporate names, usually the secretary of state, to determine whether someone has reserved or taken the name for corporate use.

6. Trademarks using The Trademark Office's free database— *http:www.uspto.gov/web/menu/tm.html* or a commercial trademark database, which also shows trademarks registered under state trademark laws. To be completely thorough, use an attorney specializing in trademarks and patents

☞ **ALERT** ☜

If you plan to use a name other than your own, you will need to register and protect your business name. If you're going to be highly visible, it's also wise to get the domain name for your own name. We obtained *paulandsarahedwards.com*.

want to answer during particular hours of the day or night. And a separate line will help avoid phone conflicts and misunderstandings with others living in your household.

33. Do you have the office equipment and supplies you need to work most productively?

Fortunately, prices for home-office equipment are priced like commodities. When the prior edition of this book was published in 1996, it cost nearly $3,000 to get a computer, monitor, and laser printer. Today for less than $1,000, you can get a computer infinitely more powerful and a color laser printer. While software is no longer bundled with computers as it once was, it still costs less to have technology that gives you the capability of a staff of employees for less than what many start-up businesses spend on marketing their first year.

34. Have you established a work schedule for yourself?

During what hours of the day and week do you plan to work? Customers, suppliers, clients, and family members need to know your hours, and you need to have at least a general work schedule in mind to make sure you don't inadvertently slack off or overwork.

For those working part time:

If you plan to do everything involving your part-time business on weekends, you'll invariably find that personal and family activities will arise to thwart your plan.

For those working full time:

Make sure you don't schedule clients so tightly that you find yourself working morning, noon, and night. A rule of thumb for establishing your work schedule is to set up your week so that you will have either the morning, afternoon, or evening free.

☞ ALERT ☜

Eight hours a week is generally the minimum time investment needed to get a part-time business under way. Fifty to sixty hours a week is typical for a full-time business, which is about the same number of hours a corporate executive puts in.

---

35. If you have young children, have you made arrangements for needed supplementary child care?

Sometimes parents overestimate how much productive work they will be able to get done with young children at home. Although some men and women can work with toddlers playing underfoot, many parents simply can't concentrate sufficiently to complete certain tasks. Therefore, if you have children under six, we recommend that you arrange an alternate source of child care for those times of day or night when you need to work without interruption.

By working from home, you have many more options for child care and much greater flexibility than when you are away at an office. In *Working from Home,* we outline seven child-care options to consider along with guidance for what level of supervision is required while working from home for children of various ages. In *The Entrepreneurial Parent,* you can see how dozens of parents organize their days in real life with "A Day in the Life" descriptions.

36. Have you lined up a team of professionals to whom you can turn for help if you need it?

Establish a relationship with the following professionals whom you can call upon when you need them. Here is a list of the kind of professionals you may need to call upon:

___ Accountant or tax adviser, to help make sure you can qualify for and take all tax deductions to which you are entitled and to help you avoid or resolve tax problems

___ Computer consultant, to help you get up and running with new equipment and software and to help you with problems

___ Information researcher, to track down key information when you need it

___ Insurance agent, to assist you in finding the best insurance coverage at the lowest possible cost

___ Investment counselor, to help you make the most of the money you make

___ Lawyer, to advise you on legal matters such as contracts and collections

___ Marketing consultant, to help you make advertising and other marketing decisions that will result in the maximum amount of business for the lowest possible price

___ Professional organizer, to assist you in setting up your office so you will have a functional place for everything and will be able to find it when you need it

___ Public-relations specialist, to assist you in achieving high visibility for yourself and your business

___ Web designer to create your site or to do other Web tasks you need help with

37. Do you have a support network of professional colleagues and friends? Nine out of ten people who go out on their own to work from home are glad they did and say they would do it again. But there is one thing missing from most home offices, and that's other people—colleagues, mentors, co-workers, business associates, and peers. To keep from feeling isolated and to make sure you keep abreast of current developments, you'll need to take the initiative to make sure you have ample contact with colleagues, peers, and mentors. For example, here are the types of social interaction that usually occur automatically when you're employed by an organization and that you typically need to duplicate:

- the ability to brainstorm ideas with a colleague
- the chance to commiserate with a fellow worker who knows what you're up against
- the occasion to celebrate a victory with someone who can appreciate what you've accomplished
- access to a grapevine that will keep you abreast of the latest developments and inside scoop in your field or industry
- the ability to turn to a mentor who can show you the ropes, introduce you to the right people, cheer you on, and guide you to success

To develop such relationships, we recommend joining or creating, and participating actively in, one or more of the following types of groups:

Trade and professional associations. You can join a professional association in your own field and/or the field to which you are marketing your product or services. Such associations are invaluable routes for meeting colleagues and peers, gatekeepers and mentors, keeping abreast of the latest developments and needs of the field, and building your reputation. Should you be one of the many people who are moving to less populated states or communities and find that there is no chapter in your area, consider establishing a chapter. Names of such associations are included when possible for the computer-based businesses profiled in part 1 of this book. We also suggest getting involved in the online communities found on association sites, in professional forums, newsgroups, and discussion groups found on the Web.

Civic, business, and community organizations. If you are serving a local clientele, becoming active in civic and community organizations such as the chamber of commerce can become a valuable route for meeting potential clients, gatekeepers, and mentors, and for building business relationships. An increasing number of communities have home-based business associations. These groups are another route for self-employed individuals to meet peers, get referrals, and support one another. An up-to-date list of home-business associations is available on the Working from Home Forum on CompuServe Information Service.

Business-referral organizations. Today most communities have one or more networking organizations, the sole purpose of which is for members to refer business to one another. Such groups customarily meet for breakfast once a week and, to prevent competition, limit membership to only one person from a given type of business. In this way, members become gatekeepers for one another.

One key to benefiting from such a referral network is to make sure the one you join has members who would come in frequent contact with your potential clients and customers. Another key is to be sure to give ample referrals yourself to people in your group. Your referrals to them will engender goodwill, and so they will want to return the favors. The largest business-referral organization is Business Network International, with chapters all over the world: (800) 825-8286, *www.bni.com*.

Web Options
Online forums can be found on virtually any topic from accounting and animals to yachts. Participation in forums can help a business. During the fifteen years we operated the Working from Home forum on CompuServe, among other things we saw invaluable information exchanged, referrals made, businesses team up for projects, lucrative contracts obtained from contacts made, and not infrequently people who lived within blocks or a few miles of each meet for the first time and then form business relationships. But such things happened only for people who actively contributed and did not overtly market their businesses. So if you join a forum, check out the forum's etiquette before jumping in.

Social networking sites help form networks and communities of like-minded people. Some are purely social; some, such as *ecademy.com,* Fast Company magazine's Company of Friends (*www.fastcompany.com/cof/*), *ryze.com,* and *tribe.net* include relating around business and career. However, as a means of developing one's business, experience is showing that while social-networking sites can be of value to some people, online forums and local organizations and networks will usually yield better results. See more about social networking on pages 340–341.

38. Are your cards and stationery designed and printed?

Your business cards and letterhead can serve as minibillboards for your work. If they are done well, they will help you get business and be taken seriously. Therefore we suggest that you make the effort to create a professional overall graphic identity for your business and use this graphic image on all your printed materials.

You may be able to design and even print your cards, letterhead, and stationery yourself using software and equipment described in Part 2 of this book. If you do not have a keen design sense, however, or the right equipment, we suggest that you make the investment to use the services of fellow self-employed individuals who specialize in desktop publishing or graphic design. Once you have created your graphic image, you can use the same artwork to create invoices, mailing labels, proposal covers, postcards, etc., as your budget allows.

39. Do you have adequate insurance to protect your business property and liability?

When you set up your moneymaking venture in a home office, the cost of insuring your business from loss and liability should be minimal, or at least far less than setting yourself up in an outside office. The chart on page 239 will help you determine what you need.

40. Have you made plans for obtaining health coverage if you are leaving behind the health insurance you had at a job?

Concern about how to get adequate health insurance for an affordable cost keeps many people from going out on their own full time. Next to getting enough paying work, it is the most common concern for self-employed individuals. We, the self-employed, suffer more than most groups under our troubled health-care system. More than one in four self-employed workers report not having health insurance; as prices have skyrocket, the percentage rises.

HOME OFFICE INSURANCE WORK SHEET

Use the following work sheet to identify which types of insurance you think you Have Already (H); Don't Need (D); Should Get Now or in the Future (G). You can then review your insurance needs with your attorney and/or insurance agent. To find the best price for insurance, get quotes from several agents.

Type of Insurance	Coverage	When Needed	Note	Costs Quotes
—— Liability (related to your home office)	Covers cost of injuries to business-related visitors while on your property	If you ever have deliveries, personnel, clients, or customers who come to your home	May be a rider or endorsement on your homeowner's policy or a separate "in-home business policy"	
—— General Liability	Damage you are responsible for on the premises of others	Your work takes you on to others' premises		
—— Business Property	Protects you from damage or loss to your business property	If value of equipment greater than the minimal coverage provided with your homeowner policy, typically $2500	May be a rider or endorsement on your homeowner's policy or an "in-home business policy"	
—— Small-Business or Business-Owner's Policy	Covers general liability, losses to inventory or equipment, business interruption and lost earnings, errors and omission, and product liability	When you have more inventory or equipment than you protect by adding a business rider or endorsement to homeowner's insurance	An umbrella policy covering multiple risks	
—— Business Interruption	Losses when you are not able to work because of disasters	If you live in an area subject to natural disasters; manmade mishaps are also covered	An "in-home business policy"	

Type of Insurance	Coverage	When Needed	Note	Costs Quotes
——— Computer	Losses of hardware, software, and data	If you store client information, regular backup is also vital.		
——— Malpractice, Errors and Ommission, or Product/ Professional Liability	Claims arising from your services or products	If the work you do could inflict injury or loss to your customers or clients		
——— Worker's Compensation	Injuries to those you employ	If you employ others		
——— Disability	Loss of income due to illness or injury	If your type of work produces work-related disabilities, e.g., medical transcription	Premiums are based on age, income, and your physical condition	
——— Partnership	Protects against losses from suits of other partners	Whenever you're in business with someone else		

Nevertheless, we believe health insurance is a necessity. A major illness or accident can wipe out even a successful home business. Many self-employed individuals find they can get the best coverage at the lowest price through a group policies offered by organizations. Here is a list of possible sources of group policies you may be eligible to get if you affiliate with them:

- A professional or trade association
- Your local chamber of commerce

- College alumni association
- Labor union
- Business organizations like the National Federation of Independent Businesses (*www.nfib.org*)
- Regional or state organizations like these in New York State:
  - Support Services Alliance, (800) 836-4SSA, *www.ssainfo.com*
  - Working Today's Portable Benefits Network, *www.workingtoday.org*

Other sources of health insurance include:

- Health-maintenance organizations, which are generally priced below Preferred Provider Plans (PPOs)
- Health Savings Accounts (HSA) with a policy covering catastrophic illness. These are usually best for single, healthy individuals.
- Individual coverage you find through insurance agents, some of whom specialize in health coverage or Web sites that provide price comparisons for individual policies and then link you to the companies or agents that sell them, such as *eHealthInsurance.com*, (800) 977-8860, and *quotesmith.com*, (800) 556-9393
- Coverage you obtain by working through a Professional Employer Organization (PEO) / employee leasing company. You can find PEOs by occupation or state at the Web site of the National Association of Professional Employer Organizations (*www.napeo.org*).
- Some states, such as California, Colorado, Connecticut, Maryland, and Texas, provide guaranteed issue of policies for small businesses and/or allow them to form their own insurance pools. More cities that recognize the importance of small business to their local economies may do or be willing to do what San Diego has done in sponsoring a group health plan for small businesses with two or more employees.
- Medicare, if you are sixty-five, *www.medicare.gov*. For other government-funded health coverage, see the site of the Centers for Medicare & Medicaid Services (CMS), *http:///cms.hhs.gov*.

41. Have you written down specific measurable goals for your business with a target date and action plan for each goal?

Research sponsored by the Ford Foundation showed that people who write down specific goals are considerably more likely to achieve them. We believe this is particularly true when you are working from home in a business of your own. Use the form on page 243 to articulate your goals.

42. Do you have realistic expectations?

A Canadian study of successful businesses found that people who have realistic expectations for themselves and their businesses have a higher success rate. For example, those who are realistic about how much money they can earn and how long it will take to build a clientele or customer base are more successful. They don't buy into the start-a-business hype that suggests they can quickly make tons of money with little work. They don't think of self-employment as utopia, a solution to all their problems from financial to family. They realize that building a business income and a new lifestyle takes time and that they will have to invest some money and lots of energy.

To help gain a realistic perspective of your expectations, think about what others with a background and experience similar to yours have been able to accomplish over what period of time. The experiences of others can serve as a baseline for what's realistic. Success is a process that has a schedule of its own, however, so if you can see a way to do things more quickly or better, don't limit yourself to what you've seen others do. On the other hand, if you're not progressing as quickly as someone else, don't necessarily throw in the towel. How long it will take you to succeed depends upon how ready the market is for what you offer and how ready you are to seize the opportunities that await you.

The work sheet on page 244 can help you determine how realistic your plans are.

Most of our unhappiness comes from comparing ourselves unfavorably to other people.

GOALS WORK SHEET

Review the reasons you checked in Question 1 about what is motivating you to make money with your computer at home. Enter these reasons below:

_____

_____

_____

Describe how you will know when you have achieved these goals: (Be specific: What will your life be like, precisely how much money will you make, what work will you be doing, etc.?)

_____

_____

_____

By what date would you like to have achieved your goals?_____

What are the first ten steps you need to take to achieve your goal, and when do you plan to have each complete by:

Steps	*Date to be Completed*
1.	
2.	
3.	
4.	
5.	
6.	
7.	
8.	
9.	
10.	

43. Are you willing to read, take courses, study, use consultants, and otherwise learn what you need to learn to succeed on your own?

Research studies show that those who are willing to make the investment in learning as much as they can about what it takes to succeed are more likely to do so. Those who succeed, for example, are more likely to spend from six to nine months planning what they're going to do and how they're going to do it. They use this time to test out the feasibility of their plans as well.

HOW REALISTIC IS WHAT YOU EXPECT?

This work sheet is designed to assist you in assessing how realistic your estimations are as to what you will be able to accomplish over what period of time.

How Ready Are You?

Rate yourself on a scale of 0 to 10 for each of the following points. (0 = virtually none; 10 = abundant)

____ Your Experience Level. How much do you know about marketing and operating on your own? How familiar are you with the field you're entering?

____ Your Contacts. How many people do you know now who need and are ready to pay for your service? How many people do you know now who are in a position to refer business to you?

____ How Much Money You Have on Hand to Capitalize Yourself. Will you need to bootstrap all your costs? Will you need to finance some of your costs?

____ Your Credentials. What credentials do you have for doing what you're offering that establish you as qualified to do what you do in the eyes of potential clients or customers.

____ Your Results. How good are the results you produce for your clients? Just how vital or dramatic are they?

____ Time. How much time do you have before you need to be supporting yourself full-time?

Scoring: The higher your score, the more likely you are to succeed over a shorter period of time. The lower your score, the longer it could take you to establish yourself and therefore the more time you will need to build your business.

How Ready Is the Market?

Check the statements that apply to your situation. Is the product or service you're offering:

____1. Ahead of the market? Are you anticipating a trend or offering something so new, different, or unusual that people are as yet unaware of it and why they need it? If so, you will need to educate them about the benefits of what you offer. That will make getting clients and customers slower and more time-consuming.

___2. Right on the market? Is there a strong, unmet demand right now for what you are offering? If so, you may find getting business easier and quicker and the lower your own readiness score needs be.

___3. In a growing market? Are the number of people who need what you offer expanding beyond the ability of what is now available to handle it? If the market is expanding, your growth could be quick and easy even if your own readiness score is not particularly high.

___4. In a stable or declining market? Are most of the people who need what you offer already using another product or service? Are there fewer people needing it? If so, you will need to be highly competitive in order to take the existing business away from others or carve out new markets, and the higher your readiness score the better.

___5. A fad? Might what you're offering be a passing fancy? If so, you may do well quickly but should anticipate that the demand for what you're offering will dwindle quickly, too. You'll need to be ready with something else. If you're on the tail end of a fad, watch out!

___6. An evergreen? Is what you're offering something that lots of people have needed for a long time and will probably always need? If so, the lower your readiness score, the longer it may take you to get established, but once you do, you could become secure.

___7. In an oversaturated market? Are there more people offering what you do than there are people who need it? If so, the higher your readiness score needs to be and the longer it may take you to distinguish yourself from the crowd.

___8. Without a market? If you have to create a demand for what you do, you can expect it will take you a much longer time to get under way, and there is the risk that you may not be able to. A very high "results" score above could speed up your success, however.

Those who succeed are also more likely to ask for and use the advice of experts. They don't assume they know everything they need to know, nor do they just blindly move ahead. They educate themselves in aspects of business with which they are unfamiliar. They take courses, buy books and tapes, and attend conferences and seminars. One added benefit of taking seminars and courses is that you may find clients, mentors, and gatekeepers through the instructors or other students you meet.

44. Where will you turn to obtain the additional information and expertise you need?

Of course, your personal support network and various trade and professional organizations will be sources of much information and expertise, but there is a wealth of information available today for self-employed individuals. Here are just a few places you can turn to build your skills and knowledge about everything from marketing to tax issues.

Resources

ENTREPRENEUR magazine, *www.entrepreneur.com*, (800) 274-6229

MANUFACTURING EXTENSION PARTNERSHIP (*www.mep.nist.gov*)—a nonprofit for small and medium manufacturers (New technology will enable manufacturing to be done at home probably within the decade.)

MINORITY BUSINESS DEVELOPMENT CENTERS: Find local offices at *www.mbda.gov*.

REGIONAL ECONOMIC DEVELOPMENT ASSOCIATIONS. Find one near you on the Links page at the site of the National Association of Development Organizations, *www.nado.org*.

SCORE (Service Corps of Retired Executives); *www.score.org/*

SMALL BUSINESS ADMINISTRATION. You can access resources and find a local office at *www.sbaonline.sba.gov/*.

SMALL BUSINESS DEVELOPMENT CENTERS. Find one near you at the site of the Small Business Development Center National Information Clearinghouse, *http:sbdcnet.utsa.edu/sbdc.htm*.

THE AUTHOR'S WEB SITE and its links, *www.workingfromhome.com*

45. Are you willing to experiment until you find the combination of products, services, pricing, and marketing methods that will work for you?

Ultimately, success on your own is not about how much money, experience, or contacts you begin with. Nor is it the result of carefully following a set of rules (unless you've purchased an already proven franchise or business system, and even then there is likely to be a learning curve). Creating a business is an experiment. It involves knowing what you want to accomplish, doing what you think you need to do, tracking the results you get, and modifying what you do accordingly until you get the results you want.

Ultimately, if you're providing a product or service that people need and you can offer them satisfying results as long as there are enough such people and you let them know about you, then, over time you will succeed. But let your results be your guide. If you're getting the results you want, keep doing what you're doing; if not, experiment further. Try different marketing methods, different pricing, different ways of describing what you do, different aspects of what you offer, until you start getting the results you want.

"Insanity is doing the same thing over and over and expecting to get different results."—Albert Einstein

46. Do you have or are you willing to develop the traits necessary to manage yourself and make your business a success?

We are frequently asked what kind of person is suited to self-employment. Having personally met thousands of successfully self-employed individuals, we can say with confidence that you do not need to be a born entrepreneur or even to have grown up in an entrepreneurial household. We have seen people succeed from all walks of life, all backgrounds, all ages, and various levels of education and experience. They are the living proof that anyone who is willing to learn, persevere, and experiment can ultimately succeed on her or his own. We've noticed that the most successful self-employed people tend to share several qualities they have already or develop along the way—all of which can be acquired by setting one's mind to it. How well do these qualities describe you? Are you:

____1. **Broad-minded.** On your own, you need to be able to let go of preconceived, limited notions and be open to a wealth of possibilities, both those you want to attain as well as those you want to avoid.

____ 2. **Competent.** Being good at what you do is a given when you're on your own. Nepotism or favoritism might get you started, but they won't keep you flying over time and mediocrity will stall you or keep you sputtering along.

____3. **Courageous.** Because most of us have been raised to believe economic security lies in having a paycheck, the act of going out on our own requires the courage to believe in ourselves and the value of our work.

____4. **Fair-minded.** Trust is at the core of most business transactions, so clients and customers must believe you will be fair-minded and consider their needs and circumstances.

____5. **Honest.** Honesty is another aspect of attaining trust. Clients and customers need to trust that you will be forthcoming and ethical in your business dealings.

____6. **Imaginative.** Since making it on your own is basically a matter of taking an idea and turning it into a living, you have to be able to see what could be in addition to what already is.

____7. **Inspiring.** When you're on your own, you need to be able to inspire your clients and customers to believe they will benefit from your products and services. You also must be able to inspire yourself to believe in your goals and keep yourself going.

____8. **Intelligent.** Sometimes people think intelligence means having a high IQ or doing well on standardized tests. Studies show that having an unusually high IQ is not necessary to succeed on your own, however. In fact, people with very high IQs don't always do well in business—possibly because they don't relate well to the perspective of their clients and customers. But the *Random House Dictionary* defines intelligence as "the capacity for learning, reasoning, and understanding." This we do believe is vital for making it on your own and, fortunately, we all have the capacity to develop our abilities for learning, reasoning, and understanding.

____9. **Straightforward.** It's hard to make it on your own if your potential clients and customers can't understand what you do and how you operate. They need to be clear about who you are, where you stand, and what they can count on you for.

____10. **Self-directed.** To work on your own, you have to know where you want to go in life and what you want to accomplish. You can't wait for something to come along or for someone else to tell you what to do.

____11. **Goal oriented.** Not only do you need to have a clear idea of where you're going and what you want to accomplish; you also have to be able to make plans for how you will get there, then follow through on them.

_____ 12. **Tenacious.** We've discovered there needs to be a little Scottish terrier in anyone who wants to succeed on his or her own. Scottish terriers are renowned for their ability to grab on to whatever they're chasing and never, never let go. Sometimes that's what you need when you go out on your own—the ability to relentlessly pursue your goals until you attain them.

We have a different kind of self-scoring Self-Assesment for Self-Employment quiz on our Web site, *www.workingfromhome.com,* where you can check your readiness to go out on your own. It's accessible from several places on the homepage.

47. Are you willing to stick it out and persevere until you succeed?

Most people who start thinking about and exploring starting a business also at some point think about giving up on it or chucking it. This is normal and not necessarily a reason actually to do so. Some people have initial success in landing a lot of business but along the way hit a "sophomore slump." Others encounter a longer learning curve than they expected. According to Small Business Administration studies, one-third of people who end a business do so after it's become financially successful. At some point, if you're tempted to give up, ask yourself what's really going on. Is it because you're:

- Not getting enough business? If so, try new ways of marketing or improve your skills or both.
- Not profitable? Consider if you can you lower your costs? Perhaps there's new technology that will reduce your costs. Or maybe you get lower prices for what you need on the Internet or from a local supplier.
- Feeling burned out? Do you get enough sleep or need a vacation. Can you delegate things you hate doing? Do you need to wind down your current business while you ramp up something new that is more to your liking?

As you proceed through the ups and downs of creating your own home-based business, keep this thought from our book *The Secrets of Self-Employment* in mind:

Your fate is the hand life deals you; your destiny is what you do with that hand.

PART III

Using Your Computer in Business

Technology has not only improved the productivity and bottom line of my business but also enhances the quality of my life.

DAVID LAM,
Winning the Paper Chase

WHEN YOU MAKE MONEY with your computer on a consistent ongoing basis it means that you're "in business." Running a successful computer-based business from home, even if it is only part time, involves managing it the same way a Fortune 500 company would. That includes handling administration, marketing, sales, customer service, and accounting. The difference is that you are probably the only employee and must do all the work yourself. How can you accomplish everything you need to do to keep your business running smoothly and at the same time do the work that brings in the money? You can do this by putting your computer and other high-tech office equipment to work for you. A well-equipped office with a computer and appropriate software is like having a corporate executive team working with you. Scheduling and organizing programs become your administrative assistant; database, contact-management software, and your Web site are your public-relations staff; financial software acts as your accounting department; and online databases help you carry out your research and development (R & D) efforts.

Here's a partial list of the things your computer can do for you:

- Keep track of your appointments and meetings
- Maintain records on all your clients and contacts
- Create brochures, slides, and many other presentation documents
- Create a presence on the Web with a Web site
- Make and receive phone calls through the Web
- Teleconference through the Web
- Create reports, business proposals, and all types of documents
- Send and receive faxes
- Send and receive e-mail
- Store and file all or most of your important papers
- Create artwork, drawings, graphs, tables, and maps
- Calculate your income and expenses and manage your financial data

- Print checks and log phone calls, visitors, transactions, and time spent on projects
- Record and diagram the steps needed to manage your projects
- Prepare your business and personal taxes
- And much, much more!

Your computer works tirelessly for you, costs only pennies a day to operate, and is always open to new ideas and new ways of doing things. In Part 3 of this book, we will show you how you can use your computer, the Internet, and other home-office equipment to solve problems and manage many critical functions of your day-to-day operations. We identify one-by-one the important routines and tasks that home businesses typically need to do or should be doing, and show you what technology exists to help you improve the way you work. Section 3.1 discusses the "ideal home office."

Section 3.2 reviews how you can manage your money with your computer, from check writing and accounting to preparing your taxes.

Section 3.3 features software programs that can help you keep track of the many administrative tasks involved in running a home-based business.

Section 3.4 discusses how you can use your computer and other technology to help you market yourself and keep a steady stream of business coming your way. We'll examine programs that allow you to keep up-to-date information about your clients and help you keep your name in the forefront of their minds. All the tips and recommendations in this section help you to stay in touch with your clients and create a professional image.

Finally, Section 3.5 explores the world of online information and how with your computer, you can obtain valuable strategic information to identify, attract, and keep clients. We will discuss how you can verify financial information on potential contacts and how you can research any topic, including how to track down money owed to you. You'll also get a primer on the Internet and the Web.

You will see that the benefits are enormous if you can learn to take advantage of the computer technology available to make your home office work for you.

3.1: The Ideal Home Office

When we say "ideal" home office, we mean setting up the equipment and furnishings so that your work space is efficient and allows for maximum productivity. Everyone has different needs—so there is no single recommendation that applies to all. Some businesses will need more specialized equipment than others.

Here are our recommendations for the essential and basic items most home offices should have:

Computer Equipment

If you are reading this book, you probably already own a computer, but you may be considering upgrading your older model in order to start your business. No matter how much you spend on a computer, the technology will likely be better and the prices lower just a few months down the road. However, waiting a few months to save a few hundred dollars may not be wise because you may risk losing a few thousand dollars in income. The best advice is to buy what you need when you need it.

If your dilemma is not knowing whether to buy a Windows-based or an Apple Macintosh computer, the choice is less problematic. Personal taste and to some extent the type of business you are in and what your clients use will dictate which platform you choose. However, in this book we largely focus on Windows-based computers, since they are more widely used in the business world. In this section we talk about the different components you need to think about before you go shopping.

Central Processing Unit (CPU)

The Central Processing Unit (CPU) is the brain of the computer and the main information processor. It interprets and carries out software instructions, performs calculations, makes logical decisions, keeps track of the current step in the execution of the program, and communicates with the rest of the computer.

When it comes to processing information, speed is important. Computer speeds are measured in Megahertz (MHz). The higher the number, the faster the microprocessor runs (theoretically, that is; other factors can affect the speed at which a computer functions). It's wise to buy the fastest PC you can afford.

Hard Drive

The hard drive is where you store your files. Consider it like a filing cabinet: The more room you have, the more files you can store. Hard drives boil down to capacity and speed. It's important that your hard drive have a large-enough capacity to store your programs and data files. How much is enough? One rule of thumb is to add up the hard-disk memory required to store all the programs you expect to use in the future (and don't short-change yourself, since you may want to use a graphics or database program down the road, even if you don't now), then add 50 percent of that figure to determine the space needed for your data files, and then double or triple that total to allow yourself room to grow. Also, if your business has any special needs, such as storing graphics files or large databases, it's likely that you will need to plan for an external storage device. Most hard drives available today provide you with plenty of storage, but look for 60 to 80 GB drive as the minimum.

Random Access Memory

There are other factors that affect a computer's speed. In addition to processor speed, you need to be aware of how much RAM (Random Access Memory) your computer has. Every time you open a program, it is loaded from the hard drive into the RAM. It's faster to read a program from the RAM than from the hard drive. The more RAM your computer has, the more data can be loaded from the hard drive into the RAM, which helps to speed up your computer. The CPU delivers its data at very high speed, and often the regular RAM cannot keep up with that speed. Therefore, a special RAM type called cache is used as a buffer or temporary storage. This cache is an extremely fast memory chip that helps the computer operate faster by temporarily storing frequently accessed or recently accessed data. An internal cache is built into the CPU, and an external cache is on the motherboard. When the CPU needs data, it first checks the internal cache, which is the fastest source. If the data is not there, it then checks the external cache for it.

Monitors

Monitors come in a range of sizes. While you can get a fifteen-inch screen, a seventeen-inch screen is preferable. This larger screen significantly reduces eyestrain, improves the amount of text you can see at once, and makes paging and moving around documents much easier. You will definitely want an even larger screen, such as a nineteen-inch one, if you are doing desktop publishing and need to see large blocks of text all at once.

The resolution of a monitor is measured in pixels. In general, the higher the number of pixels, the sharper the image and the more you can see on the screen at once. Your monitor should be capable of a resolution of at least 1024 x 768.

Optical Drives

Computers use two basic forms of optical storage: compact disk (CD) and digital versatile disk (DVD). Compact-disk storage was derived from the same media that we use from audio compact disks. The storage space averages around 650 to 700 MB of data per disk. CDs can contain audio, data, or both on the same disk. Most software for computers is distributed on CD formats. DVD was the development for a compact digital video format that also spun off into the data storage arena. DVD is seen primarily for video. DVD drives are still backwards compatible with CD formats, however.

Optical drives can come as read only (ROM) or as writers (designated with an R, RW, or RAM). Read-only drives allow you to only read data from disks that already have data on them; they cannot be used for removable storage. Writers or burners can be used to save data, create music CDs, or even in some cases video disks that can be played in DVD players. CD recorders are very standardized and should be compatible with almost all the equipment out there.

CD-ROM

We consider it essential for a home-business computer to have a CD. Most new computer systems come with a built-in CD and CD burner, but if you are having a system built be sure to include this piece of hardware. A CD drive is required for today's multimedia software and software packages. A CD burner is a powerful tool that enables you to archive your data files, back up software, and record audio CDs.

DVD-ROM

DVD (digital versatile disk) is an optical storage format that stores approximately 2.6 gigabytes in its most basic form, or about 4 times the storage of a CD-ROM. The term *DVD-ROM* can refer to the DVD media itself, or to the disk drive that is used to read DVD media. DVD-ROM drives are versatile devices that can read DVD disks and all types of CDs. With a DVD-ROM drive, your computer can display movies from DVD video disks as well.

All optical drives are rated by a multiplier that refers to the maximum speed at which the drive operates. But what does it all mean? Read-only or ROM drives can list up to two speeds.

For a CD-ROM drive, there is typically a single speed listed, which is the maximum data-read speed. Sometimes a second CD "ripping" speed will also be listed. This refers to the speed at which data can be read from an audio CD for conversion to a computer digital format such as MP3.

DVD-ROM drives will typically list two or three speeds. The primary speed is the maximum DVD data-read speed, while the secondary refers to the maximum CD data-read speed. Once again, an additional number may be listed that refers to the CD ripping speed from audio CDs.

Optical burner drives (used to create and copy CDs and DVDs) have even more numbers listed. Typically for CD recordable drives there will be three numbers listed. The first number is the maximum rated speed that the drive can record data to a CD-R optical disk. The second refers to the maximum rated speed that the drive can record to a CD-RW optical disk. The drives will still be limited to the speed of the media you are using. The final number refers to the maximum speed for reading data from a CD. DVD burners will have an additional speed listed, which is the primary recording speed to DVD media. (Multiformat DVD drives list a speed for each format type.) They also have listed the same three numbers as the CD writers.

The following chart suggests drives based on the type of computer tasks you want to perform.

Task	Drive Type	Minimum Drive Speeds
Word-processing tasks	CD-ROM	24x
Surfing the Web	CD-ROM	24x
Playing digital music	CD-RW	24x/10x/24x
Playing games	CD-RW	40x/12x/40x
Watching DVDs	DVD-ROM	4x/24x
Any combination of above	CD-RW/DVD Combo	24x/10x/24x/4x
Creating digital videos	DVD Burner	Multiformat (-/+RW) 2x

DVD Writers

As we write this book, DVD writers are a very fast growing segment in the storage industry and are poised to become the preferred storage method because the size restrictions of the optical CD storage are becoming quickly outdated. Add to that the ability to generate your own digital-quality movies, and it's no surprise. But does all this mean that now is the time you want to go out and buy one of the latest technologies? There are two advantages to DVD writers: storage and digital video. Most DVD standards out there today will store 4.7 gigabytes or more of data on a single disk. This is eight times the storage capacity of the standard compact-disk media on the market. If this optical drive is meant to create backups of data from hard drives, it means that there are fewer disks to maintain for storage compared to those produced from a CD writer. If making or editing videos is part of your business, then the concept of computer video editing and burning videos to DVD is something to look at. Most of the DVD writers on the market will allow some form of encoding of digital video from a computer or other source to a DVD medium that can be played back in most DVD players. This flexibility and durability mean that you can take old VHS tapes and convert them to DVDs for more permanent storage or create more compact DVDs that can be easily sent through the mail to friends and relatives.

It's hard to decide which format is the best one to use when making your videos or backups. Currently there are at least four competing formats for the DVD writer market: DVD-R, DVD+R, DVD-RW, and DVD+RW. Each format has its advantages and its disadvantages. The biggest drawback to all of them is that no one given format is guaranteed to work in all DVD players on the market. Even though you select one of the more compatible formats, it does not mean that it will work with the particular player or DVD-ROM drive that you or others have.

Price is also one of the drawbacks. CD-recordable disks are relatively inexpensive compared to the average price for a similar DVD medium. While the price of DVD medium works out to about the same price per megabyte as the CD medium, if write failures or mistakes occur, it can end up costing a lot more money. As with all technology, once the format becomes generally popular the costs will drop.

Multimedia Equipment

Video Card

When choosing a monitor, you also need to take into account the video card that drives the monitor's graphic capability. The video card is simply another circuit board that plugs in to the motherboard. It determines the clarity, or resolution, of your screen. Video cards also come with their own RAM in which images are stored for even quicker access time. If you expect to do a lot of graphic-design work or video editing, you will want a few more features with the video card. For graphic designs you'll need a higher-resolution capability. Many high-end displays can support 1,600 by 1,200 resolutions or higher, allowing for more visible detail. Another feature that may be of interest is multimonitor support. This allows the graphics card to support two computer displays at once, thus expanding the graphical work space.

If you are going to do video editing your needs are more specialized. The key to video editing is a feature called video-in/video-out or VIVO. This allows a video source to be plugged into the computer for digitizing of analog video sources such as TV or VHS tapes as well as exporting a video signal back to those devices. If the video card does not support this capability, it is possible to add this capability with external devices. Cards from ATI's *All-In-Wonder* series are excellent for digital video work.

Multimedia equipment is not absolutely essential to the basics of business computing, but it sure helps. A good sixteen-bit sound card, such as the industry standard *Sound Blaster* from Creative Technologies, and a pair of good speakers will not only liven up your computing experiences; they also take on a new level of importance when browsing the Web or running multimedia applications on your CD-ROM drive. Sound cards and speakers are standard with many computer systems these days. Buying a system with multimedia already bundled will save you money over buying and installing the components separately.

Notebook Systems

Notebook or laptop systems continue to grow in popularity due to their increasing performance and portability. If your business is one in which you need to be mobile and having access to your computer as you travel is important, you may want to consider purchasing a notebook system. Some home-business owners exclusively use a notebook; others have both a notebook and a desktop system. Here are some considerations when choosing a notebook:

Size and Weight: Weight and size are among the main attractions of a notebook, and they vary. When shopping for a notebook, pick up the system and be sure that it's something you are willing to carry around.

Processors: Notebook processors still lag behind desktop CPUs (although they are getting better all the time), but they make up for that with their energy efficiency. To decide which CPU is right for you, think about the purpose of the system. If it is going to be a mobile Web browser, e-mail, word processor, or even a DVD player, any CPU above 800 MHz should be sufficient. If your notebook is intended to replace your desktop, it should have a high-end processor rated at least 2.0 GHz or higher.

Displays: When you are buying a notebook, considering the size of the screen is important. A large-size screen is generally preferred, but some large screens have such high resolutions that standard fonts can be difficult to read. The size of the screen also has an impact on the size of the notebook. Systems with seventeen-inch screens tend to be very large and are therefore more difficult to carry.

Drives: Hard-drive size is straightforward in notebooks, but the choice of optical drives is important. One of the great advantages of notebooks these days is their ability to become portable DVD players. With a DVD-ROM or CD-RW combo drive, you can watch DVD movies through the computer or even plug it into a home-theater system. Many ultraportable notebooks often lack an internal optical drive to save on space.

Networking: Connecting to the Net is integral to most notebooks today. Look for systems that include a built-in 56Kbps modem and Fast Ethernet. This allows you to log in for most situations. If you want ultimate portability, look at getting a notebook computer with an integrated wireless adapter. More and more locations are available with wireless "hot spots" for connectivity.

Battery Life: How useful a notebook is directly relates to the life of the battery. Find out what the manufacturer's listed battery life is for the standard battery. We recommend a system with at least two hours of battery life under normal conditions. If you need extended time unplugged, look for notebooks with media bays that can double as extra battery slots.

Warranty Plans: Because notebooks are mobile, they take more abuse than desktops and are more prone to breakdowns. When you purchase a system, make sure it comes with at least a one-year warranty from the manufacturer. Some systems offer a three-year warranty; if you will use your notebook heavily, that may be right for you but will be more costly.

Fax Machines or Fax/Modem Boards

The fax machine is a vital home-office item. There are essentially two options for fax technology. The first option is to purchase an external machine that allows you to fax paper documents, photos, drawings, and any other kind of preprinted material. You can buy a unit that only faxes or a multifunction machine that not only faxes but also serves as a copier and/ or printer and perhaps a scanner too. The other option is a fax "board" that sits inside your computer's motherboard and is controlled by your computer. The advantage of an internal fax board is that you can type a document on your word processor and fax it directly from your computer without printing it out. You can also receive a document directly into your computer when the fax board is connected to your phone line. The disadvantage of an internal fax board is that you cannot fax a printed item you haven't created in your computer, such as a newspaper article that you might have clipped or a hard-copy invoice, without first scanning the item into your computer with a scanner.

Some people have both kinds of fax options, using the internal board to fax documents they've created themselves on their computer and the external machine to send and receive all other documents. Since a fax board is often combined with a modem, it's an easy and inexpensive way to supplement an external fax machine.

Printers and Multifunction Devices

If you regularly need to print, copy, scan, and fax, you should consider a multifunction machine that combines all these functions. Canon, Hewlett-Packard, Lexmark, and other manufacturers offer a variety of multifunction printers. There is a wide variety of different models with different capabilities available. Because technology is improving all the time and pricing is changing, too, we recommend that you visit your retailer to find out which model suits your needs and pocketbook.

Scanner: A scanner is useful if you are working in any field related to desktop publishing, Web design, graphics, or other businesses in which you may need to use preprinted materials in your documents. If you intend to produce a newsletter or maintain a Web site as a marketing tool for your business, you also might want to invest in a scanner. With OCR (optical character recognition) software getting better all the time, any business should consider the purchase of a scanner. OCR software allows you to scan documents, such as incoming invoices, business correspondence, contracts, etc., into your computer where you store them as database entries or word-processing documents and can simplify your accounting and filing procedures. Scanners vary considerably in terms of capability and price, but any business that deals with printed material as its final product, such as graphic designers and desktop publishers, will need flatbed scanners with the highest resolutions that scan in color. Web designers and multimedia and desktop-video professionals typically don't require as high a resolution.

PhotoCopier: Some home offices can benefit greatly from having a small copier or personal copy machine. If you end up going to a copy store every few days and wasting two to three hours per week in traffic and waiting for your copies, a copy machine pays for itself in just a few months.

Modems: For any computer-based home business, a connection to the Internet is a vital link to the valuable resources of online information. You can get cable modems or modems that use dedicated digital telephone lines that let you communicate at warp speed. Modems can be internal and fit inside the computer or external and therefore more portable and easier to share with another computer. Modems, like everything in the world of computers, change and evolve. Depending on what services are available in your area you can choose to connect to the Internet via a cable modem or via a dial-up telephone line. Contact your Internet service provider to find out what equipment you need to use their services.

Telephone System, Answering Machine, and Voice Mail and Computer Telephony: We will discuss telephone systems, including voice mail and computer telephony, in greater detail in Part 3.5. We believe strongly, though, that professional telephone hardware and components are critical to the success of a home-based business. From maintaining a separate line for your business to having a high-quality answering system for calls while you are away, and having a separate line for fax and modem, your phone system is an important link in your business.

Putting together the Pieces . . . : You can buy a computer preassembled as a package or as separate components that you install yourself. Unless you have experience working with computer hardware and are comfortable building your own system, purchase your equipment from a reliable source. But what source? Should you buy from a department store, a "big box" warehouse, a specialty computer store, or even from an online computer store?

Buying from a department store or warehouse means that you get "bundled" systems that often include a selection of popular software as well as the various hardware components. Big department stores are usually very good at customer service and the price points are attractive, but often the sales staff is not knowledgeable about what they are selling. Then there are the warehouses. These can be excellent places to buy peripherals and various components such as a pair of speakers, a modem, video cards, etc. You can also get good deals on bundled systems, but the personnel are often as uninformed as in the department stores. If you know exactly what you are looking for and are only shopping for price and the ability to return defective and/or unsuitable items, the warehouse stores can be a good choice.

In the smaller computer specialty stores you'll get more knowledgeable staff, though not necessarily a large selection or price. As with any small business, the salespeople usually know a lot about their product and will bend over backwards to help you. Often these small shops can match or beat the big stores' prices. Even if they can't quite match the big guys' prices, they usually make it up in other ways, such as after-sale support and service. You'll want to make sure that if you shop the "little guy" that they have been in business awhile and have a good track record.

Protecting Yourself from the Computer's Occupational Hazards

Unfortunately, using a computer can be hazardous to your health. While millions of people use their computers without noticeable distress, others suffer from eyestrain, headaches, backaches, skin rashes, problems with fatigue and concentration and, most seriously, repetitive-motion injuries. Luckily, most of these ills can be prevented or reversed if caught early enough.

Here are the key problems to be alert to. Remember, unlike in a company where an employer is concerned about health-insurance claims, worker-compensation costs, and OSHA requirements, the only person caring for you is you.

Carpal Tunnel Syndrome (CTS): Carpal tunnel syndrome is common among computer keyboard users. It can strike anyone, and its consequences are serious. The most common cause of CTS among computer users is repetitive motion. When you flex your hand or fingers the flexor tendons rub against the walls of the carpal tunnel. If you allow your hand time to recover, this rubbing is not likely to lead to irritation. The amount of recovery time you need varies from fractions of a second to minutes, depending on many circumstances, including genetic and health factors, as well as the intensity of the flexing and the extent to which you bend your wrist during flexing. Awareness of the problem and its causes is crucial to preventing CTS. With proper ergonomics you can help prevent it, and with early detection and treatment it need never become debilitating. The first step to prevention is to work at a desk that enables your keyboard to be between twenty-three and twenty-eight inches high. Ways to get your keyboard at the right height include placing it on an extension arm extending from your desk or putting it on your lap resting on a keyboard pillow or wrist-support pad.

You can take several other steps to lower your chances of developing CTS. Some of these steps center on the configuration of the workplace, or "ergonomics." Others have to do with human factors. Proper seating is important to good ergonomics. The height of your seat and the position of your backrest should be adjustable. The chair should be on wheels so you can move it easily. Armrests on the chair, though optional, are often helpful. Consider the following:

Table Height: To make sure your chair is adjusted properly, you need to check the height of the table or desk surface that your keyboard rests on. On the average, a height of twenty-seven to twenty-nine inches above the floor is recommended. Taller people will prefer slightly higher tables than do shorter people. If you can adjust your table, set your waist angle at

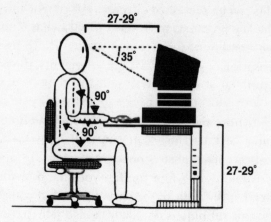

ninety degrees, then adjust your table so that your elbow makes a ninety-degree angle when your hands are on the keyboard.

Wrist Angle: A keyboard that requires you to bend your wrists is a common cause of CTS. When your keyboard is in the correct position, your wrists should rest comfortably on the table in front of it. Some keyboards are very thick, and this means that you have to bend your hands uncomfortably upward to reach the keys. Placing a raised wrist rest on the table in front of the keyboard will help.

Elbow Angle: With your hands resting comfortably at the keyboard and your upper arms vertical, measure the angle between your forearm and your upper arm (the elbow angle). If it is less than ninety degrees, raise the seat of your chair. If the angle is greater than ninety degrees, lower the seat. Try to hold your elbows close to your sides to minimize bending your wrists sideways, as when reaching for the Z key.

Waist Angle: With your elbow angle at ninety degrees, measure the angle between your upper legs and your spine (the waist angle). This, too, should be about ninety degrees. If it is less than ninety degrees, your chair may be too low (and your knees too high). Otherwise, you may need to alter the position of the backrest or adjust your own posture by sitting up straight. (**Note:** If making your waist angle ninety degrees changes your elbow angle, you may need to readjust the height of your chair or table.)

Feet: With your elbows and waist at ninety-degree angles, your feet should rest comfortably flat on the floor. If they don't, adjust your chair and table height and repeat the steps above. If your table isn't adjustable and your feet don't comfortably reach the floor, a raised footrest can help. Otherwise, you should consider a different table.

Backaches: Your chair and desk are keys to avoiding back problems. Your chair needs to provide good low-back support, and it should have an adjustable seat. More expensive chairs have armrests that are adjustable. A chair should also have five legs for greater stability. Your desk needs to provide you with adequate clearance for your knees.

Eyestrain, Blurred Vision, and Headaches: To avoid eye problems, first pay attention to the positioning of your monitor so that light sources are not producing glare and reflections. If your monitor does not have a built-in antiglare filter, you can add one or use a visorlike hood on your monitor that will protect against glare from overhead lighting. Indirect lighting is usually best, however.

Full-spectrum compact fluorescent lights and incandescent bulbs made with neodymium relieve eyestrain by being more like natural outdoor light and save on energy, too. Also, do not face an unshaded window because the difference in brightness between your screen and the window will be uncomfortable.

The center of the screen should be level with your eyes to twenty degrees below eye level. If you wear glasses, you may need a prescription that is adjusted for the distance to your screen. Make sure that your glasses, particularly bifocals, don't cause you to tilt your head into an uncomfortable position. If your eyes feel dry, blink often because staring at a computer monitor causes us to open our eyes more widely and to blink less frequently. It's also important to take frequent breaks.

Electronic Magnetic Radiation (EMR): The harmfulness of electromagnetic radiation is still being debated. By staying eighteen to twenty-eight inches away from your monitor, however, you can avoid the most potentially harmful rays. Be aware, too, that monitors vary in the amount of EMR they transmit, so it's wise to consider the EMR rating in choosing a monitor. Computer radiation filters that you just hang over your computer screen can be purchased from retailers that sell computers. They block out or reduce exposure to a very low level. They also reduce eyestrain and fatigue.

First, a Word About Software Suites

On the following pages we will discuss how computers and computer software can make your life easier as a home-based business person. We've identified four major aspects of doing business in which computer technology can be of greatest help: Money Management, Administrivia (we'll define this term in Part 3.4), Marketing and Promotions, and Communications.

We're not the first to have delineated these aspects of doing business. Corporate giants like Microsoft have identified the same basic needs. Their way of addressing these needs has been to bundle software applications into "suites." Typically, a suite of products includes a word-processing program, a presentation or graphics program, a spreadsheet program, and a database-management program. Sometimes other smaller programs are included as well. Suites generally come in two levels: a higher-end one for business and a more consumer-oriented lower end. For example, Microsoft offers the *Microsoft Works* suite as their consumer-oriented package and *Microsoft Office*, in its several editions, as their higher-end package. Lower-end suites usually contain scaled-back versions. For example, the word-processing program contained in the *Microsoft Works* suite is not as powerful as the full version of *Microsoft Word*, which is offered in the higher-end editions of *Microsoft Office*.

Suites generally include a "shell" program that allows documents and data created in one program to be seamlessly imported to another. For example, you can enter a client's address into a suite's database program. If you need to send the client some correspondence, you can import his or her address directly into the word processor, where it can be used in the letterhead and printed on the envelope so you won't have to retype it. The address and other data on the client can also be used in your spreadsheet program for billing, job tracking, etc. There are countless other time-saving scenarios.

For the remainder of Part 3, we will focus on the four areas of doing business where your computer will be of greatest help. These pages will be equally helpful whether you use individual software programs to help you in each of these areas or if you use a suite of programs.

3.2: Using Your Computer to Manage Your Money

One of the things that people fear most when they think about becoming their own boss is looking after the finances of their business. Many people don't enjoy this activity and are concerned about their ability to do it well. Unfortunately, some home businesses fail or their owners struggle needlessly because they don't know how to handle the financial aspects of their businesses. Studies that identify the reasons for small-business failures reveal that while some problems are caused by inadequate planning, frequently it is how people manage their money in business that is a major factor, including:

taking on too much debt
poor budgeting
bad cash management
taking too much money out of the business
confusing net income with cash flow
not keeping up with billings, and
errors in paying one's own bills.

One of your computer's most valuable assets is the ability to help you organize, manage, and otherwise run the financial aspects of your business. With the right computer software you can avoid all these problems and many more with surprisingly little effort on your part.

Finding a Simple Way to Manage Your Money

Problem
Basically there are only five financial tasks most home-based businesses need to accomplish when it comes to managing their money:

1. figuring out how much money to charge for your product and service
2. keeping track of your income and how much you spend each month
3. analyzing your profitability and seeing what products or services produce the most income
4. keeping track of your invoices and making sure your customers pay you on time
5. keeping sufficient records to pay your estimated and year-end taxes accurately and on time while claiming all the deductions that you are entitled to

Computer Solutions

In most cases, your computer can help you carry out these five financial tasks quickly, easily, and accurately. In fact, you can choose from a variety of software that is designed to help you perform your own financial record keeping, estimating, and analysis. With the huge variety of accounting software that's available on the market today, it's important that you choose a program that's right for your business needs. Here are some things to consider:

Suitability: Out-of-the-box accounting software is most suitable for small businesses that have standard accounting needs. If your business needs unique data reports, make sure the accounting software you choose offers customizable reports. If you run a service-related business, you may need a features such as time and billing modules.

Ease of Use: Does the accounting software allow you to print or electronically send checks, purchase orders, and invoices? Does it have Internet connectivity so you can bank online? Is it integrated with other software that you use, such as Microsoft *Office*? Is it able to convert data from other accounting programs or databases? In other words, will the accounting software be able to meet all your needs, now and in the future?

Learning Curve: Although all accounting software claims to be user friendly, you'll still need to take some time to learn how to use it. Take a close look at the accounting software before you buy it. Many trial or evaluation programs are available online so that you can test out the software. Is the user interface intuitive and comfortable? Will you be able to sit down and learn it on your own, or will you need further training (which means an additional investment)?

Support: Online help comes with most software applications and is an important feature. Does the accounting software include features such as screen tips, a searchable help index, and demos, to get you started? Are there print and online manuals available? And how accessible are the company's technical-support people?

While there is a mind-boggling variety of products to choose from, here is an overview of some of the most popular packages:

Microsoft Money Small Business: *Microsoft Money Small Business* enables you to use one program to manage both business and personal finances. It is integrated with Microsoft Outlook and a "Business Resource Center" on the Web and facilitates invoicing by e-mail. See *www.microsoft.com*.

Quicken *Premier Home & Business*: With Intuit's Quicken® *Premier Home & Business* you can get an instant overview of your business and see everything in one place, including unpaid invoices, upcoming bills, accounts receivable, and more. You can track multiple jobs, send out customized invoices, track your taxes, and generate business reports. At this writing, the *Home and Business* edition comes only in a Windows version.

Quickbooks®: Intuit's *Quickbooks*® is a popular family of accounting and payroll programs designed for small business. *Quickbooks*® is available in several editions including, Simple Start, Basic, Online, Pro, and Premier. The Premier edition includes management and planning tools such as building a business plan based on your finances and a financial analyzer. *QuickBooks*® *Simple Start* is an easy-to-use program specifically designed for first-time users of business-management software. It includes a tutorial on how to use the software and is very intuitive. For more information see *www.quickbooks.intuit.com*.

Peachtree Complete Accounting Software: Peachtree offers a range of accounting software products for small businesses. For home businesses with basic accounting needs *First Accounting* provides fast start-up, easy invoicing, convenient check writing, and over thirty-five customizable reports. For information about Peachtree products, see *www.peachtree.com*.

Determining What You Need to Charge and How Much Business You Need to Generate

The Problem

No doubt you know or can calculate how much money you need to bring in to support yourself and your family. For many it is more difficult to figure out how much you should charge and how much business you actually must generate each month to meet your income needs after paying your expenses and other costs involved in getting and doing business. If you have been used to living on a salary, you probably haven't had to make such projections. It doesn't take long to realize that because you have to

Basically there are two methods of accounting and two methods of bookkeeping. Each meets different needs. Here's an overview of all four.

Two Accounting Methods

Accounting is essentially a process of determining and demonstrating the financial health of your business. There are two basic methods for doing this: accrual basis and cash basis.

Accrual Basis: In accrual-based accounting, income is recorded when a service is performed or when a product is sold, regardless of when the cash is received or paid. So, in using this method, if you perform a job today and mail out your invoice, you have "received" income even though you didn't get the money yet. Similarly, an expense is logged when services or goods are purchased, not when you actually pay for them. Accrual-based accounting is most frequently used by companies that have inventories because it allows them to manage their accounts better and recognize income and expenses on a timelier basis.

Cash Basis: In cash-basis accounting, income is recorded when you get paid, and expenses are incurred when you write a check or pay cash for them. Do not confuse cash basis, however, with paying in cash; you can still write checks or use credit cards when using a cash-basis system. The terminology has to do with the method of accounting, not the method of payment. Cash-basis accounting is generally the preferred method for home businesses, since they seldom have extensive inventories or employees, and usually their financial picture is most accurately determined from the balance of money that has come in and gone out rather than what's been billed or acquired.

Two Bookkeeping Methods

Bookkeeping is basically a method of recording information about your business's financial situation, and as such it is secondary to accounting. That is, first you choose the accounting method by which you want to demonstrate the value of your company; then you pick the method by which you will record the information. As with accounting, there are also two basic bookkeeping methods.

Double Entry: In using double-entry bookkeeping, there are dozens of accounts on which the business keeps separate records, and each account uses a two-sided grid as shown here:

debit | credit

For every transaction, you always need to log two accounts, with one recorded as a debit and the other as a credit. This is why the bookkeeping method is called double entry, and why the method is preferred for reducing errors and making sure that everything always balances out. What makes double-entry accounting confusing is that sometimes a debit is an increase and sometimes it is a decrease; similarly, sometimes a credit to an account is an increase and sometimes a decrease, depending on whether the account is an asset, a liability, or an owner's equity account. Programs like *QuickBooks* simplify this, using positive and negative numbers in Amount columns.

Double-entry bookkeeping is useful because it makes it easier to track mistakes. It also works better with the accrual-accounting method in which businesses are usually tracking their assets, liabilities, and equity in great detail to portray what they own, what they owe, and various intangibles such as depreciation, deferred charges, and goodwill. Double-entry bookkeeping can become quite complex, however, and can take a lot of time to learn and master. For this reason, most home businesses prefer the single-entry method.

Single Entry: In using single-entry bookkeeping, you only need to log each transaction of income or expense once, in the way *Quicken* and other check-writing software programs work. A transaction in this method is simply an increase or a decrease in one main cash account that you maintain. You do not track corollary accounts for the company's assets or liabilities. For example, if you were to buy inventory, you only record a payment to the vendor as an expense. You don't record both a payment to the vendor and an increase in the inventory asset account, as you would in a double-entry system. Single-entry methods are therefore most appropriate for small service businesses in which your primary objective is to track cash flow, not assets and liabilities of the company like inventory or debt.

Errors inevitably develop in a single-entry system, however, because even the most careful person makes mistakes, so it's important to reconcile a single-entry system regularly.

Congratulations on completing Accounting 101! In a nutshell, if you are like the owners of most home-based businesses, you can restrict yourself to using cash-basis accounting with a single-entry bookkeeping system—and this is all you really need to understand.

spend money to make money, too often it's your living expenses that come up short.

Computer Solution

You can use your computer to prepare a budget that will help project how much you need to charge and how much business you need to generate. Using a computer to calculate expected income and expenses saves a lot of time in recalculating your projections and will actually make your budget projections more accurate.

Most programs like *Quicken* or *Microsoft Money* have budgeting capabilities that help you make the projections you need. In general, begin by identifying the recurring expenses you anticipate and establish a category for each type, such as those we listed on pages 205–206 in Part 2 (salary, travel, office supplies, phone, insurance, and so on). *Quicken* and other similar programs make this easy because they have predefined categories for common businesses expenses. You simply check them off to include in your budget, or you can add your own categories if you have special expenses. When preparing your budget, be sure to include all three classes of expenses we mentioned in Part 2: your personal living expenses, your direct costs, and your overhead. We find that many home businesses do not account fully for their overhead expenses when setting their prices or fees, and that's why they may be working long hours but not making enough money.

Once you have selected your categories, you can estimate the amount of money you believe you need to spend each month in each category. The software will tally the numbers for you and give you a total budgeted expenditure. This is the amount you need to make that month to pay for your supplies, your overhead, and your salary.

Then, if you are trying to determine how much to charge per hour for your services, you simply take the total amount from your budget and divide it by how many hours you expect to bill that month. The result is equal to how much per hour you should charge. For example, if you add up all your costs and see that you will spend $4,000 per month including your salary, direct costs, and overhead, and you know you have to charge around $40 per hour to be competitive, it follows that you will have to bill out one hundred hours to generate sufficient income. You can then develop your marketing efforts accordingly.

We realize that sometimes new businesses must accept whatever work they can generate or accept a smaller fee than they'd like to, at least in the beginning. So, of course, your budget is simply a "projection." However, a budget of estimated income and expenses benefits you in three ways:

1. The numbers you derive are useful in giving you a realistic idea of how much to bid on a job.
2. Budget projections give you a clear target to aim for. You can use them to motivate yourself to keep marketing aggressively until you have all the clients you need to cover your projections. Without budget projections, it's too easy to lull ourselves into thinking "Well, I'm busy so I must be doing okay."
3. Budget projections provide a barometer to measure your progress and evaluate how close you are to achieving your goals.

You may want to perform more sophisticated analyses on your budget projections than check-writing programs like *Quicken* or *Microsoft Money* allow for. For example, perhaps you want to see what would happen to your budget if you doubled your expenditures on advertising. Could you increase your billable hours by thirty? Such "what if" scenarios are more easily handled by spreadsheet programs like Microsoft's *Excel*. A spreadsheet program allows you to examine many different options at the same time. These programs are quite easy to learn to use; often they incorporate an internal "intelligence" that does some of the work for you. For instance, in some programs, when you type "January" in the first space of a row, the program automatically types in the remaining months in the rest of the row.

Once you've used a spreadsheet to project various scenarios and selected your optimal projections, you can put the final data back into a budget in your program to track actual income and expenditures against your projections.

☞ **ALERT** ☜

Be conservative in estimating the number of hours you will be able to bill. Many consultants, professionals, and technical people, working fifty to sixty hours per week, will only be able to bill twenty to thirty hours each week. Marketing and managing a business take time!

Keeping Track of Your Money

The Problem

Many home businesses operate essentially with their bank statement as the only source of information about where they stand financially. In some cases (although we recommend against it), the home-business owner has not even set up a separate business bank account for his or her company. Instead he or she mixes his or her personal checking and savings with the money from the business. In either case, the bank statement provides little useful information about how your business is really doing. Without additional information, you may find yourself making decisions in the dark and end up in debt or having to put off making purchases that would actually increase your income because you may assume that you can't afford it.

Computer Solutions

By using programs such as *Quickbooks® Simple Start*, *Quicken*, *Microsoft Money*, or a general ledger or spreadsheet program, you can monitor your financial situation in much greater detail than a bank statement can provide. In fact, by having identified categories for your projected income (e.g., types of projects, services, or clients) and expenses (e.g., marketing costs, insurance costs, etc.) when making out your budget, you have already done half the work of tracking your money.

From that point on, all you need to do when recording your income or paying your bills is to indicate which categories each deposit or payment applies to as you enter it in your check register. Then at month's end, the software can generate and print out a report that clearly shows where you made your money and where you spent it, category by category. Some programs also allow you to establish subcategories for even more precise information such as tracking income or expenses by client name. You can generate a printout to compare your projection in each category against your actual income and expenses as well. You can also graphically display how well you did, where you may need to cut back, and where you could expand.

By creating a report of your income and expenses in this fashion, you are, in effect, examining your "cash flow," that is, how much is coming in versus how much is going out. This computerized record provides useful history that you can call upon when bidding on projects or making estimates for a flat fee. You no longer have to rely on guesstimates or intuition to estimate your costs, thus assuring that your projects are profitable.

Such information can also help you make a case for turning down business that won't be profitable.

Once you are in the habit of recording your finances, you can easily move on to preparing the many other kinds of reports that most financial software programs will do. For example, you can create reports that account for all the invoices you have sent out—that is, your accounts receivable—and track how long it takes to get them paid. Most of the software packages we discussed can create and print out account-receivable reports that are formatted either by client or by date showing which accounts are thirty, sixty, and ninety days overdue. And should you need one, you can also generate a "balance sheet," which shows your company's assets, liabilities, and owner's equity.

All these programs can create charts and graphs that let you plot your data in various ways. You can also export your data to a spreadsheet program that has a graphics module. Seeing where you are making money and where you are losing money on a bar graph helps you to see patterns in your business, such as recurring seasonal downturns or relying too heavily on one client. It can also help you in making wise tax-planning decisions.

Analyzing Your Profitability

The Problem

Most home businesses operate with limited resources. You have only so many hours you can bill out; you can charge only so much to still be competitive; and you have only so much money to spend for equipment, marketing, and other aspects of running your business. Many of us end up spending most of our time, money, and energy on activities that are not necessarily the ones that give us the best results. We get bogged down responding to the most bothersome clients, trying to break into the most difficult-to-penetrate fields, or going after the most complex projects. The truth is that often 20 percent of your clients generate 80 percent of your money, or 20 percent of your services will produce 80 percent of your income, or 20 percent of your marketing expenditures bring in 80 percent of your clients. This is known as the Eighty/Twenty Rule at work.

How do you know where to direct your time, energy, and resources to get the best results? For example, should you take the time to submit a complex proposal for a shot at a big contract or would it be better to devote more time to your existing smaller, ongoing clients? Is it better to attend the upcoming national conference in your field or upgrade your laser printer? These are the kinds of strategic decisions that challenge us all day in and day out.

Computer Solutions

Computerizing your finances means that you can analyze the profitability of various activities and more easily correlate your efforts with what actually produces your income. When you track your hours and expenses and compare them to your income, you can recognize if you have fallen prey to the Eighty/Twenty Rule and then redirect your energies at once. For example, you can determine if the time you spend on a particular project is worth the fee you are charging, and whether the time and money you are putting into a particular marketing activity is paying off.

Good time-tracking software pays for itself. Being able to precisely track the time you spend on projects allows you to manage your time more efficiently. Here is an overview of time-tracking software programs that are also easy to learn and use, and also include reporting and billing features. Generally, you can download trial versions or view demos of the software at the vendor's Web site.

TimeSlips: *TimeSlips,* by Best Software, is a well-established program that has a user-friendly interface. Tracking time and expenses is a simple process. You can use the stopwatch timer to track your activities or simply enter all your time at once. A unique "Slip List" displays your work in one location with totals and includes only the users, clients, and date ranges that you specify. *TimeSlips* also offers capabilities for printing bills. The accounts-receivable module included allows you to quickly and easily enter bill payments and other transactions such as write-offs, credits, refunds, and funds transfers. It contains over 100 predefined reports and includes the ability to create custom reports and graphs. For more information see *www.timeslips.com/products/summary/default.asp.*

Track-IT light: *Track-IT light* time-tracking software from Dovico has excellent features and is relatively inexpensive. The program allows many types of time entry; handles multiple projects; and lets you create a variety of reports for employee productivity, invoicing, and also expenses. It produces invoices, too, and allows data to be exported in a variety of formats. For more information, see *http:www.dovico.com/time_and_attendance.html.*

Project Clock™: *Project Clock™* is a project time entry system by CyberMatrix Corporation. *Project Clock™* is useful for anyone who needs to record time billed to different projects. It has custom reporting and time-sheet entry features. It is also an easy-to-use time-tracking and billing system with invoicing and expense-management features. Data can be exported for use with other programs to create customized reports. You can access it over the Internet. For more information see *www.cyber-matrix.com*.

TraxTime: *TraxTime*, by Spud City Software Co., is inexpensive, can handle unlimited projects, and has a punch clock metaphor that makes it easy to use. You can also append memos to the time entries and create customized reports. For more information, see *www.spudcity.com/traxtime/traxtime.htm*.

Responsive *Time Logger:* Responsive Software's *Time Logger* lets you track your time while you're working. You can customize reports on-screen by dragging and dropping, use time-record data in other applications, customize invoices, and track expenses. For more information see *www. responsivesoftware.com*.

TimeWriter: XSO's *TimeWriter's* entry screen is a weekly grid that displays one week of hour entries at a single glance. This makes it easy to enter hours worked quickly. Data can be exported in a variety of formats. This time tracking program has more administrative features than some other single-use programs. For more information, see *www.timewriter.com/en/ index.php*.

Programs like *Quicken* and *QuickBooks* can also be useful in helping you to analyze your profitability. For example, once you define your income and expense categories (for example, type of client, type of expense), you can have *Quicken* print a Project or Client report that compares your income and expenses across all categories for both clients and projects. This information readily tells you the extent to which one project is worth more to you than others.

Let's say, for example, that it's time to renew your membership in a professional association and you must decide whether to rejoin or to use the $400 you would spend on your membership to expand your newsletter mailings. On the one hand, the phone always rings with new clients after your newsletter goes out and, on the other hand, you can't remember getting many new clients from networking at the association meetings. So you are leaning toward postponing or dropping the membership in favor of sending your newsletter to a larger mailing list. But by printing out a report of the sources of your income over the last year and another report of your marketing expenditures, you can find out which activity is really paying off. You could discover that while the newsletter brought in more clients, the clients you got through referrals from the association brought in larger sums and did more repeat business. In other words, the newsletter could actually cost more to produce per-client dollar than the dues for the professional association.

Or, let's say that you attend four trade shows every year because industry wisdom has it that "everyone needs to be at these shows." By analyzing the business produced from each show, however, you might learn that two of the shows have never actually paid for themselves. You decide to cut back to only the two shows that are producing results.

Making Sure You Get Paid

The Problem

Home-based business owners, especially new ones, may have to wait sixty or ninety days or even longer to get paid. If your clients are large corporations that have long payment cycles, this is often the case. Even for home businesses with a track record, being a small sole proprietor can mean your invoices end up low on the priority list for getting paid. Unless you stay on top of your invoices you can spend hours on the phone tracking down your hard-earned money. Getting paid ends up costing you money because you have to waste so much time finding out what's holding up the money you've already earned.

Computer Solutions

To get paid promptly it's important to invoice your customers as soon as you finish a job or can bill a partial fee. Your clients will take your invoice seriously if you use a professional-looking one that commands immediate attention. Your computer can help you to keep track of billable time for each client as each job progresses. With a notebook computer you can even bill your invoices in the field by recording expenses as they occur.

Invoice Details: An invoice not only tells your customer how much money is due but also details tax information. Both you and your customers need to be able to keep track of the amount of taxes paid or owed. A basic invoice should include the following information:

- Your business name
- Invoice date

- Business number (if applicable)
- Purchaser or customer's name
- Description of the goods or services performed
- Total amount of goods delivered or services performed
- Indication of taxable items or services
- Total amount of taxes payable
- Terms of payment

Note: Avoid using phrases like "Payable upon receipt" or "Due within thirty days." You don't necessarily know when your customer is seeing the invoice—even if you e-mailed it. All the invoices you send out should state a specific expected date of payment, such as "Due on November 6, 2005." Clients are more likely to pay attention to a specific payment date, and it eliminates the possibility of any misunderstanding. You can encourage prompt payment by offering an incentive to pay on time. Many businesses, for example, offer a discount for paying within ten days of an invoice date. A discount of 2 percent for payment within ten days is common.

The accounting software programs we discussed previously in "Finding a Simple Way to Manage Your Money" can generate your invoices for you. You can also purchase software designed specifically for invoicing. For example, programs like *Invoice2go* (*www.invoice2go.com*) and *Quick Invoice* (*www.quick-invoice.com*) are simple to use and create professional-looking results.

Quickbooks Pro's time-tracking feature alerts you when an invoice due date arrives so that you can follow up on overdue accounts. For customers who say they can't find your invoice you can instantly e-mail or fax them another one. In fact, you can e-mail or fax a second copy of any overdue invoice with a polite reminder.

It's a good idea to have templates for a series of collection letters that are progressively more firm. You can quickly customize them as the need arises. Such repetitive reminders serve to let the client know that you mean business. Software programs like *3001 Business and Sales Letters,* by Write Express™ (*www.writeexpress.com/sales-letters.html*), provide samples of collection letters (as well as many other types) that you can modify for your own use. You can also use your computer to access online databases that can help you find out about the financial stability of prospective clients and those who owe you money (see Section 3.5 in Part 3).

Preparing Estimated and Year-End Taxes

The Problem

Tax preparation can be time-consuming and frustrating when you're busy focusing on getting business and serving your clients and customers. But every quarter, you must take time out to calculate how much your net income has been over the past three months and pay your estimated taxes. And, of course, you must take out time once again to tally your year-end totals and prepare your final tax return. You could end up working several days for the IRS or alternatively having to pay an accountant thousands of dollars of your hard-earned money to do it for you. If you don't keep track of your taxes throughout the year, it will take even more time at tax-filing time to get everything ready. And, if you should happen to be audited and have to document everything for the IRS, even more time is involved!

Computer Solutions

Preparing your taxes is one of the best reasons to use a bookkeeping and financial record-keeping program. Most of the programs described earlier make preparing your taxes almost routine. When you set up your business categories, you can tailor them to correspond with IRS Schedule C for businesses and log your actual expenses and income throughout the year by category. Thus, you can lay the groundwork for quickly preparing your taxes.

Many of the financial record-keeping programs allow you to export your data directly to tax-preparation software such as *TurboTax*, by Intuit. If, in addition to entering expenses you've paid by check, you enter deductible expenses paid in cash or with a charge card, the export procedure practically wraps up your taxes. All you need to do is write a check. If you prefer, you can print out reports in conjunction with doing either quarterly estimates or year-end summaries, and then prepare your taxes by hand or give them to your accountant. In either case, by using a tax program you save a lot of time and may be able to save money on the amount of professional tax-preparation help you need.

No matter how computerized you become, remember that the expenses you deduct must be ones that are acceptable to the IRS, and since computer entries can be altered, you still must maintain a paper trail of all your receipts and other transactions.

3.3: Computerizing Your Administrivia

Most home-business owners dislike "administrivia." That includes filing, record keeping, scheduling, keeping track of appointments, deadlines, names, phone numbers, e-mail, notes and project details, making copies and getting things into the mail—the list seems endless—all the little detailed, repetitive things that someone has to take care of. Unfortunately, chances are that the only person who can do them now that you're on your own is YOU.

The amount of administrative tasks involved takes many home business owners by surprise at first. If you worked in an organization with administrative support staff, you relied on others to take care of things that might become time-consuming roadblocks to getting your work done. Things like creating and sending letters or making appointments to meet with clients . . . all these previously simple tasks could devour our days.

Today most of the tasks that slow us down can be streamlined by computer, fax, online connections, printers, copy machines, telephone, and other home-office technology. With today's constantly changing and improving technology we can get many of these administrative tasks done with the ease and speed of a well-trained staff. No longer do you have to run out to the paper store: You can go to a Web site, order online and have what you need delivered by mail or courier. You no longer have to hand-address mail or even feed envelopes into your printer: One press of a button, and the computer feeds in and prints out envelopes or mailing labels.

By taking advantage of the many administrative tasks the computer can handle, you free up hours and even days each month for income-producing activities instead of spending your time bogged down in administrative chores you don't enjoy anyway. In this part we'll address how you can use your computer to streamline four of the most time-consuming and frustrating types of administrivia that we all face.

Organizing Tasks and Responsibilities

The Problem

In the hustle and bustle of operating a one- or two-person business, it's easy to feel overwhelmed as you try to keep up with the many demands of a given day. You may be trying to finish a project while responding to incoming calls, or trying to make a key marketing arrangement while dealing with an emergency with a new client—all right at the time when your estimated taxes are due and your new printer is being delivered.

Somehow, you often wish you could be more productive and better organized. You know that if you were more on top of things you could not only get more business but also do it more efficiently and have more time left over to play. Sometimes, of course, procrastination or too many distractions and interruptions keep us from being more productive, but more frequently it's a matter of simply having too much information to track and too many priorities to handle. Organizing these tasks and responsibilities is a perennial problem even for the most dedicated and committed home-business owner.

Computer Solutions

Fortunately, many software programs are directly aimed at helping people better manage their time and information. Depending on your needs, you can select from a variety of calendar and appointment-tracking programs or from more robust "personal information managers" (PIMs). Here's a brief description of these two types of technologies and how they can help take the hassles out of your day.

Everyday Essentials for Managing Information in Your Computer

If there's one housekeeping program we can't do without, it's *Windows Explorer* and for Mac users, *Mac Explorer.* Randy Caruso describes *Windows/ Mac Explorer* as being as important to managing the information in your computer as Internet Explorer (or whatever browser you're using) is to navigating the Web.

You can bring up *Windows Explorer* simply by pressing your Windows key + E. We keep *Windows Explorer* on our Start menu and run it constantly. It's the program for creating new folders and for reorganizing your files much more easily than it is to reorganize paper files. When a project grows too large, you can create new folders.

A question people frequently ask Caruso is "How many folders can I create on my computer and where?" The answer is: As many as it takes. We have literally hundreds, and using the file-finding capability (Windows Key + F), we can identify even "lost "information with a minimum of grief. When you want to back up an important file, just grab that one first folder you created and copy to another folder, or a disk, another drive or another device—wherever you want.

A program for managing any kind of information—such as e-mail, research notes, name and addresses, virtually anything—is *askSam,* a free-form database without peer in the view of its enthusiastic users.

MindManager (*www.Mindjet.com*) and *ResultsManager* (*Gyronix.com*) are programs that enable you to use mind-mapping technology to keep track of your world. *Personal Brain* (*TheBrain.com*) and *Grokker* (*Groxis.com*) are programs that also take visual approaches to organizing information, such as that collected from Web searches. For written guidance on organzing your office, *Winning the Paper Chase,* by David Lam (Joy Life, ISBN: 0974119768), is a helpful resource.

For viewing files people send you that your software doesn't recognize, *DiskJockey File Viewer* handles this source of frustration. It is also a Zip tool, encryption utility, and file manager.

Calendar and Appointment Programs: These programs are particularly useful if you want to automate your calendar, appointment schedule, and address book. They have a wide variety of features ranging in complexity from simple to highly sophisticated.

Microsoft's *Outlook,* for example, not only can manage and organize e-mail messages but also help you to schedule tasks and organize notes, contacts, and other information. Plus, it can work in conjunction with other programs in the Microsoft *Office System.* (**Note:** Microsoft *Outlook Express* is included as part of Microsoft's *Internet Explorer* and *Windows* operating system and is a basic e-mail program. *Outlook Express* allows you to send and receive e-mail messages, but it doesn't provide the advanced functionality of Microsoft Office *Outlook.*) Lotus *Organizer* is an electronic day planner with tabs for each section and pages that turn. You can use it to set up appointments, track your business and personal contacts, and create to-do lists. Auto dialing is another time-saving feature. When you access a phone number in the program's address book, you can tap a key or two and the software will dial the phone number for you. You need to have a modem connected to your computer for this feature to work. You can even share calendars online to set up meetings and trade schedules through the Internet.

There are dozens of other programs that allow you to view your calendar in different ways such as two days at a time, a week at a time, a month at a time, or a whole year at a time. Many of these programs link up to database programs and address-filing programs to help keep even greater track of whom you need to see, when, and where. Some will even interface with your e-mail and send out as well as receive scheduled e-mail correspondence. Many of these programs are available to download from the Internet for free or at a small cost. One of the best places to search for a calendar program to suit your needs is at *www.tucows.com.* This Web site offers thousands of different types of programs you can download and also reviews of them.

Personal Information Managers (PIMs): PIMs are a step up from calendar and appointment programs. They typically offer more powerful features. In fact, PIMs are actually specialized database programs that let you make "records" of information far beyond simple names, numbers, appointments, and dates, although the programs have those capabilities as well. For example, with a PIM you can take lengthy notes, write personal profiles, store references to magazine articles, make lists of all kinds, and link them all together in groups so you can correlate related topics. Then, whenever you need to find something, you can search through all the information you've stored using keywords or phrases, and any record that contains those words will appear on your screen.

ECCO Pro (*www.compusol.org*) and *Time & Chaos* (*iSBiSTER International*) are examples of excellent PIMs. Most of these programs are "free-form databases," which means that you are not restricted to predefined fields for your entries. For example, with *Infoselect*, a popular program by Micrologic, you can find data in an instant, no matter where or how you entered it.

We'll also discuss a related kind of software called "contact-management programs" in the next part. Contact managers are better suited to keeping track of clients and customer contacts while PIMs are best for storing, accessing, and using information.

PDAs and Handheld PCs: One of the drawbacks to keeping your calendar, agenda, notes, etc., in your computer is that a desktop PC is a little awkward to carry to meetings. Even notebooks can be cumbersome. Personal digital assistants (commonly known as PDAs) or handheld PCs are small, fully functional computers that you can hold in one hand. They easily fit into a briefcase, purse, even a coat pocket. Information entered into a PDA can be quickly downloaded into your office computer. For example, appointments can be streamed into a calendar program, meeting notes converted into a word-processing document, and new addresses and phone numbers transferred into a database program. You can also import information the other way: from your office PC into your PDA. You can send e-mail and browse the Internet from anywhere you happen to be. A wide variety of software is available for these miniature computers.

Making Time to Do What Needs to Be Done

The Problem
Finding time to do everything that needs to be done is no less daunting than keeping track of what we need to do. We frequently have more to do than will fit into an eight-hour day. Chances are, in times like these, we either get diverted by the many administrative tasks that demand to be done, or after having ignored them long enough, we get bogged down because they haven't been addressed.

Computer Solutions
Technology is a time-saving tool when it comes to administrative matters such as typing letters, getting out a mailing, making phone calls, preparing

faxes, and so on. Here's a list of ways technology can help you save time by taking over and streamlining many common administrative tasks:

Use integrated software (suites) when you need to make intermittent use of multiple software programs. With integrated software like one of Microsoft's *Office* suites you get a word processor, a spreadsheet, presentation graphics, and a database program as well as many other modules. All these components have similar command structures and tool bars so you can learn them quickly. You also can move simply and easily from one to another and transport information or data between the various applications. (See the our introduction to suites at the beginning of Part 3.)

Find it online! No matter what you are looking for, just about any fact or product is available online. Save time by using the Internet to buy items and make reservations, or just compare prices and features before you buy. Before you look anywhere else, log on and try to find it online.

Use macros. When using a word processor, macros save time by stringing together sequences of keystrokes that can be activated by entering one short command. Each sequence—be it several words, a sentence, or a paragraph—is associated with just one or two keys that you can press to get the entire sequence. For instance, you might program your word processor so that whenever you press the Alt and C keys simultaneously, it writes out a standard closing for your letters, for example:

Sincerely,
Paul and Sarah Edwards

Automate as many functions as possible. Programs such as *AutoMate*, from Network Automation (*www.unisyn.com*), allow you to set up a schedule of tasks the program will automatically perform for you, such as backups, close routines, or other tasks you routinely do.

Use templates for standardized documents. Many programs like Microsoft *Word* have predefined templates or style sheets for business letters, faxes, memos, proposals, and more. Desktop publishing packages like Microsoft *Publisher* and Adobe *PageMaker* also have predefined templates for creating newsletters, cards, catalogs, etc. When you use one of these templates for a letter, for example, the program automatically inserts the date, sets up the "Dear . . ." salutation, lets you select from a library of names and addresses you've already keyboarded, and signs "Sincerely" and [Your Name], thereby saving you hundreds of keystrokes.

Use "wizards." A wizard, such as those that are included in Microsoft's desktop publishing program *Publisher,* helps you to quickly and effectively create professionally designed brochures, business cards, flyers, etc. You can choose from among various document designs and customize information like your business name, address, and the text you want to include.

Use the outlining feature of a word-processing program that lets you move entire sections of a report around just by moving the title associated with that section.

Use the spell checker, grammar checker, dictionary, and electronic thesaurus that come with many word processors and save time in looking up words in reference books.

Link documents if you are operating in a Windows environment. With linking, anytime you revise the numbers in one document like a spreadsheet, they can be automatically updated in your other documents like reports, overheads, or proposals that have incorporated those numbers.

Use the automatic addressing and envelope-printing utility that comes with most word-processing programs or purchase an add-on utility with additional powers like *Office Accelerator,* by Baseline Data Systems (*www.baselineconnect.com*). You'll save keystrokes since you don't have to type a name and address twice, or spend time setting up your printer for an envelope.

Use a separate label printer such as Avery's *Personal Label Printer.* These dedicated label printers also enable you to print out labels for file folders and make index tabs for proposals. If you use Microsoft *Outlook* as your e-mail program, Avery also offers their *Pro Write* software that lets you create mailing labels for your contacts in just a few clicks. You can download a trial version at *http:avery.nereosoft.com.*

Use form-design software for your standard business forms. Packages like *FormDocs* let you quickly design, fill in, print, automate, and organize the forms that your business uses. A demo version can be downloaded from *www.formdocs.com. Business-in-a-Box,* by Envision SBS, offers over 1,250 in its library of business document templates. You can download a demo at *www.envision-sbs.com.* With these programs you can print out and use these forms or you can save paper by filling them out on your computer screen, for example, while interviewing or collecting information by phone. Using electronic forms is saving some companies over 70 percent of what they would be spending to print paper forms.

E-mail documents instead of using traditional mailing, when possible. You can e-mail documents with text or graphics anywhere in the world. This saves a great deal of time and expense for approving terms and conditions on contracts, approving content for publications, and any form of business or personal correspondence. Keep in mind, though, that graphics files are considerably larger than text files and, depending on the type of Internet service, the graphics may take a very long time to download. Also, some people are limited in file space allowed by their Internet service providers and large files can be rejected.

Add an internal fax board or fax/modem so you can fax directly from your computer instead of having to print out a document and manually feed it into your fax machine.

Turn incoming faxes into text files so you can edit and revise them or capture them to use in your own documents. The technique used to accomplish this is called optical character recognition, or OCR. Programs such as *PhoneWorks Pro* enable you to easily turn your faxes into documents compatible with Microsoft *Office Word, Excel,* and other popular applications. Without this type of software, your computer simply considers a fax to be a graphic image, like a piece of art, and you cannot manipulate or edit it, or use it in a document of your own.

Use your fax machine as a copier. If you don't have a copy machine you can make one or two quick copies with your fax machine and save the time of having to run out to a copy shop. Most fax machines can make small numbers of copies with plain paper.

Speed up your printer with a print-enhancement software program like *SuperPrint*, by Zenographics (*www.zeno.com/Products/SuperPrint*).

Eliminate the need to manually load or feed envelopes, letterheads, or other special papers into your printer by investing in an envelope and/or paper feeder that will do it for you.

Use special precut and preprinted papers to speed up making indexes, printing brochures, and creating reports. Such special paper products and printing supplies are available from mail-order supply houses like Paper Direct (*www.paperdirect.com*) or in stationery stores in many metropolitan areas. See Part 3.5 for additional information on sources of specialty papers.

Back up your hard drive. You probably have all your important information stored on the hard drive of your computer. Unfortunately, you may lose that data for various reasons. For example, your hard disk can crash, catch fire, or suffer water damage, theft, electrical problems, computer viruses . . . Many things can go wrong. You need to protect yourself by

---

HERE ARE SOME BACKUP OPTIONS

- An extra hard drive or hard card can back up data several times during a day.
- USB flash drives are about the size of a car key and weigh about as much as a stick of gum. They are easy-to-use devices and store approximately 2 gigabytes of data.
- Tape drives quickly store anywhere from a few hundred kilobytes to several gigabytes. Their transfer speeds also vary considerably. Fast tape drives can transfer as much as 20MB (megabytes) per second.
- Removable drives such as Iomega's Zip Drive securely store your data magnetically. They are durable, portable, easy to use, and very efficient. One Zip 250MB disk can store the same amount of data as 173 floppy disks.
- With a CD writer, you use inexpensive CD-R (compact disk recordable) media, which offers large data storage, fairly fast access, low cost, and portability.
- Digital Versatile Disk (DVD), a writeable CD technology, allows you to store over 4.5 gigabytes on a disk.
- DAT (digital audiotape) is still another option.
- You can also still store small amounts of information on floppy disks, although some of the newest computers and notebooks no longer have diskette drives.

---

keeping a copy of your files somewhere else as well. The backup files should be stored somewhere safe, preferably in a different location. If you are the victim of fire or flood and you've stored your files in the same location, you have lost both your original and backup files.

Probably the most important thing you can do to prevent data loss is to stick to a consistent backup schedule. Software like *Norton Ghost,* by Symantec (*www.symantec.com*), is designed for home businesses and is an easily administered backup tool. With this program you can set up an automated backup routine. Whether your data changes daily or just once a month, *Norton Ghost* can be configured to ensure that your changes are backed up in a timely fashion. Should things go wrong, *Norton Ghost* can retrieve and bring back your entire system. At the same time, it's flexible enough to recover select files. *Norton Ghost* is also compatible with almost any kind of media, CDs, DVDs, a USB device, or you can even choose to save your backups to a network location. If you are unfortunate and experience a system crash, Norton *GoBack*™, by Symantec, is a recovery program that can return your entire system to its precrash state. It also helps you recover inadvertently deleted or overwritten files, and it offers you a list from which you can choose a rollback point.

Cut down on the time and difficulty involved in drawing up business contracts by using software that contains contract templates that you customize to your needs. For example, you can find such contracts for writing partnership agreements, engaging professional service, employee agreements, nondisclosure agreements, permission to use copyrighted material, and consignment agreements. Sources of such contracts include *Quickform Contracts* (*www.quickforms.net*).

Planning Large Projects

The Problem
If you are involved in large or complex projects that involve many steps or components, inevitably something can go wrong if you miss a step or forget a task. Such mistakes can cost you money and time, and even future business.

Computer Solutions
Project-planning and flow-charting software can help you manage many of the problems associated with large projects. Programs like Microsoft *Project* and *Visio* are tools that use flow charts and diagrams to help you to cre-

ate business and technical diagrams that document and organize complex ideas, processes, and systems. You can use different shapes (triangles, boxes, rectangles, etc.) to visually represent individual aspects of a project and sequence or arrange them into time lines or action plans; then you can track your progress along these chains knowing that you won't miss an important step. These programs also provide analysis capability to notify you of time or resource conflicts you may have mistakenly assigned to the project. Good project-management software should also be able to actually provide you with options to the problems that data analysis points out. Many also allow you to quickly and easily send memos and write reports on a given project's status, and even connect to the Internet so that these communications can be instantly sent wherever they need to go.

Managing Your Computer

The Problem

Like many computer users, you may find that your computer soon becomes overstuffed with multiple programs, along with hundreds of Windows files and other UFOs (unidentified file objects) you can't remember creating. When your computer gets to this stage of clutter, it can become as self-defeating as a hopelessly disorganized desk or an overstuffed file cabinet. What you thought would save time now eats away at your time as you try to figure out how to access what you need, remember what you named it, or where you put it on your disk. The best way to think about computer management is that in running a business, your computer becomes your staff in a box. Instead of managing people, you must start effectively managing the contents of your computer to get the most out of them.

Computer Solutions

There is a wide variety of "computer-management" software available to help you solve your computer woes. One of the most well known programs is *System Works,* by Symantec (*www.symantec.com*). This robust program is really several utility programs bundled together. It features a "One Button Checkup" that lets you quickly identify and fix common PC problems and a virus protection program that updates automatically. Also included in the bundle is *Norton Utilities.* This program can optimize and improve your hard drive's performance, and can detect and fix many Windows and disk problems automatically. It also continuously monitors your PC to spot problems before they occur.

Once you invest the money and take the time to select and learn to use the types of software and other products available today, your computer can provide you with the same capabilities as a talented and dedicated support staff, freeing you from hours of drudgery to do the work you do best. But there is more, because not only can your computer help you administer your business more easily; it can, as you will find out in the next part, also help you bring business in the door without breaking your budget.

Protect Yourself: Computer Security Issues

ANTIVIRUS SOFTWARE

The Internet is a valuable business tool for e-mail and accessing the Web, but it can cause problems too. When you are working online, you are exposed to potentially disastrous viruses that can damage or even wipe out your important files. Never go online without the latest antivirus protection. Fast-spreading mass-mailing viruses, "worms," and Trojans like Mydoom, Bagle, and Sasser can easily infect exposed PCs over dial-up or broadband connections. They can forward themselves to your e-mail contacts and even help remote hackers hijack personal information. McAfee's *VirusScan* is a popular program that automatically scans your e-mail, attachments, shared disks, and downloads, then immediately starts to clean or quarantine infections.

Identity theft is another potential problem. Internet hackers can break into vulnerable PC systems and steal private files, credit-card information, tax records, passwords, and Social Security numbers. Programs such as McAfee's *Personal Firewall Plus* provide a secure barrier between your computer's hard drive and hostile Internet threats. Another top-selling program is Symantec's *Norton Internet Security.* This bundled software package includes *Norton AntiVirus* to protect against viruses, Norton *Personal Firewall* to keep personal data in and hackers out, and *Norton Privacy Control* and *Norton AntiSpam* to safeguard your PC from other common online risks.

3.4: Using Technology to Market Yourself and Increase Your Business

Once you decide to make money on your own, your first thoughts will be to how to attract customers as quickly as possible. When you do get some business, you need to turn that business into a steady flow. To achieve this, you must market yourself and your business to keep the customers coming.

Most home-business owners have limited funds to spend in attracting business and usually little expertise or interest in marketing and sales. However, to keep business coming your way, you need to continuously market your business even after you're busy working with new clients or customers. And somehow prospective customers have to be able to reach you even while you're out marketing and serving your clients.

Fortunately, your computer and other wisely selected home-office equipment and services—from Internet service providers (covered in Part 3.5) to the latest telephones to voice-mail systems, faxes, modems, copiers, and scanners—can become your marketing partners. You can produce affordable, cost-effective, high-quality marketing materials and maintain communications to virtually anywhere. In our book, written with Laura Clampitt Douglas, *Getting Business to Come to You*, we describe thirty-five of the most effective, low-cost marketing methods used by successful home businesses. While this part won't explain the ins and outs of using these methods, it will show you how your computer and other technology can assist you in using almost every one of those marketing methods more easily and effectively. Just as your computer can help you manage your money and office administrivia, this part demonstrates how your computer can be an invaluable tool for getting and keeping plenty of customers.

First we'll address how you can use hardware and software to initiate and expand your client and customer base, and then we'll discuss how to equip yourself so you can make sure that you're accessible to your clients.

THE BEST MARKETING METHODS

Getting Business Fast

- Turn your ex-employer into a client.

- Ethically take business with you when you leave your job.

- Get referrals from your competitors for work they don't want or are unable to do.

- Respond to classified ads and convince prospective employers that you can do a better job as an independent professional.

- Directly solicit business by phone or in person whenever you have free time. The worst thing that can happen is that you will make a new contact that doesn't need your services at this time.

Generating a Steady Flow of Business

To generate a steady flow of business you need to identify and get to know potential clients and their needs, then attract them to your product or service and keep them coming back to you. Although such marketing efforts take time and energy initially, the momentum they generate can get business coming to you with only a minimal amount of ongoing effort. Your computer can help you launch your initial marketing effort; then make a regular habit of continuing to reach out and stay in touch.

For example, you can use desktop publishing, Web publishing, and powerful word-processing software to create your own display ads, newsletters, flyers, Web sites, brochures, cards, and stationery. You can use brain-extending software like *IdeaFisher*™ (*www.ideafisher.com*) to develop creative and effective ad and brochure copy. You can use contact-management software to communicate with prospective clients every month so you are never "out of sight, out of mind." In this section we will outline how you can use your computer to accomplish the three most time-consuming and challenging administrative tasks involved in getting and maintaining a steady flow of business.

Keeping Track of Your Growing Sphere of Business Contacts

The Problem

Each day you're in business you are in contact with people who represent potential business or access to business. This ever-growing base of contacts can be your most valuable resource and lifeline to a source of business. Unfortunately, however, we often find ourselves too busy or too disorganized to take advantage of these contacts. For example, you might meet twenty or thirty interested contacts at a speech, trade show, or exhibit. Though some of these contacts may turn into business from that first contact, a larger number could potentially become clients if you continue to make contact with them. Perhaps you run an ad and receive 100 phone calls that turn into five new clients. Many of the other ninety-five callers could also become clients later if you are set up to send them a mailing at regular intervals in the future. For most people, out of sight equals out of mind.

If you are a one-person business and don't have administrative help, it's easy to lose track of contact information such as business cards or notes that represent valuable contacts you've made. But if you could keep track of all the contacts you've already made and stay in touch with them regularly, you could increase your business manyfold and reduce the time and energy you need to exert continually to make new contacts.

Computer Solutions

With your computer you can create a complete record of all your vital business contacts—potential clients, present clients, past clients, gatekeepers, and other referral sources, so you can easily identify and contact them regularly by phone, e-mail, or regular mail. You can use personal-organizer software or a personal-information-manager program like those described in Part 3.3. Or, you might consider using mailing-list software, or contact-management software, or even a full-fledged database program. We'll describe each of the additional methods here so you can decide which will best meet your needs.

MAILING-LIST SOFTWARE

The simplest way to create a contact list is to use a mail-list manager, such as, *My Deluxe Mail List* by Avanquest (*www.avanquestusa.com//index.htm*).

These programs are actually simplified database programs that are "pre-formatted" with only ten or twelve fields to fill out for each person, such as Name, Address, City, State, Zip, Phone, and so on. The software also enables you to print out the letters and mailing labels complete with Zip bar codes. It also sorts first-class and third-class mail to save you money with bulk mailings.

When looking for a mailing-list program, make sure it has the capability to export data into word-processing documents for mail merges (discussed below) and into larger database programs. Although you may not need this feature currently, as your business grows you'll be thankful that all the hard work you put into compiling your mailing lists isn't stuck, immovable in your mailing-list program.

CONTACT-MANAGEMENT SOFTWARE

Another alternative for setting up and maintaining a list of your clients and contacts is to use a specialized type of database program: contact-management software. Contact-management programs combine mailing-list management and mail-merge capabilities with other features such as calendar and appointment logs, notepads, automatic phone dialing, record

PERSONALIZING MAILINGS WITH MAIL MERGE

Mail merge refers to the ability to link your mailing list to letters and other documents so that you can send the same letter to individuals on your list with each one personally addressed. The mail-merge function automatically goes through your mailing list and inserts the proper name, address, salutation, and other information into a template document that you have designed.

Full-scale word-processing programs such as Microsoft *Word* have mail-merge capabilities that may make it easy for you to create your customer lists and write letters without even purchasing a mailing-list program.

Mailing-list programs, however, usually don't provide the features to create and sort your list by your own categories, nor do they have features such as calendars for scheduling activities, alarms that alert you to whom you need to follow up with, or notepads for recording discussions you have with those on your list. But if your needs are primarily to send out regular mailings of various kinds to your entire list, a mailing-list program may be your best bet.

keeping of calls, alarms that alert you when to follow up with contact, daily to-do lists with priority settings, and even faxing and e-mail capabilities. The power of contact managers is that all these functions are integrated and linked in an easy-to-use format.

With contact-management software you can contact those in your database by e-mail. Many programs even offer features such as "docking," which allow you to work off line (in the car, on planes, in hotels, etc.) and then use docking to synchronize databases, mail, and appointments when reconnecting to the Internet through your office computer. Another powerful feature allows you to record timed events such as customer calls or consulting time in either the record history or a notepad. When the scheduled appointment date and time arrive, the software sends an audio or visual "alarm," to remind you of the appointment. A click of your mouse button can provide you with a snapshot overview of your day with appointments, tasks due, unread mail, next alarm, and more. Many programs even allow you to drag an e-mail message to your calendar and create an appointment automatically.

Some of the popular contact-management packages include Microsoft's *Outlook* (*www.microsoft.com*), *Best* Software's *Act!* (*www.act.com*), and *Maximizer*, by Maximizer, Technologies, Inc. (*www.maximizer.com*). Most contact-management programs also offer features such as mail merge for quickly sending out customized letters, quick label and envelope printing using addresses already stored in the records, and alarm mechanisms you can program to beep at a given time if you need to be reminded about an upcoming appointment or call.

DATABASE SOFTWARE

Mailing-list-management and contact-management software are actually specialized database programs that provide a predefined structure for keeping track of client contacts. Another way to keep track of all your contacts is to use a full-fledged database program. Popular database programs include Microsoft *Access*, *FileMaker Pro* (*www.filemaker.com*), and *Alpha Five* (*www.alphasoftware.com*). You can also use the database modules associated with Microsoft *Works* or other integrated packages.

To use a database program for contact management you define what you want each client "record" to contain. Because most database programs are graphically oriented, this process is quite easy and requires simply laying out the different "fields" or types of information you want to store: e.g., Name, Address, Phone, E-mail, Fax, Notes, etc., on an on-screen index card. Once you define fields of data, you then enter the information for each contact you have and continue updating your database as you add new contacts. There is also a type of database software known as "free-form," in which you do not need to specify your fields in advance. Instead you see a totally blank screen onto which you can write anything you want in any order, and call it a record. Then when you want to look something up, you can search through your records using easy commands such as "Get Fred Smith," and the program will find all the records that contain the name Fred Smith. Many people find these kinds of database programs much easier to use, since they don't have to remember any specific method of keying in information or searching. Popular programs of this nature include Micro Logic's *InfoSelect* (*www.miclog.com*). Because there are so many programs available that offer similar features, we recommend that you obtain as much information as you can about any program you're considering. You'll find that online many software companies offer free demos or evaluation versions so you can test out the product to make sure it fits the specific needs of your business.

No matter which type of software you select, the biggest hurdle to using it effectively may be finding the time and making the effort to enter the information you want to keep track of. Whether you do the data entry yourself or hire someone else to do it, once the initial work is done, on an ongoing basis you can update your data and expand it with ease.

Making Sure Your Clients and Customers Keep You in Mind

The Problem
When someone needs what you offer, typically she or he turns to whoever comes to mind first. You have to make sure that it's you. We call this "top-of-the-mind marketing," and we know firsthand just how important it can be. Here's just one example.

One week, you contact a company to discuss some work you might do. They're interested but not at this time. Of course, you tell them that you'll be glad to work with them when they are ready, and you leave feeling optimistic about having them as a client sometime in the future. A few months later, however, you hear that one of your competitors is working with that company, doing exactly what you were proposing to do.

In cases like this you may actually have done the sales job for someone else who walked in at just the right moment. The most frustrating thing about this is that it happens all too often—more than you know—but, of course, you can't be everywhere at once.

Technology Solutions

If you've created a database of all your business contacts and selected the right software for it, you can use your computer, laser printer, fax, and modem; you can make sure that every person on your list receives something from you by phone, fax, e-mail, or regular mail as often as necessary with minimal time and energy on your part. Your software can track and inform you of who needs follow-up. You can use your computer to design and produce materials that you can easily reproduce and send to everyone on your list.

Here are some ways that you can use your computer hardware, software, and supplies that enable you to do "top-of-the-mind" marketing without breaking your budget or your work schedule:

Customize Your Brochures and Flyers. You can use your computer to send prospects and clients professional-looking brochures tailor-made to address their needs. Preprinted papers formatted for brochures, flyers, certificates, and letterheads like those available from Paper Direct (*www.paperdirect*) or Idea Art (*www.ideaart.com*) allow you to produce full-color items using a printer or copier. These papers have high-quality designs printed in color on them. If you use them with a high-quality laser printer, you can produce documents that are virtually indistinguishable from an expensive full-color print job from the best printer in town. For a truly special effect, use your word processor and its mail-merge function to customize the language on the brochure, flyer, or envelope for each individual or company you wish to contact. Vary the greeting, the price, and the services you indicate as your specialty, whatever you think will best demonstrate what you can do and appeal most to their needs.

Create special postcards. You can send your clients and potential customers a quick postcard every six to eight weeks to remind them about your services or to let them know about any specials you may be offering. You can create postcards economically with your laser printer and desktop-publishing software. Many desktop-publishing packages like Microsoft *Publisher* and Adobe *PageMaker* have predesigned templates for postcards and most of the other marketing materials described in this part. You just fill in the copy and any additional art you wish to use. Then, using your contact-management software, organizer, or mailing-list software and your laser printer, you can quickly print out the cards and the mailing labels to send off dozens of cards in just a few minutes.

Send personalized messages via regular mail. You can create and send personalized announcements, thank-you notes, greeting cards, and other attention-getting messages to clients, prospects, and referral sources. For example, Idea Art offers a variety of laser papers preprinted with cartoon and graphic word art such as "Thanks," "For Your Information," "News," and "Attention." Paper Direct has a line of attractive, blank prefolded holiday greeting cards that you can run through your laser printer with your own message on the inside. Microsoft *Publisher* has a template for creating your own attractively designed thank-you notes or greeting cards.

Send personalized messages via e-mail. These days, people check their e-mail more frequently than their regular (snail) mail. Sending personalized, informal e-mail messages is an effective way to keep potential customers thinking of you. Direct e-mail marketing and the use of e-mail for information delivery have become increasingly popular. But people hate getting "spam" messages (overtly commercial offers), so we don't recommend sending e-mail to someone unless you have already established contact in some other way. With e-mail, the more personalized the better. Most contact-management software allows you to e-mail right from their programs (if you have an Internet service provider), so it is relatively easy to keep track of what you sent to whom when.

While many people have questioned the effectiveness of e-mail marketing due to the rapid increase of unsolicited e-mail in recent years, it still proves to be a very effective means of promotion on a budget. As the popularity of this marketing strategy has taken hold, so has the range of auto-responder and mailing-list-manager software packages available. Because there are so many products to choose from, we suggest that you research a few and decide which one best meets your needs. Some examples of auto-responder software are: *Intellicontact Pro* (*www.intellicontact.com*), *Send-Studio* (*www.interspire.com*), and *FollowUpXpert* (*www.xtreeme.com/followupxpert*).

Publish Periodic Newsletters. Other than a check or an order, nothing is more likely to stand out amid the volume of postal and electronic mail every business receives each day than a newsletter that's chock full of important information or free advice. Whether your newsletter is a single sheet or an eight-page booklet, you can produce this effective marketing tool easily with desktop publishing programs like Microsoft *Publisher*. Most desktop publishing programs also include HTML templates or easy-to-use HTML coding so you can quickly convert your printed newsletter to an online version for the Web. If you plan to send an online version of a newsletter, look for a contact-management or mailing program that will allow you to do mass e-mailings.

Most desktop-publishing and word-processing programs come with preformatted newsletter templates. All you need to do is enter your text, and import a piece of clip art or scan in a photo, and there you go . . . a professional newsletter ready to print out on your laser printer or at your local print shop. And once again you can quickly print mailing labels from your contact-management, database, or mailing-list program and get your newsletter to the mailbox.

Of course there is the cost of postage if you use "snail mail," but a newsletter not only pays for itself with the first call it generates but also may bring thousands of dollars in additional business. If you have developed a list of prospects and clients who use e-mail, you can use the Internet to distribute your publication without incurring the cost of postage. Whichever method you decide to use, at the very least it keeps your company in mind for future business.

Communicate on the Internet. Online gathering places such as users' groups, newsgroups, Web sites with "chat" rooms, and discussion groups can serve as important connections to your colleagues, customers, and potential clients. Through these sources you can obtain news and updates on trends in your business by communicating with other people online. If you are a financial planner, for example, you can find literally hundreds of places online to talk with your peers, discuss trends with providers of financial products, find out about the latest productivity tools, market your services—you name it, and it's probably out there. The information you gather online may prove valuable in obtaining intelligence regarding your market and industry. You may find new ways to target new clients or get the edge you need in a competitive situation. Networking online is also a great way to obtain leads for new business. The growth of the online virtual world is shrinking the size of the actual business world. Networking online frees you from the confinements of geographic markets. Because of the Internet, most home-based computer businesses can service clients anywhere in the country, or even the world. Find where you can locate groups sites on page 340 under the topic "Overcoming Isolation."

Blogging is the current rage, and 8 million people at this writing read blogs. If this medium, a sort of public journaling, appeals to you, JotSpot (*www.jot.com*) is a tool that enables you to use Word to write blog entries but then enables other people to edit them. Yahoo! has introduced a combination of blogging and social networking.

Obviously, to use online resources you need a subscription to an Internet service provider (ISP). Most ISPs offer fairly inexpensive basic monthly rates. However, you may need to pay user fees to log onto private bulletin boards.

Send out professional news releases. Public-relations (PR) efforts using the media are important marketing tactics of any successful business. If a news release features your business, you have the double benefit of "free" (not counting the expense of producing and mailing the kit, see below) exposure and a recommendation from a trusted impartial source. People give far more credence to the judgments of a publication's editorial content over its advertising content.

Instead of having to spend huge amounts of money on the services of a professional PR agency you can use your computer to help you create your own PR campaign. While it takes practice and time, it is possible to produce a top-notch media kit yourself from your home office. You must begin with a clear understanding of what is newsworthy about what your goods or services offer. Keep the emphasis on news. If your kit looks like an overt marketing presentation about your business, no one will want to pick up your story. Concentrate your press release on how your product or service helps people. Answer questions like: Who will it help? How will it help? Is it part of a trend? Is it trend setting? When you've determined the content of your news release and media kit, use your word processor to write a news release. You may want to use your desktop-publishing program, clip-art software, graphic-design software, and a scanner to add any graphs, illustrations, or photos that might enhance your presentation. You can print out your materials on your own laser printer, create a CD, or transmit the material over the Internet. Finally, you can package your news release and accompanying material in a professional-looking folder such as those available in office-supply stores.

To learn how to write effective news releases and create a successful media kit, see Part 2 of *Getting Business to Come to You*, which we wrote with Laura Clampitt Douglas.

The next step is getting your kit or news release into the hands of the right people. You can have your news release distributed via fax by PR Newswire (*www.prnewswire.com*), 810 7th Ave., 35th floor, New York, NY 10019, (800) 832-5522 and Business Wire (*www.businesswire.com*), 44 Montgomery

Street, 39th Floor, San Francisco, CA 94104, (888) 381-9473. You can also e-mail your release to both of these services, and they will distribute it, for a fee, to hundreds of online news-gathering organizations such as America Online, Cnet, and others.

Bacon's Press Distribution Service (*www.baconsinfo.com*) also offers mailing labels as well as printing and distribution for news releases. You can contact them at 332 S. Michigan Avenue, Chicago, IL 60604, (312) 922-2400. *Gale Database of Publications & Broadcast Media (http:library.dialog.com/ bluesheets/html/bl0469.html)* has detailed information on thousands of newspapers, magazines, journals, periodicals, directories, newsletters, radio, television, and cable stations and systems.

Creating a Professional Image for Your Business

The Problem

Succeeding in today's fast-paced, competitive economy means that you must command respect and convey a positive professional image at all times. Many home-based businesses fear that clients, vendors, and business institutions may discount home-based businesses or automatically assume that someone who works from home cannot do as good a job as a larger company. To overcome any stigma associated in people's minds with your being a home-based business, you must project the image of a professional business that will get the job done with the highest quality possible.

Technology Solution

Once again, home-office technology comes to the rescue. With today's technology everything you produce can be indistinguishable from what comes out of a Fortune 500 corporation. There is an onslaught of technology and resources that will enhance your professional image and add a glow to your business. Whether it's a computer-based slide presentation, a memo, or a final report, that glow will go a long way in capturing your clients' attention and making sure they feel that you have gone to the end of the road for them.

Here's a list of cost-effective suggestions for how you can use your computer, software, and printer to give your work a 100 percent professional image:

Create a Distinctive Graphic Identity for Your Business

Design your own logo. Whatever business you are in, it pays to have smartly designed letterhead and/or company logo that distinctively identifies your business and makes people take notice. An appealing, dynamic letterhead or logo for your company solidifies your unique professional identity and adds to the positive impression clients will have about your company. Your distinctive graphic identity should appear on all of your stationery including letterhead, envelopes, business cards, Web site, and just about anything else you present to the public.

Desktop-publishing software offers templates, clip art, and wizards to help you design, print, and publish all your marketing collateral including newsletters, brochures, and even a Web site. While you can use expensive professional programs such as Adobe's *InDesign* or *QuarkXPress,* scaled-down software packages like Microsoft's *Publisher* and Broderbund's *Print Shop Deluxe* (*www.broderbund.com*) are low-cost and don't require the steep learning curve of the pricier professional software. However, Adobe's *InDesign* is integrated with other Adobe products such as *Photoshop* and *Adobe Acrobat.* If your business involves designing materials for others, do budget for a professional program.

If you have a freelance designer do the work for you, be sure to get the image scanned and saved as a graphic file so that you can take it home and add it into your own computer where you can use it with your word processor or desktop-publishing program on everything you produce. In this way, you can put your company logo on every document that leaves your printer—even your mailing labels, invoices, notes, postcards, and memos.

Don't forget your business card! Face-to-face contacts are still among your most important encounters, and a business card is essential. Make sure that your business card coordinates with the design elements of your stationery. Design software comes with professionally predesigned templates that you can modify to create your own unique business cards.

Software can help you keep track of all the cards others give you. For example, *CardScan,* by Cordex (*www.corex.com*), is a desktop device that quickly and accurately scans the printed information from business cards into the correct fields of a searchable electronic address book. In seconds, *CardScan* enters more cards than you could type in hours. I.R.I.S.'s *CardIRIS* (*www.irisusa.com*) and NewSoft's *Presto BizCard* (*www.newsoftinc.com*) software are also well-regarded programs that scan business cards right into your database and other programs.

Custom-design your forms. Use desktop publishing or form-design software to produce distinctive invoices and other forms that make your company stand out from the rest. Add an inspiring message or thank-you to standard forms using an intriguing typographic that lets your clients know you appreciate their business. You can create custom multipart order forms and invoices and print them on carbonless paper with your laser printer. Such forms can be ordered from distributors like LLT Bar Code and Label (*www.lltproducts.com*), (800) 882-4050.

Give envelopes and mailing labels a distinctive look. Use your software to print envelopes and labels on your laser or ink-jet printer. The more individualized your envelope appears when it arrives, the less likely it is apt to be thrown away unopened. Avery offers a wide variety of labels to choose from, including larger die-cut mailing labels such as their 557 that can be printed with your logo at a local printer.

Print your checks. When you pay suppliers or vendors, print your checks with your printer, using customized checks available with one of the financial programs. Intuit's *Quicken* or *Quickbooks* automatically fill in the check with the name of the payee and the amount—just as you entered the last such transaction.

CREATE MEMORABLE MARKETING MATERIALS

Use special fonts, photos, or clip art. There's no longer any reason to produce bland, boring documents when most word processors and desktop-publishing software offer scores of font choices. (If you're unsure—and many people are, including manufacturers—about the difference between a font and a typeface; a typeface is a printing term and refers specifically to physical "type" that must be set by a machine; a "font" is simply the digital equivalent of a typeface. Computers and computer printers use fonts, not typefaces.) You can use special fonts on your brochures, flyers, and other marketing materials to capture attention and enhance your company image.

Consider getting one or two inexpensive software font type packages. Bitstream offers a selection of font packages that provide literally thousands of special fonts in scaleable point sizes. These font add-ons work with Windows's print manager and can be output on any brand or type of printer you may use. Bitstream's *MyFonts* is an easy-to-use Web site that provides over 35,000 that you can try and buy online. For more information, see *www.bitstream.com*.

Use a high-quality printer. Your marketing documents represent your company identity, and so top-quality printing announces that you are a professional who takes business seriously. What kind does your home office need? If you need to print high-quality color documents regularly, then you'll need to invest in a top-of-the-line color printer for your home office. If not, you may be able to get away with a black-and-white printer. If you only occasionally need documents such as full-color brochures printed, it may be more economical to get your high-quality documents done by a professional printing company. Laser printers still deliver crisp text and graphics at top speeds, and they are less expensive to operate than ink jets. Ink jets offer low-cost color printing, but they are slower than lasers and the cost of ink cartridges and paper can quickly add up. Overall, the output quality is better, print speeds are faster, and prices for printers are lower than ever and continue to be more and more affordable. You have a great many choices for business. We suggest you visit your local retail outlet to find out which printer will best meet your needs.

About color: Inappropriate use of color or special effects can detract from the professionalism of your materials. A good cook knows just how much salt to use to make a recipe taste great; too much salt will kill the flavor of any dish. If you are in the least unsure of your color choice or design sense, skip the color or effect. If you are not a visually-oriented person, we recommend you give the business to a fellow home-based designer or desktop publisher.

Use special paper. You don't have to limit yourself to plain white paper. You can print your marketing materials on special papers from companies like Paper Direct (*www.paperdirect.com*, [800] 272-7377) or at your local office-supply outlet. You'll find paper specially formatted for brochures and flyers with colorful frames, exotic designs, background patterns, and "faux finishes" like parchment, marble, and granite that already include color borders and designs around which you can place your text for an instant professional look.

Consider alternatives to printed materials. Some people can be better reached through other media, such as e-mail with attached files, audio-cassettes, and videocassettes. So why not produce an electronic brochure? Presentation software like Microsoft's *PowerPoint* allows you to create dynamic, interactive presentations and save them to a disk that you can send out. Microsoft's *PowerPoint Viewer* allows those who use *PowerPoint* to share their presentations with people who do not have *PowerPoint* installed on their computers. When you e-mail or post presentations on the Internet, you can include the *PowerPoint Viewer* to expand your online audience to people who might not have *PowerPoint*. To add even more punch, you can purchase attention-grabbing disk and cassette labels available for use with your laser printer. You can color-coordinate with your letterhead and stationery, including "hot" colors and metallic foils that you can print, cut, and stick on anything. You can also create premiums and other gift incentives ranging from T-shirts to mouse pads that you can customize with your company logo or motto, using laser-printer transfer toners and metallic foils available at many retailers.

MAKE IMPRESSIVE PROFESSIONAL PROPOSALS, REPORTS, AND PRESENTATIONS

Format your documents for distinction. Whenever you need to give a client a written document such as a proposal or report, use your software to format and lay it out so that pages are attractive and easy to read. You can incorporate useful graphics, charts, and even artwork. If you need to write many such documents, we recommend using a word-processing program like Microsoft *Word* that allows you greater flexibility in formatting. For very lengthy documents with lots of charts or graphics, you might want to port your word-processed file over to one of the desktop publishing software packages discussed earlier in this part. These programs give you even greater flexibility in laying out text across pages, as well as in formatting them if you need to vary the fonts, margins, columns, and other components of text-heavy documents.

To add borders or artwork to your proposals and reports, you can buy any number of clip-art programs that provide you with thousands of images from which to choose and integrate into your report. You can also draw your own artwork using drawing programs like *CorelDraw* (*www.corel.com*), Adobe *Illustrator* (*www.adobe.com*), or any number of useful shareware art programs (check out *www.jumbo.com* or *www.tucows.com*), all of which let you download art into a word processor or desktop-publishing program. These drawing programs also give you hundreds, sometime thousands, of clip-art pieces you can use as is or customize for your presentations.

Add visuals for impact. If you are preparing a slide presentation or proposal requiring many bulleted charts and graphs, use a software program like Microsoft *PowerPoint* to create high-impact, colorful slides and charts quickly and easily. You can then print out overheads for your presentation on your laser or color printer using special transparencies or you can transmit your output online over the Internet to special photo labs like Chroma Copy ([201] 796-2444) that can make up color slides for you and ship them to you in a twenty-four-hour turnaround.

Present proposals, reports, and samples in elegant folders and bindings. Excellent selections of plastic sleeves and envelopes, presentation folders, binders, slipcases, notebooks, and other supplies for presentations are available from companies like Avery and Paper Direct, as well as at your local office supply store.

Making Sure Clients and Customers Can Reach You: The Telephone

Unlike a retail shop, your prospective clients most likely will not be dropping by. No matter how great your marketing efforts are, if your potential and existing clients and customers can't reach you when they need you, you may not get their business. Considering that your fax machine and online access also utilize the phone lines, your telephone connection is your lifeline to getting and doing business. Whether you need to follow up on an overdue invoice or negotiate a new contract, chances are many of the key transactions with your clients will be by phone.

You need to make sure that you don't miss incoming calls even though you may frequently be away from your office providing services to others engaged in marketing activities. You also won't want to miss calls coming in while you're talking with others. You need to decide how you will manage personal and business calls as well as how to deal with your fax machine's and modem's need to use the phone lines as well. Most phone companies are eager to help small and home-based businesses find solutions to all their telephone needs, and they have developed a wide variety of services to meet almost every conceivable need. Your telephone system can make you virtually indistinguishable from a Fortune 500 company. Today the choice is yours, and the only problem becomes finding out and selecting among the many telephone options open to you.

Here is a variety of telephone solutions to the five biggest challenges involved in making sure that you don't miss calls for new business and that your clients and customers can reach you when they need you. You can review these various options and then consult with your local telephone operating company about the best way to meet your needs. Not all these services are available from every telephone company, and some call the services we describe by different names; but if you describe what you need the service to do, they will most likely be able to tell you how they can meet that need.

Taking Messages When You're Busy or Out of the Office

The Problem

Missing a call can mean missing the opportunity to sign up a new client or the chance to serve a current customer. Having a reliable way to get calls or take messages while you're out is crucial. In addition, there will undoubtedly be times when you don't want to be interrupted by incoming calls, times when you're meeting with a client, working on a deadline, or completing a highly demanding project.

In these situations, you need your telephone system to serve as a dependable receptionist, capturing your messages reliably and accurately. Unfortunately the most common solutions—having an answering machine or an answering service—have significant limitations. Also, as we all know, answering machines sometimes break down unexpectedly, cut off the caller's message, or simply have poor sound quality. On the other hand, hiring a traditional answering service can be equally frustrating, as many services are impersonal, distant, and prone to making mistakes.

Another drawback of both of these options is that you will most likely end up spending time playing telephone tag with your contacts and clients, because busy people can spend days leaving messages for each other without ever talking personally.

Telephone Solutions

The following is a list of more versatile options for taking messages so you can return calls when it is most practical and productive.

Voice mail. Voice mail answers your calls and takes messages like a sophisticated answering machine, but it offers additional advantages. First, since most large companies use voice mail, a home business with voice mail becomes virtually indistinguishable to callers from a Fortune 500 company. And in many ways voice mail is like having a receptionist because it can carry out so many of the tasks a receptionist would provide. For example, in addition to simply leaving a message, callers can choose from among a variety of options. They can listen for a list of your services, get directions to your office, or obtain instructions for ordering a product. Having such information available on a prerecorded message saves you the time of returning such calls and provides your callers with immediate access to frequently requested information.

Also, voice-mail systems usually offer the ability to set up different outgoing messages that can be programmed to run at various times of the day. Voice mail enables you to set up individual "mailboxes" where you can leave private messages for different people in addition to your generic greeting. Each mailbox has its own ID-coded extension, which you can assign to people who call you frequently. You can leave detailed messages for any individual with whom you may need to communicate and thereby avoid playing phone tag with hard-to-reach people.

As with an answering machine you can pick up your voice-mail messages from wherever you are by dialing into your own number. And as you will see below, voice mail can also take calls while you're talking on the phone, forward selected calls to you at other locations, or even have you paged so you can call in to receive a message.

Here are three different ways you can set up a voice-mail system for your business:

Voice mail through your phone company. Most local telephone companies offer voice-mail service for a modest monthly charge with your telephone service. These services include the ability to set up a number of mailboxes and take messages while you are on the line. As with an answering machine you can access your messages from a remote location, save some of the messages to replay at a later time, and erase others. Contact your local telephone company to find out what voice mail features they offer.

Private voice-mail services. If voice mail is not an option through your phone company or they don't offer the features you need, another choice is to sign up with a private voice-mail service. In fact, in Part 1 of this book, you'll note that we have described Answering/Voice Mail Service as one of the computer businesses you might even start.

In the short term, using one of these two methods is probably the most simple, effective, and least expensive option for most home businesses—with one exception, which we'll discuss directly.

Voice mail on your computer. Another cost-effective solution might be to receive voice mail in your e-mail in box and listen to messages through your computer speakers or headphones. You can set up a voice-mail system on your computer using specialized software and a voice-mail card that you install in your computer. When a call comes in, it is picked up by the voice-mail card, the caller hears your greeting, and the person's message is recorded on your hard disk. Many new computers come with simple voice-mail software packages included as part of their "bundle." You can also buy voice-mail systems separately.

Since, like an answering machine, your voice-mail system will need several seconds to reset between incoming calls, a system that will handle two lines is an advantage for people receiving a heavy volume of incoming calls. As with any other computer technology, there is a wide range of voice-mail products offered with a wide variety of prices and capabilities. We recommend that you discuss your needs with a consultant at a computer retailer in your community.

Call forwarding to a homebound assistant. Another option for taking your phone messages is to have your calls forwarded to a reliable individual who will take your messages for a reasonable charge.

Fax in or fax back. Since callers often want either to leave or obtain information of some kind, you might want to consider using your fax to respond to certain calls when you can't answer the phone. For example, your voice-mail or answering-machine message can inform callers that they can fax certain information to you that you can respond to upon your return. Or by using a fax-back service, your callers can select an option to have information like a price list or service descriptions faxed to them automatically.

Caller ID. If you have too high a percentage of hang-ups when callers get your recorded message, Caller ID is an ideal service. This device records and displays the phone numbers of callers, even those who hang up. You can call these individuals back to ascertain interest in your service.

DO YOU NEED VOICE MAIL?

If you answer yes to any of these questions, you probably will benefit from voice mail:

- Is it important that you disguise the fact that you are a small, one-person, or home-based business? Voice mail makes you virtually indistinguishable from a Fortune 500 company.
- Do you have an aversion to call waiting but believe you are missing calls while you are talking on the phone? Voice mail will take messages while you're on the phone.
- Do you find yourself frequently playing telephone tag? Voice mail can allow you to leave personalized messages for people who would otherwise be hard to reach.
- Do you spend a considerable amount of time conveying the same information to caller after caller? Voice mail can allow your caller to select a prerecorded message containing frequently requested information.
- Could your clients place an order or request information without talking with you personally? Voice mail allows callers to receive instructions for placing orders or requesting written materials like a catalog or product list.
- Do you need to have a variety of messages for different types of callers? Voice mail allows your callers to select specific types of messages.

Receiving Calls When You're Out of the Office

The Problem

Sometimes taking a phone message, no matter how reliably, is not enough. There may be times when you need to get your calls immediately even though you are not in your office. You can't afford to pick up your messages later if you need to make appointments, take orders, handle emergencies, or respond to customer needs on demand.

Telephone Solutions

Using telephone services and equipment, you can be available to your business callers literally anytime, most anywhere, no matter what you are doing. Here is a variety of ways to have your calls follow you when you're out of the office:

Call forwarding. Call forwarding sends your calls to another telephone number wherever you are. For example, you can have your calls forwarded to a meeting you're attending, to a client site where you're working, or to a cellular phone. A number of other options may also be available if you subscribe to call forwarding, for example:

Delayed call forwarding will automatically forward your calls to another number after four rings, so you don't need to take the time to program your phone for call forwarding each time you leave the office.

Remote call forwarding is an added feature offered by some phone companies that enables you to program call forwarding remotely from one location to another, so you can direct your calls elsewhere when you are not in your office.

Priority call forwarding is offered by some phone companies. If you don't want all your incoming calls forwarded, you can forward calls only for specific phone numbers you designate.

Cellular telephones. If you routinely work at various client sites during the day, travel a lot in your work, or spend considerable time making deliveries or sales calls, a cellular phone is practically a necessity for conducting business. There is a wide variety of cell-phone features and cellular service plans available, and they are changing all the time. Contact your mobile-service provider to determine which cell phone and service plan best meet your needs.

A paging system is another alternative for remaining accessible to your clients. The paging service takes your calls and then pages you through a remote unit that you carry with you. The pager service provides you with a telephone number for your pager that you can give out to your clients and have put on your business cards so they can call your pager directly. By entering their phone number when they reach the pager, you can see the number on the pager screen and can call them back immediately without having to call the service.

Of course, you can combine several of these technologies to arrive at the best solution for your business. For example, you can leave a voice-mail message that includes instructions to call your pager or cellular number in case of an emergency. You can refer callers to a homebound assistant to take orders or schedule service. Some phone companies even offer a call-forwarding service that first forwards a call to your cellular phone (or any other number you designate). If the call is not picked up after a certain number of rings, it is forwarded again, this time to your pager, or other number. You can add several numbers in this chain.

OTHER HANDY AND HELPFUL PHONE FEATURES

Automatic redial. Tired of dialing a busy number over and over? Automatic redial will do it for you. You hang up your phone and you're notified when the number you're calling is available.

Three-way calling. This is the residential version of conference calling. This feature allows you to connect with one party, flash the switch hook to call a second party and, after the second party answers, flash the switch hook again to allow all three parties to be connected on the same line. You can also enlarge the conference to up to thirty parties if the people you call also have three-way calling because they can also add people to the conference.

Call wake-up. While this service is designed for wake-up calls, it can equally be used as a reminder for telephone appointments and prearranged conference calls that can be programmed up to twenty-four hours in advance. The phone will ring to remind the subscriber to initiate the conference call.

Call timer. Do you want to know how much telephone time to bill to a particular client? It's easy to underestimate how much time you've spent on the phone. Call Timer will provide that information for you when you're talking on the phone. While you can do this with software like *TimeSlips* or have it as a feature on your phone, you can also get it as a service from many phone companies.

Call blocking. Tired of being hounded by a particular salesman or other frequent but uninvited caller? Some phone companies allow you to specify originating numbers that will not be able to get through to your number.

Handling Incoming Calls While You're on the Line with Someone Else

The Problem

If your phone line is tied up between your voice calls, fax use, and computer online time when others need to reach you, a repeated busy signal can turn away potential business and frustrate existing clients and customers. Of course you don't want to be in the predicament of having to stay off the line just in case someone calls. You need a way to pick up calls while you're tying up the line.

Technology Solutions

Fortunately, you don't need to miss other calls while you're on the phone. Here is a variety of ways to pick up incoming calls.

Voice mail. One of the best features of voice mail is that it picks up incoming calls while you are on the phone, so your callers never get a busy signal. Most systems have an audio cue, such a subtle beep to let you know that there's a call coming in. This feature is typically available with voice mail provided by the phone company as well. If you don't have this feature, you won't know you have a second call coming in until you check to see if any calls came in while you were on the phone. With a message-waiting indicator light on your phone, however, you'll know immediately.

Call waiting, cancel call waiting, and three-way calling. With call waiting you can tell when another is call coming in and, if you wish, you can interrupt the call you're on to answer the incoming one. Essentially, you are putting your first caller on hold while you find out who is calling. You can then either handle that call or put the second caller on hold while you wrap up your initial call. The problem with call waiting is that it does not interact well with online communications. If you are online and a call comes in, the call-waiting beep or audio cue can sometimes knock you off line. This is not desirable if you're talking with someone online or downloading a file.

Some people find taking another call in the midst of a phone conversation to be rude and disruptive, but if you generally like call waiting except under certain circumstances, you might want to use a feature called cancel call waiting. It enables you to enter a code that will cancel call waiting when you want to place a call or while you are in the midst of an important phone call—or while online!

Three-way calling enables you to talk to two people in different locations at the same time—no matter who placed the call. Using these three features together gives you the equivalent of having two incoming lines and two outgoing lines all with one telephone line, and the monthly charges for these services are minimal.

Call return. This feature will automatically redial the number of the last person who tried to phone you. So if you're in the middle of a vital conversation and don't want to interrupt it by responding to call waiting, you can still let the incoming call go by and call return will call the number of the call you missed when you hang up.

Busy call forwarding. If you don't want to use call waiting, you can use "busy call forwarding" to forward your incoming calls to a second phone line when you are on the phone. For example, you can send incoming calls to your residential line or to a second business line. If you place an answering machine on your residential line during working hours, your business callers will never get a busy signal. Not all phone companies have busy call forwarding available for forwarding to a residential line, however.

Call forwarding of call waiting. If you want to use call waiting under some circumstances, but not others, call forwarding of call-waiting will forward your call-waiting callers to a second line when you don't pick up on the call-waiting signal.

Call hunting. If you have more than two lines, you may be interested in call hunting, a service that will seek out or hunt for the free line when an incoming line is busy. By having voice mail or an answering machine on the lines, you can avoid missing incoming calls. This hunting feature is not always available for crossing over to a residential line, however.

SCREENING CALLS WHILE YOU ARE ON THE PHONE
If you had a full-time assistant and two lines, he or she could screen your calls while you're busy talking on the phone. Well, you can do almost as well without the assistant using several phone services in conjunction with one together. By having **Call Forwarding of Call Waiting** and **Caller**

ID, along with a telephone that has a message-waiting indicator light, you can see the phone numbers of incoming calls and pick up special calls before they are forwarded to your voice mail.

SCREENING CALLS WHILE YOU ARE WORKING

Incoming phone calls, as vital as they are, can be highly disruptive when you need to stay focused on income-producing work. You can easily respond to many if not all calls at a later time without unduly inconveniencing the caller. But we usually feel compelled to take our calls because any call could be "the" important one. Screening calls while you work is an excellent solution to this dilemma. Here are two ways you can screen calls while you're working:

Use an answering machine. Turn on the answering machine; set the volume to a tolerable level, and listen to the incoming callers as they leave their messages. If a call is a "must take," pick it up. Allow the others to complete their messages so you can return their calls later at a more convenient time.

Special call acceptance. Some phone companies offer this service as a way to screen calls. To use this service, you enter the numbers of those calls you want to receive even when you're not taking other calls. When you receive a call from one of these numbers, the call will ring through to you while other callers will hear a recording requesting that they leave a message.

VIP alert. Another feature that enables you to screen for priority calls is VIP Alert. It announces with a short-long-short ring that someone is calling from a list you have designated. Usually up to twelve numbers may be chosen for this treatment.

Not Enough Telephone Lines

The Problem

For those of you who are starting out in your first home-based business, if you have only one phone line, you don't have enough phone lines! Think of all the personal phone calls you get, not to mention those you make. Then add the business calls. The more your business succeeds, the more calls there will be. Then add the faxes you will need to send and, of course, those you will receive—and then there is your online time. How much time you spend online depends on your business, but chances are that it will be significant. Never underestimate the importance of being connected to the world via phone lines.

To ensure that there are adequate connections, many home businesses simply pay the price for extra lines—several for business, one for residential, a spare line for a teenager, and so forth. But often it's not that simple. Some homes are not wired for multiple lines. Multiple lines are more expensive, and a business line is more costly than a residential line. And, of course, you don't want to go running around the house from room to room answering various phone lines. Nor do you want to have your desk loaded down with multiple phones, answering machines, and faxes.

Technology Solutions

Today's technology offers an amazing variety of solutions to these problems. If you want to start out handling multiple types of calls on one line, there are practical options for doing that. If you're ready to go for two or even three lines, that's possible too. Here is a checklist of options.

1. PUT ONE LINE TO MULTIPLE USE
Here is a variety of ways you can get multiple uses from your one line:

Mixing Personal and Business

Distinctive ringing. Although different companies call this service by different names, distinctive ringing enables you to use one line for up to three different incoming phone numbers. For example, if you have only one phone line coming into your home, your family might use one phone number, while your business uses another. This way, your teenager won't pick up your business calls when he or she hears the distinctive ring. Or if you and your partner have separate businesses, you can give each one a separate number and a distinctive ring. You could also use a separate number for different aspects of your business as larger companies do: for example, one number to reach your "order line," another to get your "business office."

But, since you have only one physical line coming into your house in this arrangement, distinctive ringing still has a drawback: You can't do two things on the one line at the same time. So you can't send a fax while you're talking on the phone. And callers to one of the numbers will still get a busy signal whenever the other line is being used. However, if you have call waiting on both phone numbers, each of your numbers has a distinctive call-waiting beep, so you can tell which number is receiving the call.

This can be a good stopgap measure, but having a separate business line is still the best arrangement for most home-based businesses. A separate line for your business assures your business callers privacy and also makes it easier to track phone expenses for tax purposes. If you decide to use this option, talk to your phone company about how you can make sure that the distinctive-ring number you use for your business can be transferred to a business line in the future if necessary.

Mixing Voice, Fax, and Modem

These are your options for using one line for receiving all types of business calls on one line:

1) A variety of programs like those offered by GotVMail Communications (*gotvmail.com/solutions*) can manage phone, fax, and modem communications easily and efficiently. Their *VirtualOne* solution is designed with a variety of features that make a small business look more professional and attractive to potential customers and provide small businesses with a communications system that functions similarly to those used by Fortune 500 companies. *VirtualOne* combines a unique toll-free number with a variety of features and acts as a virtual attendant. It provides employee and department extensions/mail boxes, call forwarding, message notification, pager notification, and more.

2) *Distinctive ringing.* You can use distinctive ringing on your business line. Assign one ring to your business voice calls and the other ring to fax calls so you are prepared to receive a fax if your phone setup requires that your fax machine be answered manually.

3) Use line sharing devices such as Command Communication's (*www.twacomm.com*) *ComShare* to share telephone lines with telephones, faxes, modems, and other devices.

4) *Fax/phone/voice-processing combination.* With this combination, you can have one line serving three purposes. When you are unavailable to answer your phone, the machine answers incoming calls and detects if the incoming call is a fax or a voice call. Voice calls trigger the answering machine, and if it's an incoming fax, the fax machine receives it. This type of technology is available as a stand-

alone system or integrated into your home computer. Many modems come with software that allows for fax/phone/voice-processing combinations.

5) *Fax/modem switches.* If you already own a fax machine or are using an internal fax/modem board inside your computer, the combination unit described above won't help you. Instead, you can buy a fax/modem switch that enables you to use the same phone line for both voice and fax/modem transmissions.

6) *Use the Internet to make inexpensive long-distance and local calls.* Several years ago, dozens of companies offered software to make free long-distance phone calls over the Internet through technology called Voice over Internet Protocol (VoIP). All you needed was a sound card, a microphone, speakers or a headset, and an Internet connection, and you could call any other PC that was online and also using the same software. VoIP worked by breaking up your voice into tiny data packets and carrying them over the Internet. Although with this technology you could make free or very inexpensive phone calls, the packets did not always reassemble perfectly, often resulting in poor transmission. Today, however, VoIP technology is so advanced that PC-to-PC calls sound almost as clear as those made on telephones, and the calls are still free. There are a number of companies offering free PC-to-PC calls, such as the Swedish company Skype (*http:skype.net*). You can download the program (which runs on Windows 2000 or XP) for free. Because privacy is a concern, Skype encrypts your calls end-to-end to ensure that no one can eavesdrop on your conversations.

Besides free PC-to-PC services, you might consider PC-to-phone services, especially if your prospects or clients don't have computers. While these services aren't free, they are less expensive than traditional long-distance phone calls. Companies such as iConnectHere (*www.iconnect here.com*), Net2Phone (*www.net2phone.com*), and DialPad (*www.dialpad.com*) are very affordable.

2. ADDING ADDITIONAL PHONE LINES: BUSINESS VERSUS RESIDENTIAL

We strongly recommend adding a separate line for your business as soon as you can, and we recommend that your second line be a business line, as opposed to a second residential line. Without a business line, you usually can't get a yellow-pages listing; so when clients call information for your phone number, the operator likely will not look for you in the residential directory. In some states utility commission tariffs preclude your using a residential number in business advertising, including on your business cards, letterhead, and stationery. When arranging telephone service, ask your telephone company what their regulations are.

3. INTEGRATED EQUIPMENT

Between business and personal lines, fax/modem lines, answering machines, and fax machines your home office could start looking more like an electronics store than a residence. But today's phone equipment is getting smaller and smaller, and one piece of equipment may do what it once took two, three, or more pieces to do. Using such integrated equipment can save you money as well as desk space.

While integrated equipment doesn't save you the cost of installing a second or third phone line, it does reduce clutter on your desk, improve your efficiency, and save you the cost of buying multiple pieces of equipment. You can choose from a growing selection of space-saving integrated telephone equipment such as:

TIP

ANSWERING MULTIPLE LINES IN MULTIPLE PLACES

Once you get two or more lines, you don't want to have to be running back and forth from home to office to answer them. Here are three solutions for being able to pick up your lines wherever you are in your home.

1. Multiple extensions. Identify the places where you expect to be spending major blocks of time and install extensions in each of these places.

2. Two-line phones. Install a two-line phone on each floor or area of your home so you can pick up either business or residential calls wherever you are.

3. Call pickup. This service allows you to answer any other ringing line within your designated pickup group, usually with a one- or two-digit code.

- two-line phones and two-line cordless phones
- speaker phones, single or two line
- telephone-answering machines
- fax phones, some with built-in answering machines
- computer phones utilizing sound or fax card, speakers, and microphone

By shopping at office superstores that sell home-office electronics, you'll find a wide selection of these integrated products. Before you shop, however, analyze what your needs are. The range of options is almost overwhelming, and each choice has its own advantages and disadvantages. To benefit most from one device or another, you may also need to have other options such as those we discuss throughout this section.

4. ONE HOUSE-WIDE PHONE SYSTEM

Few home offices want the expense or complication of having the entire house wired for a phone system like those you find in office buildings. But once you've grown to the point that you need multiple phones with three or more lines, you may want the convenience of a system that links all your phones. You can use a modular telephone system like AT&T's Partner Phone Systems, Sieman's Gigaset, or ones from Panasonic, VTech, and Motorola. They link all the phones and all the lines (up to four) in your home without requiring a special closet or room for the "brain."

Here are some tips to consider when you are ready to install a new phone system for your home-based business.

- Buy a system that's big enough with room for your business to grow into it.
- Make sure to get a warranty.
- Make an actual drawing or plan of which lines you want where. This helps when coordinating with phone companies.
- If the manufacturer of the phone system offers training on how to operate the system, take it!
- Used equipment is available, but be very wary.

To select options that will truly work for you, we suggest you call your local telephone operating company. They likely have their own version of the services we've mentioned and are willing to assist you in determining the best approach for your business. Also Hello Direct offers a compre-

FULL-FEATURED PHONES

Telephone hardware is keeping pace with all the new telephone services and offering a myriad of useful features for complementing and making these services easier to use. You can buy a telephone with a variety of combinations of the following features:

- **Caller ID** display shows the phone number of your caller.

- **Redial** calls back the last number you called.

- **Recall** calls back the last number that called you.

- **Call-forward indicator** reminds you that your calls are being forwarded to another number.

- **Hold** puts your caller on hold. Some even play music.

- **Speakerphone** allows you to dial numbers and have conversation while keeping your hands free.

- **Call-on-hold indicator** tells you that you have a caller holding.

- **Message-waiting indicator** tells you that you have a voice-mail message.

- **Programmable memory keys** provide one-touch dialing to frequently called numbers or immediate access to phone features like call forwarding, three-way calling, or call waiting.

- **Call log** stores incoming phone numbers so you have access to the phone numbers of people who have called you.

hensive catalog of telephone products (*www.hellodirect.com/catalog*), (800) 435-5634.

As you can see from this part, your computer is a valuable tool in marketing yourself and your business—from contact managers and other kinds of specialized database programs that help you track the people who can make a difference in your business, to "top-of-the-mind" marketing techniques and software programs that can help you establish and maintain a professional image. Getting full use of your computer is like having an entire corporate staff working for you.

3.5: Using Your Computer to Go Online to Find Customers, Collect Money, and Get the Information You Need to Compete

Getting Online

The Internet is the most powerful, accessible, and affordable information and marketing resource the business world has ever known. It provides you with marketing channels that might otherwise be unavailable to you. In many ways the Internet is the great equalizer among businesses both large and small. As a home-based business entrepreneur you have the same access to the same information and resources that multimillion-dollar corporations do.

If you are not connected to the Internet, you should be, and here's why:

- The Web gives you access to a wealth of information, as well as suppliers and customers.
- With your own Web site and a custom domain name (a domain name locates an organization or other entity on the Internet, e.g., the domain name *www.mybusiness.com*) you can establish a presence to sell your goods or services. You don't need a "brick-and-mortar" storefront.
- You can advertise around the world easily and inexpensively.
- E-mail lets you communicate with others throughout the world day or night. You can send and receive information at virtually no cost.
- If you are not already online, you are placing your business at a real disadvantage. Information that your online peers, allies, and competition have at their fingertips will take you hours, perhaps days, to access—if you can find it at all.

You can use your computer and the Internet to gather the key information you need to:

- select a name for your business that attracts the right customers
- evaluate what to charge and set your prices to maximize your profits without turning potential clients away
- study your customer base to learn what media they use most often so you can plan your advertising or promotional campaign
- figure out what and how well your competition is doing

- learn about new developments in your field so you can be prepared for the future
- stay abreast of general business trends that affect the economy as a whole
- advertise, broadcast, and otherwise communicate to and with local, national, and international communities through the Internet and the Web.

Whether you are just starting out in business or have been self-employed for years, understanding the nuances of your market is an important function in the equation to attain success and maintain it. This part will provide online solutions to the common problems encountered in making contacts and obtaining information. We'll show you how to tap into valuable online information sources to gather the key information you need to make many of the most important decisions that all businesses must make.

Getting Connected

You connect to the Internet through an Internet service provider (ISP) and, depending on where you are located, there are a number of different ways to connect to the Internet: dial-up, DSL/cable, satellite, or wireless. So which type of Internet access is best for you? The answer isn't always clear-cut and often depends on where you live. Read on for an overview of the options.

Dial-up
When using a dial-up connection the modem in your computer uses your telephone line and dials a number that connects the modem to "servers" that make the Internet connection. The connection is maintained until you disconnect. If you have only one phone number, one of the main issues with dial-up connection is that while connected to the Internet you cannot make or receive phone calls.

DSL/Cable
In larger communities, telephone companies offer DSL (digital subscriber line) service. Cable-television companies also offer cable-modem services. In many larger centers you can choose either, although in some cities only one or the other is available. Both work over wires that already come into most homes and offices.

DSL uses ordinary telephone lines but, unlike dial-up access, it does not tie up the phone. It's also faster than dial-up service. DSL "lite" or "starter" services typically transfer data from the Internet at 256 kilobits per second (versus dial-up's top speed of 56 kilobits), and full-fledged DSL delivers your data at 3 or 4 megabits a second.

A cable modem connects you to the Internet over the cable that carries your television signal, but it doesn't interfere with the television signal. Speeds are as high as five megabits per second; some providers also offer a slower and less expensive service. Generally the cost is about the same. Many Internet service providers (ISPs) offer discounts to new subscribers that last for the first few months. They may also offer features such as anti-virus and spam protection, firewalls, multiple e-mail addresses, varying amounts of storage for e-mail, and so forth.

Satellite

High-speed satellite Internet service is the answer if you live outside the access area of local DSL and cable Internet providers. Its speed is comparable to other high-speed Internet services, it is always on, and you have the option of adding satellite TV service. While DSL and cable are both faster and cheaper than satellite service, their range of availability can be quite limited. If you have a clear view of the southern sky from your home anywhere in the continental United States, then you should be able to access the Internet via satellite.

Wireless

With advances in wireless Internet technology, a high-speed Internet connection is no longer limited to your stationary desktop. High-speed wireless Internet access on your notebook or Pocket PC is now available from a growing number of wireless Internet service providers.

The range of this wireless service is usually limited to around one thousand feet from local wireless access nodes, which are typically found in areas like hotels, airports, cafes, and the like. Though wireless Internet is not "everywhere," it likely will be available in the places where you need it most while traveling in the United States.

For most people, no one technology is the clear winner. The choice depends on where you live and the services available there.

Choosing the Right ISP (Internet Service Provider)

Choosing the right ISP for your needs is just as important as choosing which accounting-program package to buy. The right ISP can make your online life much easier. How do you decide? The first thing to do is identify your own needs in terms of services. Whenever you are looking for a new supplier, it's important to know the right questions to ask. It is particularly true in this age of Internet "techno-speak." Consider the following factors:

> **Speed of connection (throughput speed).** Can the ISP offer the speed that meets your current and future needs?
> **E-mail hosting.** How many e-mail boxes come with the services offered? Can that number be increased?
> **Security features.** What kind of security measures (e.g., firewalls, virus protection) does the ISP include for Web sites, e-mail, etc.?
> **Flexibility, scalability.** Can the options offered adapt to changes in the needs of your business? Are you locked into a contract? Can you make changes to your plan? How long does it take to do so?
> **Support.** Does the ISP offer technical help twenty-four hours a day? Do the support people talk to you in simple language or in difficult-to-understand techno-speak?

The best way to compare Internet services is to visit several ISP Web sites and compare their service offerings. Most libraries have computers with Internet access for public use, and many towns and cities have "Internet cafes" that rent time on Internet-connected computers.

Internet and Online Glossary

In case you are not familiar with the terminology frequently used in discussing online systems, this short glossary is intended to clarify the most frequently used terms.

Bandwidth—The biggest technological issue concerning the Web today is bandwidth. Bandwidth is simply the amount of digital "space" transmissions take up. Bandwidth is measured in bytes. A small Web site with few graphic images takes up relatively little bandwidth and can be quickly accessed by viewers. The really exciting stuff on the Web—like video, audio, animation, and high-resolution images—takes up much more bandwidth.

Browser—Browsers are software programs that allow you to navigate the Internet, especially the Web. Browsers are really a seamless interface that reads HTML, JAVA, and other Web languages and translates the information into graphics and text combinations. The leading browsers today are *Microsoft Explorer* and *Netscape Navigator*. Browsers can be enhanced by using "plug-in" applications. A plug-in is a software program that extends the browser's capabilities. For example, a plug-in gives you the ability to play audio samples or view video movies from within your browser. Two of the most popular plug-ins that let you to view video and audio streams are *Windows Media*, by Microsoft, (*www.microsoft.com/windows/windowsmedia/default.aspx*), and *RealPlayer*, by Real Networks (*www.real.com*). The basic program can be downloaded free of charge.

Database—A database is a collection of records, each of which may be the full text of an article from a magazine, journal, or newspaper; or it may be simply a brief summary (called an abstract) of an article along with a listing of the original author, name of publication in which the article appeared, the date of publication, and several key words that the computer uses to classify the article for searches. Other databases may also be composed of factual and statistical information, such as tables and lists of numbers, rather than text, such as CENDATA (*www.census.gov/population/www/socdemo/foreign/cendata.html*), which is a database based on U.S. Census data. A database may be compiled from one publication or from articles originally printed in hundreds of publications.

Database Vendor or Information Service—As online services continue to expand the amount information they offer, database vendors have grown increasingly specialized. Ebsco Host (*www.ebsco.com*), for example, provides online access to more than one hundred databases. Generally database vendors offer comprehensive databases of information focused on a particular topic or service.

Domain Name—The domain name is the most important part of the URL (uniform resource locator), the global address of documents and other resources on the Web. The *www* component is easy to remember, but the domain is tricky. Having a memorable domain name for your site is like having a memorable phone number. With a memorable domain name, people can find you more quickly. Most businesses use their business name, for example: *www.microsoft.com*. You can obtain your own unique name by registering it with interNIC (*http:rs.internic.net*), the official registrar of domain names. There is a one-time registration fee and an annual registration fee to keep your domain name current and exclusive.

FTP (file transfer protocol)—FTP allows you to both download files from FTP sites on the Internet and upload files to computers that you have access to. Files can consist of software, text, and graphics.

Newsgroups (also called Usenet groups)—Newsgroups allow you to find communities of people interested in specific topics, and you can participate in discussions on a wide range of subjects with millions of people around the world (*http:groups.google.com*).

Online Service Providers—These offer a gateway into the Internet in addition to a plethora of their own information resources. Online service providers are part library, part newsstand, part broadcast network, and part town square and meeting place. Sometimes the original content they provide is unique and separate from the Internet itself and can only be accessed by the service provider's signed-up members. Often monthly or even hourly fees are charged. Examples of online service providers are America Online (*www.aol.com*) and the Microsoft Network (*www.msn.com*).

URL (uniform resource location)—Every Web site has a unique address that allows it to be found on the network. This address is the URL. For example, the URL to our site is *http:www.workingfromhome.com*. The *http://* component of the URL signifies that the file uses in Hypertext Transfer Protocol (the protocol that allows you to see text, image, and sound simultaneously). The *www* component signifies the Web. The *workingfromhome* component is the domain name (see above), and the *.com* signifies that ours is a commercial site. Other common extensions include *.org* for organization, *.edu* for educational, and *.gov* for government related.

Web Site—A site on the Web is basically a file that contains text, graphics, and sometimes video, audio, and animation. The site itself resides on a server that is part of the Web network.

To find out more about what exactly goes into a Web site and the Web in general, read through the profiles for Web Design, Web Specialty Programmer (CGI, JAVA, HTML), Web Site Publicist, Web Publication, and the other Web-related business in Part 1 of this book.

Identifying Prospects for a Mailing List or Direct Solicitation

The Problem

Every business needs new customers, so being able to locate names, addresses, and telephone numbers of companies, professionals, or businesses that might need your services can be important to your survival and growth. To obtain such information, many businesses buy mailing-lists from mailing-list brokers. Yet buying such lists can be expensive, and generally the lists can be used only once.

Computer Solutions

By going online, you can locate names, addresses, telephone numbers, and a great deal of other information about potential clients for you to contact by phone, regular mail, or e-mail. Here is a list of some of the resources available to you:

Hugo Dunhill Mailing Lists: www.hdml.com, (888) 274-5737 provides mailing lists and mailing services.

InfoUSA: www.infousa.com, (877) 708-3840 is a leading provider of business-to-business marketing information about millions of businesses in the United States and Canada. The database is compiled and updated from multiple sources, and the information is verified by telephone for the most accurate information. InfoUSA also operates under various trade names such as Donnelley Marketing, American Business Information, idEXEC, and infoCanada. Business and consumer lists are available at www. list bazaar.com.

D&B Small Business Solutions: D&B Marketing Lists for small businesses have 13.7 million-record database to generate leads by industry and location, http:smallbusiness.dnb.com.

Edgar: This is the online database of the Securities and Exchange Commission. The site allows you to obtain federal filings for thousands of public companies (www.sec.gov/edgarhp.htm).

Mergent Online: Mergent Online (www.mergentonline.com) provides in-depth descriptive and financial information. It gives such details on businesses as descriptions, history, property, subsidiaries, officers and directors, long-term debt, and capital stock. Financial statements are presented in "as-reported" form and in native currencies, maintaining the full integrity of this critical information. Mergent Online's features and functions include the ability to:

- research fifteen years of detailed financial statements
- customize viewing and output to retrieve precisely the information you need
- export company reports and financials into software applications such as Microsoft *Word,* Microsoft *Excel* or Adobe *Acrobat Reader*
- execute accurate cross-border searches using a variety of financial and text variables
- compare multiple companies' reports
- view over 115,000 images of company annual reports

Standard & Poor's Corporate Descriptions: Standard & Poor's provides comprehensive strategic and financial information and current news on thousands of publicly held companies. These firms trade securities on the New York, American, and regional stock exchanges, the NASDAQ system, Over-the-Counter in the U.S., and on various exchanges in Canada and abroad. The files provides access to capitalization, corporate background, and financial data including annual report financials and recent interims (see *http:library.dialog.com/bluesheets/html/bl0133.html*).

Thomas Register Online: Thomas Register is an online resource for finding companies and products manufactured in North America where you can place orders online, view and download millions of computer-aided-design (CAD) drawings, and view thousands of online company catalogs and Web sites (*www.thomasregister.com*).

Obtaining Credit Information About Clients and Those Who Owe You Money

The Problem

Before you undertake work from a client, you want to know that the client is able to pay you. Determining whether a customer is a good credit risk or not means that you need to gather financial information about the company to help you decide whether or not to work for them, or under what conditions. Likewise, if you have collection problems, you may need to locate people and determine vital financial information about them.

Computer Solutions

You can often get information about a company's creditworthiness and financial track record through several online sources, including:

- **Dun & Bradstreet (D & B):** *www.dnbcreditreport.com,* **(866) 598-8696. Dun & Bradstreet's Business Information Reports contain D&B's estimate of credit worthiness.**
- **Credit.Net:** *www.credit.net,* **(888) 249-5015. The company also sells sales leads.**

Credit Reporting Services

Credit reporting services provide reports on individual and business credit ratings and are a good way to check a customer's past paying habits. A number of companies offer this service. *Business.com* provides a listing of consumer credit reporting services at *www.business.com/directory/ financial_services/consumer_finance/consumer_credit/reporting_services.*

Finding Facts Fast for Business Plans, Proposals, Reports, and Decisions

The Problem

When writing a business plan or proposal for a potential major client, you must prove that you know your field from top to bottom. You must be able to gather the most up-to-date information, or you may need information about a new competitor. To stay abreast of late-breaking news in your industry, you have to be able to access information of all kinds without spending endless hours researching.

Online Solutions

Online research is the only way to operate when it comes to obtaining timely information quickly and cost-effectively. Whatever your needs, you can find a universe of facts and information about specific companies, product lines, market trends, and potential clients in many different kinds of databases to be found online.

Here are some online sources that may be useful to you for finding the pertinent information you need to have at your fingertips:

Internet/Web Search Engines

The Web is *the* information source and clearinghouse. Before going anywhere else for information, chances are you can find it on the Web first, and for free! To locate information on the Web, you use one of the many search engines available. Search engines continuously find and compile the ever-growing mountains of information on the Web and the Internet and index it so you can find just what you want. Contrary to popular belief, search engines don't search the entire Internet; they search through their own extensive databases of Web sites, FTP sites, newsgroups, etc. To keep their databases current, they send out "spiders"—little software agents that search the Internet and bring back new information. Here are the current top-tier search engines:

- Google: *www.google.com*
- Alltheweb: *http:www.alltheweb.com*
- Yahoo: *www.yahoo.com*. To take advantage of Yahoo's strength as a directory, *http:dir.yahoo.com*
- MSN: *www.msn.com*

Meta search engines that search a dozen or more search engines can help you find information when you're not having any luck or need something on an obscure topic.

- Info.com: *www.info.com*
- Search.com: *www.search.com*
- WebCrawler: *www.webcrawler.com*

The Open Directory project is another resource that can enable you to find information you need. It is edited by thousands of volunteers: *www.dmoz.org*.

Specialized search engines can help you reach specifics sometimes more directly. For example for:

- articles, FindArticles, *www.findarticles.com*
- business statistics, *www.BizStats.com*
- scholarly resources, AllLearn: *www.alllearn.org/er/directories.cgi* and InfoMine: *http:infomine.ucr.edu*

TIPS FOR BETTER INTERNET SEARCHES

A search on any one topic can produce thousands, even millions, of results of which only a small percentage might be of use to you. However, the Internet can, and does make finding information faster and easier. How you enter a search phrase to specify what you're looking for determines how useful the search results are for you. The following tips will help formulate the best search phrases and get you right to the information you need while excluding the superfluous.

Every search engine offers its own help section, tips, and answers to frequently asked questions (FAQ). Take the time to read these over. The time and frustration you save will be immeasurable.

Many search engines also offer enhanced, pro, or advanced versions. Use these whenever possible.

Be as specific as possible in your search phrase. Avoid generalities such as *marketing,* or *graphic design.* Specific phrases such as *"October 2005 sales Mercedes statistics, Los Angeles"* or *"graphic design accounting software"* will get you to the information you're looking for much faster.

Use "specifiers" such as locations, dates, brand names, company names, etc., to make the search as exact as possible.

Use quotation marks around phrases that shouldn't be separated. Search engines look for occurrences of the words you enter. For example, if you are looking for medical software billing programs, put quotation marks around the entire phrase. This tells the search engine to find just those words in just that order. Without the quotation marks, the search will turn up every occurrence of the word *medical,* every occurrence of the *billing,* and . . . You get the picture.

Use quotation marks around inseparable phrases, and use the plus sign (+) to specify words that must be shown in every search result. For example, if you're seeking a professional association of family mediators, type "family mediators" + professional + association.

Tip* The University of California, Berkley, Library's Web site has a tutorial called *Finding Information on the Internet,* which offers a five-step search strategy. Check it out at: *www.lib.berkeley.edu/TeachingLib/Guides/Internet/Strategies.html.*

For Statistical Information

If the data you are seeking is statistical or factual in nature, you can examine many of the statistical sites on the Web. The U.S. Department of Labor's Bureau of Labor Statistics Web site (*http:www.bls.gov/bls/other.htm*) provides links to government statistical Web sites as well as other links to statistics and information from more than seventy agencies in the U.S. federal government.

Libraries on the Net

Library Web sites offer exhaustive informational resources and links to a wide variety of business and other topics. They also offer links to hundreds of online databases. *Libweb (http:sunsite.berkeley.edu/Libweb/)* is a site that lists links to libraries in over 115 countries and is updated daily at midnight, Pacific Time.

The Latest Breaking News Stories

At *PR Newswire (www.prnewswire.com)* you can gain access to breaking news from tens of thousands of organizations around the globe and get the complete text of news releases prepared by companies, PR agencies, trade associations, and government agencies. News releases often contain valuable information not found in newspaper or magazine articles.

Keeping Current in Your Field

The Problem

Whatever field you are in, chances are the pace of change is constant, and keeping up with it can occupy half your time. To stay competitive and keep the confidence of your clients, you need to keep up with all the news in your field without having to subscribe to dozens of journals or newspapers and spend your days reading instead of working.

Online Solutions

Many of the databases mentioned in the previous problem can also fulfill your need to stay abreast of general news in your profession. Daily newspapers, magazines, and journals have Web sites that you can browse through for subjects of interest in your field for free, or at minimal cost. Here's a list of some additional online solutions that you may wish to explore.

Electronic News-Clipping Services

With news-clipping services you can access articles, abstracts, and updates for a particular subject area.

> Looksmart.com lists popular electronic news-clipping services (*http: search.looksmart.com/p/browse/us1/us317916/us147927/ us269888/*).
> Some of the popular electronic clipping services include:
> Lexis Nexis's ECLIPSE (Electronic Clipping Service) lets you track and receive updates on specific news, business, and legal information and have it automatically delivered to your desktop (*www.lexisnexis.com/ currentawareness/eclipse*).
> CyberAlert also monitors Web message boards and UseNet news groups for consumer insight about companies and products (*www. cyberalert.com*).
> NewsLibrary.com archives hundreds of newspapers and other news sources (*http:nl.newsbank.com*).

New Products Tracking

> ThomasRegister (*www.thomasregister.com*) is a comprehensive and useful online resource for finding companies and products manufactured in North America where you can view and download millions of computer-aided design (CAD) drawings and view thousands of online company catalogs, and Web sites.
> ZDNet (*www.zdnet.com*) is one of the Web's leading sources of information about computer and technology products.

Finding Names and Titles for Your Mailings and Sales Calls

The Problem

As you prepare to do a mailing to a few dozen or a few hundred companies, you may discover that you do not know the names of the people to whom you should send your materials. When this happens, you need a reliable, speedy way to find out who the key people are in the companies you want to reach so that you won't find yourself sending out an expensive mailer impersonally addressed to a title like "Dear Chief Financial Officer."

Online Solutions

Many of the databases we've already cited can be used to find out the names of the officers and executives in millions of American companies. You can also refer to:

> Hoover's Online (*www.hoovers.com*), a database of millions of companies, with in-depth coverage of forty thousand or more of the world's top business enterprises.
>
> Marquis Who's Who (*www.marquiswhoswho.com*) provides information on key North American professionals, including date of birth, education, positions held during career, civic and political activities, memberships, awards, and other affiliations.

Finding a Supplier for Hard-to-Find Items and Locating Good Prices

The Problem

Selecting the most cost-effective business equipment, accessories, and supplies can be a difficult decision, given the plethora of products from which to choose. You may need to find reliable information and reviews of office equipment, computer supplies, and other items required to run your business.

Online Solutions:

- Catalogs—Google's directory of catalogs, *www.catalogs.google.com*
- Cnet—latest news about computing and technology products, *www.cnet.com*
- Drop Ship Sales Directory—suppliers willing to drop-ship their goods at wholesale prices: (212) 688-8797, *www.dropshipsales.com/indexnew.shtml*
- Liquidation.com—a marketplace of liquidated products, *www.liquidation.com*
- Power Sourcing—an online service for finding and contacting suppliers of products and services, (800) 955-6335/(614) 799-1759, *http:PowerSourcing.com*
- Thomas Register of American Manufacturers—available both on the Web and in bound volumes in libraries, (800) 222-7900, ext. 200, *www.thomasregister.com*. Another Thomas product is *www.ProductNews.com*, a source of new-product information in the industrial marketplace.

- TRACE-EM—industrial machinery and equipment, contract manufacturing services, *www.Trace-em.com*
- Worldbid.com—trade leads from companies and government organizations around the world, *www.worldbid.com*
- The Web! The Web was created for the purpose of helping people
and businesses find one another. Use any of the major search engines to search for the product or technology you are looking for.
You can also use the Web to locate trade magazines and trade shows
- ZDNet—databases useful for finding harder-to-find items and
suppliers. Notable among these is the *Computer Directory*, which
provides information on over seventy thousand computer-related
products and more than 8,500 manufacturers of hardware, software, peripherals, and data communications equipment. Information
includes pricing, phone numbers, fax numbers, and key specifications.
- For advice on choosing vendors, *A Guide to Online Purchasing* and
A Guide to Small Business Leasing are co-published by SCORE
(*www.score. org* or [800] 634-0245).

Overcoming Isolation

The Problem

In a rural area or even an urban one, no longer having colleagues or co-
workers in an office down the hall to sound out an idea or share opinions
or experiences with can leave you feeling isolated and alone when you
work from home. Throughout the day, week, or month, you may well feel
the need to get suggestions and support from colleagues and want to
avoid feeling trapped or stuck to your home office.

Online Solutions

Forums and groups abound on the Web. Each group has a theme, and
there are tens of thousands of them concerning virtually every conceivable topic. Many of them cover substantive topics and are rich sources of
contacts and business information; others are of little value. You can find
lists of forums, newsgroups (sometimes newsgroups are still referred to as
usenet groups), and listserv groups on:

- Google's Group directory (formerly Dejanews) is found at *http:
groups.google.com*
- Jump City at *www.jumpcity.com*—listing has a brief description of
group

- Tile.net at *www.tile.net*
- Listsoft.com at www.lsoft.com/catalist.html
- Yahoo! Groups at *http:groups.yahoo.com*

Most professional associations have Web sites. Check out the associations related to your business and see what's happening on their sites. In fact, the Internal Revenue Services recognizes over seventy thousand business organizations and trade groups. You can find many of these at the American Society of Association Executives' site (*www.asaenet.org*) where "Gateway to Associations" is provided as a service to the public. Many associations have forums; some associations open them up to nonmembers.

Getting Business Online

The Problem
Local markets don't always readily provide enough business to keep your cash flowing. With access to potential clients around the world via the Internet, how can someone use the Web to get work?

Online Solutions

Freelance Bidding Sites
You may find work on a freelance bidding site like *elance.com* and *guru.com* on which companies list work they need done. Work available ranges from providing administrative support like data entry, event planning, mailing list development, and transcription to multimedia tasks like video animation and converting a Web site to a downloadable workbook. The way freelance sites work is they charge a commission usually between 5 and 10 percent from what you are paid. (Do beware that some among the dozens of sites that promise to offer work don't deliver it and are just there to take your initial money.)

It's a fairly straightforward process to get work. You register at a site and provide a profile describing your specific capabilities and experience. Regularly search for work suited to you. When you find a project to your liking, bid on it in terms of what you will charge and how long you will take to complete the work. If the buyer responds to your bid, expect some negotiating.

While *elance.com* and *guru.com* are the most active bidding sites, you can find a listing of many others on the FreelanceMom.com site at *www.freelancemom.com/gigs.htm.*

Here are some things to remember when bidding on work:

1. Learn how the freelance bidding site you're using works. Read the fine print.

2. Develop a profile that shouts you're a high-quality provider. In it show your background in the field, your education, training, and credentials, the services you offer, and the range of your rates. If you need help putting your profile together or with writing it, consider posting it as a job on one of the freelance boards for a writer to help you. You'll then learn firsthand what it is to receive bids and what it takes to impress you about the bidders.

3. Put up a portfolio with samples of your work. What a photographer or graphic or Web designer uses as samples is fairly obvious, but if you're a consultant, it's still worthwhile. To provide examples of projects you've managed successfully, if you have testimonials from customers, you can show letters as a JPEG file or offer them as audio files.

4. Demonstrate you have the skills and tools needed to do the job. So if you're seeking administrative support work and you're certified in Microsoft Office Certification, say so.

5. Don't place your bids based on guesswork. Ask appropriate questions of the company or person seeking bids. Often the descriptions buyers write leave room for guesswork on your part and mind-reading probably isn't in your capability statement.

6. You may be competing against bidders from all over the planet, many of whom can and will underbid the prices most North Americans can charge. Do your market research—check to see what your competitors are bidding for the kind of work you want to do. Keep in mind wary buyers (and experienced) buyers are apt to be just as suspicious of extremely low bids as they are turned off by high ones.

7. Offer a schedule for payments and delivery of work that will make sense for you and be satisfactory to the buyer. It's usually wise to begin with a motivation to get the work done in a timely manner, such as asking for a relatively low initial down payment of 20 or 25 percent and with progress payments based on agreed-upon milestones.

8. Use your Web site to provide more depth and detail than you do in the portfolio you post. Portfolios can be too long, taxing buyers with too much to look at. Remember buyers are reviewing other bidders' profiles and

portfolios. If your bid and portfolio interest them, they'll want to know more about you.

9. If you choose to use Elance, consider becoming a select service provider. This helps the physical positioning of your bid and assures buyers that your credentials have been verified.

10. Learn from the bids you don't get, and don't stop at one or two attempts. As with most things in business, persistence pays off.

Networking Online

Many people get business online as a result of meeting people, sharing information, and developing friendships. Social networking services are designed to facilitate communication and referrals for professional purposes. Here's how it works: You submit your contacts, invite friends and colleagues to be part of an "inner circle" of business or personal associates, then use the system to seek "friends of friends" or business contacts of your associates. This inner circle of contacts expands as individuals are contacted directly or as introductions are made by mutual friends and associates. Just as services such as MySpace.com and Friendster.com bring singles and groups together based on mutual interests, business-networking services like LinkedIn.com (*www.linkedin.com*) and Ryze.com (*www.ryze. com/*) provide the same offering in the professional world. These services typically have sign-up steps that help you to create your online identity. Some business networking sites enable you to join specific community discussion groups. With your account set up and contacts entered, a network of individuals can easily search your personal network for relevant business contacts. This could be as simple as specifying a broad search for contacts within a specific industry. With the growing array of Web-based live communication tools, an online business networking site can offer a meeting environment where professionals can converse, face-to-face, through the site's own technologies.

Government Contracts

Federal Business Opportunities, FedBizOpps.gov (*www.fedbizopps.gov*) is the government point-of-entry for federal-government procurement opportunities over $25,000. Government buyers are able to publicize their business opportunities by posting information directly to FedBizOpps via the Internet. Through one portal, FedBizOpps (FBO), commercial vendors seeking federal markets for their products and services can search, monitor, and retrieve opportunities solicited by the entire federal contracting community.

Business Information & Development Services, Inc., offers an electronic bid-matching service for both the U.S. government's FedBizOpps.gov and Canada's Electronic Tendering Service operated under contract as MERX™. It also provides consulting services on getting government work: (716) 836-0919/(800) 440-BIDS, (*www.bidservices.com*).

To learn about state and local opportunities, check state and local government Web sites and with nearby Small Business Development Centers. A commercial service that provides this information is Onvia, (800) 331-2320, *www.onvia.com*.

Trade Shows

Since trade shows are another route to attracting business, you can find the dates and locations for trade shows, international conferences, conventions, and exhibitions using Global Sources Trade Show Center (*www.globalsources.com/TRADESHW/ALLSHOWS.HTM*).

Create Your Own Web site

The Web is one of your best resources to promote your products or services and attract business. It is the beyond the scope of this book to provide all the details of how to create a Web site, but the following information should point you in the right direction.

There are three basic steps involved in creating and posting a successful site on the Web:

1. *Creating the Site Itself*—The first step is to design the Web site. You can do it yourself with one of the commercially available software packages such as Microsoft's *FrontPage* or Macromedia's *Dreamweaver,* or you can have a professional Web-site designer do it for you. There are many excellent books available that are entirely devoted to the process of creating Web sites. See the resources section of the Web Site Design profile in Part 1, page 159.

2. *Finding a Server/Host*—When the site itself is finished, you need a server/host service that will actually store your site and serve it to the Web. There are literally thousands of companies who do this. Your best bet is to research several and find the best one to suit your needs. You may want to start with your own ISP (online service provider). Nearly every ISP provides Web hosting services.

Call at least three to four other hosting services. You can find these services by asking colleagues whom they use, conducting searches on the Web itself, and looking through computer- and Web-oriented magazines. Compare features such as price per month, speed, bandwidth, size of the site (listed in megabytes), how long the company has been in business, and their list of services. Ask any company that you are considering using to give you a list of their current business customers. Then contact some of them to ask if they're happy with the service.

3. *Publicizing Your Web Site*—Once your site is securely nestled on a server, you need to let the world know about it. Many businesses make the mistake of assuming that if "they build it, they will come," then wonder why their site is lonelier than the Maytag repairman. To get people to visit your site you have to tell them it's there. Consider hiring (or perhaps bartering for) the services of a Web-site publicist. Their business is building up the traffic on your site. If want to do the publicity yourself, start by submitting your site to all the major search engines. There are many companies that can help you, as well as software tools such as *Web Position Gold* (*www.WebPositionGoldPro.com*). Searchenginewatch.com (*http:searchenginewatch.com*) is a first-rate source of information on search engines. Articles like "131 (Legitimate) Link Building Strategies" are available free. Another useful site for keeping up with the process of doing business on the Web is *WebmasterWorld.com*.

It's a good idea to write a press release and send it out electronically and also via regular mail to trade magazines, newsletters, and any other organizations your industry and customers turn to for information. Also, ask colleagues, trade organizations, and any other relevant entities to include a link to your site from their site.

☞ **ALERT** ☜

Many ISPs offer free Web-site hosting for personal use. We recommend that you not take advantage of this for your business. The URL you receive will not indicate that your site is a business site and will detract from the professional appearance and perception of your business. We recommend that you pay the extra money and list your site as a business site for the same reasons that we recommend that you obtain a business phone line so that your business will be listed as a business in the phone directory.

Tips for Using Online Services

Know What You Are Looking For

There is a vast sea of information out there, and you can drown in it if you don't know specifically what you are looking for. Before you do any searching, think clearly about what you want to find and which vendor and database are likely to have what you want. For example, if you want a brief overview of a topic from a magazine like *Time* or *Newsweek* or a newspaper, you would search in the kind of database that offers such full-text articles. However, if you were seeking more in-depth business information, complete with financial analysis, ratios, and other quantitative information, you can log onto a database that is more oriented toward that specific information.

Scope Out Your Territory

Familiarize yourself with how each online service works so that you don't spend needless time reading menus or using help files. The best way to do this is to take advantage of the trial periods most online services offer before subscription charges begin.

Select the Fastest Internet Service Possible

Subscribe to DSL/cable or satellite Internet service if it is available in your area. If not, invest in the highest-speed modem you can afford. It will more than pay for itself if your online service charges hourly rates. Even if you pay a flat rate, a faster modem will save a great deal of your own time!

Perform Efficient Searches

Review the section in this part on conducting better Internet searches. The better your search results, the less time you will spending sifting through information you don't need.

Search Multiple Databases at the Same Time

If the service you are using offers you the ability to search multiple databases at the same time instead of one at a time, you will usually save time and money. Some services allow you to store the commands you use in making a search (your search strategy). Doing this enables you to repeat a search in another database or at another time more quickly, thus saving you money.

Use Bookmarks

Both Microsoft *Explorer* and Netscape *Navigator* allow you to mark and store a list of favorite and most frequently accessed sites on the menu bars. For example, Microsoft's list is referred to as "Favorites," whereas Netscape's is "Bookmarks." Once a marker is created you can click on it anytime and be taken to the site immediately, so you don't have to search for it again.

Know When to Sign Off

Once you get involved in the online world, you might find yourself spending more time there than necessary. Always have an idea of what you wish to accomplish online before logging on. Once you have found what you were looking for, contacted the people you need to, or otherwise accomplished what you set out to do, log off.

Save Your Search to a File

To minimize the time you spend online, download your entire session to a file in your computer so that you can review it when you are done. You not only save time by not reading while online, but you can also go back and review the files off line. Most communications software allows you to "capture" your online sessions to a file on your hard drive or on a CD or diskette.

Learn More

You can find a lot of specific information and software that will help you take full advantage of any database and vendor. If you are serious about making online resources your business partner, you can refer to the *Gale Directory of Databases* (ISBN: 078766409X, published by Thomson Gale, *www.gale.com*). It profiles thousands of databases available worldwide in a variety of formats. Entries include producer name and contact information, description, cost, and more. Each edition is composed of two volumes: Vol. 1: *Online Databases* and Vol. 2: *CD-ROM, Diskette, Magnetic Tape, Handheld and Batch Access Database Products*. Each volume is released in two parts, once in the fall and again in the spring, with the second parts being complete updates of the first. Volumes (both parts) are also available individually. It includes subject, geographic, and master indexes.

Appendix:
Additional Useful
Web Sites

Government Information
- GPO Access: from the Government Printing Office, access to federal documents: *www.access.gpo.gov/su_docs/multidb.html*
- Internal Revenue Service site for the self-employed: *www.irs.gov/businesses/small*. Canada Revenue Agency's counterpart is found at *www.cra-arc.gc.ca/tax/business/menu-e.html*.
- Laws and regulatory information for small business: *www.businesslaw.gov*
- SearchGov.com: You can reach the states and federal agencies from this site, *www.searchgov.com*.
- United States Small Business Administration (*www.sbaonline.sba.gov*) provides lists to SBA resources such as documents and links to Web pages such as compiled frequently asked questions on various topics within the Small Business Administration and business laws and regulatory assistance. Industry Canada provides access to information at *http:strategis.ic.gc.ca/SSG/me00010e.html*.

Handy Sites to Know About
- City-Data.com offers profiles of all U.S. cities with pictures, maps, satellite photos, stats about residents, geographical data, businesses, zip codes, area codes, similar cities list, comparisons to averages, and more, *www.city-data.com*.
- Ideacafe (*www.ideacafe.com*) is a fun site that offers business gossip, horoscopes, and valuable help for entrepreneurs and owners.

- Inflation Calculator: available from InflationData.com, *http:inflation data.com/inflation/Inflation_Rate/InflationCalculator.asp*
- VoyCabulary can make the nonunderstandable understandable. If you find a Web page that you think has valuable information but you don't understand the "insider" vocabulary, this site will turn the words on any Web page into links, so you can look them up with just a click in a dictionary of your choice: *www.voycabulary.com/*.
- Web-site Designs: you can use these free of charge: *http:freesite templates.com*.
- Writing Guide for the Web: provides lots of useful guidance, and it's free: *www.webstyleguide.com*.

Sources of Help for the Disabled
In your local community:

- Your nearest Small Business Development Center should have a list of programs in your area.
- State Vocational Services, California and New Jersey; Pennsylvania, Iowa, and Wisconsin have programs, and other states may also.

National organizations:
- Disabled Businesspersons Association: *www.web-link.corn /dba/dba. htm*, (619) 594-8805; *seedbiznet.org*
- National Rehabilitation Association: Self-employment for the disabled is one of their interests: *www.nationalrehab.org*, (703) 836-0850.
- Robert Dole Foundation advances workforce opportunities for the disabled: *www.doleinstitute.org*, (202) 457-0318.
- SEED offers complete programs for starting and running a small business tailored to the specific needs of people with disabilities: *seedbiznet.org*, (949) 413-1555.

About the Authors

Paul and Sarah Edwards are award-winning authors of seventeen books, including *Working From Home*, the first commercially published book on the topic. They operate the Pine Mountain Institute from their home office in a California mountain community; through the institute, they provide coaching and teach online courses based on the theme that motivates all their writing—living the life you want to live while doing the work you want to do. They also broadcast a live radio show from their home office.

The Edwardses are columnists for *Entrepreneur, Entrepreneur's BYOB, Homeofficemag.com,* and *Costco Connection.* They were named as Speakers of the Year by Sharing Ideas in 1996.

The Edwardses operate two Web sites where they can be contacted directly, *www.workingfromhome.com* and *pinemountaininstitute.com.* Updates and added content for this book will be found at *workingfrom home.com.* The authors welcome learning about resources they can add or updates for the information in the book.